ST. ANDREW'S CHURCH, WISSETT, SUFFOLK, ENGLAND

THE DESCENDANTS

OF

Major Samuel Lawrence

OF

GROTON, MASSACHUSETTS

WITH

SOME MENTION OF ALLIED FAMILIES

BY

Robert Means Lawrence, M.D.

HERITAGE BOOKS
2012

HERITAGE BOOKS

AN IMPRINT OF HERITAGE BOOKS, INC.

Books, CDs, and more—Worldwide

For our listing of thousands of titles see our website
at
www.HeritageBooks.com

A Facsimile Reprint
Published 2012 by
HERITAGE BOOKS, INC.
Publishing Division
100 Railroad Ave. #104
Westminster, Maryland 21157

International Standard Book Numbers
Paperbound: 978-0-7884-1768-9
Clothbound: 978-0-7884-9285-3

Know then thyself, presume not God to scan,
The proper study of mankind is man.

ALEXANDER POPE,

Essay on Man.

PREFACE

THE preparation of this volume was undertaken at the request of members of the Lawrence family, who wished for a reliable genealogy of the descendants of Major Samuel Lawrence, brought down to the beginning of the twentieth century.

In many cases the compiler would gladly have made the biographical notices more complete, had the necessary data been available. Great care has been taken to insure accuracy, yet errors will doubtless be found. The material herewith submitted has been obtained from replies to circulars and personal letters, supplemented by information derived from printed memoirs, biographical publications, college class reports; state, municipal, church, and probate records; county and town histories; genealogies and family registers. The particular sources of information have not usually been indicated.

It is hoped that the insertion, wherever practical, of the lineage of persons nearly allied to the Lawrences by marriage, may enhance the usefulness of the volume as a hand-book for reference.

The Rev. Anson Titus has rendered valuable aid in tracing several lineages.

By permission of the author, the interesting story of " A Minute-man " is here included. While the form of the conversations therein presented is chiefly traditional, the story itself is founded on fact.

This volume is a sequel to the compiler's " Historical Sketches of Some Members of the Lawrence Family," issued in 1888.

R. M. L.

321 DARTMOUTH STREET,
  BOSTON, MASS., January, 1904.

CONTENTS

THE DESCENDANTS OF MAJOR SAMUEL LAWRENCE

ENGLISH ANCESTRY

Sir Robert Lawrence of Ashton Hall in Lancashire was knighted by King Richard the Lionhearted, for gallant conduct at the siege of Acre, when that famous city of Syria was recovered from the Saracens by the knights of the third Crusades, A. D. 1191. According to tradition, he was the first to scale the walls and plant the standard of the Cross upon the town's battlements. From this warrior, through sixteen generations of knights, squires, and hardy yeomen, has been traced the descent of John Lawrence, a native of Wissett in Suffolk, who crossed the sea about the year 1630, and became the ancestor of a numerous kindred in New England.

His pedigree was compiled with laborious research from heraldic manuscripts, ancient deeds, charters, wills, and parish registers.

ASHTON HALL

Ashton Hall, the ancient seat of the Lawrences, is about three miles to the south of the town of Lancaster, in northern Lancashire. It is picturesquely situated, commanding fine views of the estuary of the River Lune, and of Morecambe Bay, an extensive inlet of the Irish Sea, and is noted for the sylvan beauty of its spacious park, which is well diversified with hill and vale. The mansion is a large edifice, with many of the characteristics of an ancient baronial castle, having a square tower at one end, and numerous battlements, turrets, and machicolations. Successive alterations and additions have been made at different epochs, in harmony with the mediæval type of architecture. The oldest portion is probably the tower, which is believed to date from the fourteenth century. The interior contains a fine baronial hall.

The estate remained in the possession of the Lawrences until the year 1513. Sir Robert Lawrence, of the seventh generation from the hero of the Crusades, had three sons, of whom the eldest, Sir James, heir to Ashton Hall, was knighted at Hutton Field, July 24, 1482, by Lord Stanley, "Steward of the King's House." His eldest son and heir to the estate, Sir John Lawrence, the last of the Lawrences of Ashton, was killed at the battle of Flodden Field, Northumberland, Sept. 9, 1513. His daughter, the heiress of Ashton Hall, became the wife of Sir John Butler of Rawcliffe, and their only child and heiress, Isabel Butler, married Thomas Radcliffe of Wynmarleigh. Anne, daughter and heiress of Thomas Radcliffe, became the wife of Sir Thomas Gerard (of Gerard's Bromley, Staffordshire), who was the son and heir of Sir Gilbert Gerard (Master of the Rolls, 1581–1592). Afterwards the estate passed to the Hamiltons by the marriage of James, Earl of Arran, afterwards Duke of Hamilton, with Elizabeth, daughter and sole heiress of Digby, Lord Gerard of Bromley. Ashton Hall is now the residence of J. Chamberlain Starkie, Esq.

According to researches made under the direction of Colonel T. Bigelow Lawrence, Nicholas Lawrence, the youngest son of Sir Robert above mentioned, was the ancestor of Major Samuel Lawrence of Groton, Mass. He settled at Agercroft.

Sir Robert represented Lancashire in Parliament in the years 1404, 1406, and 1414, and his second son, of the same name, was its representative in 1429–30.

WISSETT

Wissett is a small parish and village in the northeastern part of the County of Suffolk, two miles northwest of Halesworth, which is a market town on the river Blythe and a station on the Great Eastern Railway, one hundred and one miles from London. The population of Wissett in 1851 was 490, and in 1894 it was 376. The Rev. Arthur Lawrence, D. D., who visited the town in 1877, writes as follows : " The old church at Wissett is a fairly interesting structure, with one of the round flint towers not uncommon in the east of England. What might be its venerable appearance is marred by a coat of whitewash. I preached there one afternoon. The congregation had never before seen an American. Rev. Robert Kemp, the vicar, was a very aged man, who died not long afterward. The service was conducted in a very simple way. A lot of children sat on the chancel step. The old vicar, if I remember rightly, read the Lesson, sitting in a chair behind the lectern. Now and then he would doze off and go to sleep, while the congregation sat patiently until he woke up and went on again. The churchyard was full of old graves, and in the parish register were the names of many Lawrences. Archbishop Whately was once rector of Halesworth [1822], and at the rectory, Arnold, Keble, and Whately met to read the manuscript of the 'Christian Year.' The rector of Halesworth in 1877 had a very interesting history. He had been a missionary in China, where he was confined in a cage, and was crippled as a result of his sufferings."

At the present time, 1903, Rev. John Garforth is sequestrator, and in entire charge of the Wissett parish, having been appointed thereto by the Bishop of Norwich.

First Generation.

John Lawrence, a son of Henry and Mary Lawrence, was baptized at Wissett, Oct. 8, 1609. Within a few years after his arrival in America, or about the year 1635, he made his home in Watertown, Mass., married a wife, whose name was Elizabeth, and became the father of thirteen children. In 1662 he changed his residence to Groton, where he was an original land proprietor, having a twenty-acre-right. He also served on the first Board of Selectmen of whose election a record is extant.

Mrs. Elizabeth Lawrence died August 29, 1663. He married (second) at Charlestown, Susanna, daughter of William Batchelder, and had two daughters, born at Groton.

He died there, July 11, 1667, and his widow at Charlestown, July 8, 1668.

Second Generation.

Nathaniel Lawrence, the second son of John and Elizabeth Lawrence, was born at Watertown, Oct. 15, 1639, and married at Sudbury, March 13, 1661, Sarah Morse, daughter of John and Hannah Morse of Dedham. He lived in Groton for some thirty years, and served as ensign of a military company, selectman, and as a deacon of the church. He was also one of the first representatives from Groton to the General Court in the year 1692, under the charter of William and Mary. About the year 1694 he removed his residence to Charlestown, and later to Cambridge Farms, now Lexington, where he died, April 14, 1724, aged 84 years.

Third Generation.

John Lawrence, the second son of the preceding, was born at Groton, July 29, 1667. He married, Nov. 9, 1687, Hannah or Anna, elder daughter of Thomas and Hannah Tarbell of Groton. She was born June 10, 1670. They removed in 1693 to Cambridge Farms, and became members of the First Parish in that precinct, Feb. 1, 1699. He was chosen an assessor in 1701, a town constable in 1705, and selectman in 1716, serving in the latter capacity several years. His homestead was situated near the border of Billerica, on what is now called the Bedford road in Lexington, and this was the birthplace of his younger children.

John Lawrence died at Lexington, March 12, 1747. Mrs. Hannah (Tarbell) Lawrence died Dec. 19, 1732.

Fourth Generation.

Amos Lawrence, the youngest of ten children of John and Hannah (Tarbell) Lawrence, was born at Lexington, Feb. 13, 1716, and became a resident of Groton in 1742. He married, Nov. 7, 1749, Abigail, daughter of Nehemiah and Sarah (Foster) Abbott of Lexington, who was born Jan. 26, 1721. He held the rank of captain in the militia, and was elected a selectman in 1756, serving fifteen years. He was prominent among his patriotic fellow-citizens in ante-Revolutionary times, and was an earnest worker for the cause of American liberty. He died at Groton, June 20, 1785. Mrs. Abigail (Abbott) Lawrence died Jan. 6, 1784.

FIFTH GENERATION

FAMILY NO. 1

1. **Samuel Lawrence,** the third son of Amos and Abigail (Abbott) Lawrence, was born at Groton, April 24, 1754, and m., July 22, 1777, Susanna, eldest daughter of William and Sarah (Richardson) Parker of Groton, who was born Oct. 10, 1755.

Their children, born in Groton, were:

2. I. **Luther,** b. Sept. 28, 1778. Family No. 2. Groton and Lowell.

3. II. **Samuel,** b. July 2, 1781; d. May 21, 1796.

4. III. **William,** b. Sept. 7, 1783. Family No. 3. Boston.

5. IV. **Amos,** b. April 22, 1786. Family No. 4. Boston.

6. V. **Susan,** b. May 24, 1788; d. at the house of

her brother William, in Southac Court, now Howard Street, Boston, Aug. 17, 1815.

7. VI. **Mary,** b. Nov. 12, 1790. Family No. 5. Groton.

8. VII. **Abbott,** b. Dec. 16, 1792. Family No. 6. Boston.

9. VIII. **Eliza,** b. March 13, 1796. Family No. 7. Groton.

10. IX. **Samuel,** b. Jan. 15, 1801. Family No. 8. Stockbridge.

Samuel Lawrence spent the years of his childhood and youth upon his father's farm, in his native town of Groton. When the Lexington alarm sounded he was twenty-one years of age, and a non-commissioned officer in the militia company commanded by Capt. Henry Farwell. Leaving his plough in the field, he promptly answered the call. Mounting a horse, he notified the minute-men living in his circuit of the approach of the British troops. The two Groton companies, and one from Pepperell, assembled in haste, and early in the afternoon of the eventful 19th of April, 1775, they started on the march to the scene of action. Although unable to reach Concord and Lexington in season to take part in the fight of that day, they pressed forward to Cambridge, and thenceforth bore their share in maintaining the siege of Boston. These companies became a part of the newly organized Western Middlesex Regiment, and for several months Samuel Lawrence acted as orderly to Colonel William Prescott.

On the evening of June 16, 1775, a detail of one

thousand men, including the Groton companies, under Colonel Prescott, marched from their headquarters at Cambridge to Charlestown Neck, and during
the night constructed a redoubt and breastworks
upon Breed's Hill. Samuel Lawrence was placed in
command of a detachment of men from his company,
with orders to watch the movements of an English
frigate, which was lying in the harbor near by. He
also assisted in the construction of the earthworks
on the night of the 16th, and was an active combat-
ant throughout the battle of Bunker Hill on the next
afternoon. A spent grape-shot inflicted a slight
wound on his arm, and a bullet passed through his
hat, furrowing his hair. He continued in active service for more than three years, attaining the rank of
major. On July 22, 1777, having obtained a brief
furlough, he was married at Groton to Susanna
Parker. During the wedding ceremony the alarm-
bell sounded, and he was obliged to leave his bride in
haste, to rejoin his regiment.

At the battle of Quaker Hill, in Rhode Island, Aug.
29, 1778, Samuel Lawrence narrowly escaped being
captured by the enemy, having become separated
from his command. His rescue was due to the gallant
conduct of a company of negro troops, who hastened
to his support.

Honorably discharged from the army, he returned
to his home in Sept., 1778, and soon became active
in town affairs, serving at different times as selectman, assessor, and town clerk of Groton. He was
also a deacon of the church for more than forty
years, and enjoyed deservedly the confidence and re-

spect of his fellow-citizens. His death occurred at Groton, Nov. 8, 1827.[1]

Whatever relates to Major Samuel Lawrence, and especially his experiences before and during the battle of Bunker Hill, must have an interest for his descendants. Therefore it has seemed appropriate to reprint here the following affidavit, which appears in Dr. S. A. Green's "Groton during the Revolution," pp. 219, 220:

I, Samuel Lawrence, of Groton, Esquire, testify and say, that I was at the battle of Bunker Hill (so called) in Colonel William Prescott's regiment; that I marched with the Regiment to the point on Breed's Hill, which was fixed on for a redoubt; that I assisted in throwing up the breastwork, and in forming a redoubt, under Colonel Prescott, who directed the whole of this operation. The work was begun about nine o'clock in the evening of June 16th, 1775. I was there the whole time, and continued in the redoubt, or in the little fort, during the whole battle, until the enemy came in, and a retreat was ordered. General Putnam was not present either while the works were erecting, nor during the battle. I could see distinctly the rail fence and the troops stationed there during the battle, but General Putnam was not present as I saw. After the retreat was ordered, the troops retreated towards Bunker Hill, and continued over and on the side of the hill (I was on the side of

[1] A fuller account of Major Samuel Lawrence and of his American ancestry is contained in *Historical Sketches of Some Members of the Lawrence Family*, by R. M. Lawrence, pp. 7-15 52-65, 85-93, and 97-119.

the hill) towards Charlestown neck. . . . Just before the battle commenced, General Warren came to the redoubt. He had on a blue coat and white waistcoat, and I think, a cocked hat, but of this I am not certain. Colonel Prescott advanced to him, said " he was glad to see him, and hoped he would take the command." General Warren replied: " no, he came to see the action, but not to take command: that he was only a volunteer on that day." Afterwards I saw General Warren shot; I saw him when the ball struck him, and from that time until he expired. I knew General Warren well by sight, and recollected him perfectly when Colonel Prescott offered him the command, and was sorry to see him so dangerously situated, as I knew him to be a distinguished character, and thought he ought not to have risked his life without command on that occasion. No British officer was within forty or fifty rods of him, from the time the ball struck him, until I saw he was dead. I have read General Dearborn's account of the battle, and think it correct, particularly with regard to the occurrences at the gateway of the redoubt.

(Signed)   SAMUEL LAWRENCE.

COMMONWEALTH OF MASSACHUSETTS.
COUNTY OF MIDDLESEX.

June 5, 1818.

Personally appeared Samuel Lawrence, Esq., and made oath that the above declaration by him subscribed, is just and true in all its parts, according to the best of his knowledge and belief. Before me,

(Signed)   SAMUEL DANA,

Justice of the Peace throughout said Commonwealth.

The descendants of Samuel Lawrence justly revere the memory of his wife, Susanna (Parker) Lawrence, whose sterling virtues, shown as a patriotic maiden, wife, and matron, deserve to be held in lasting remembrance. To her strength of Christian character, and to the moulding force of her precepts and example, her children owed much How well they have repaid the debt, these pages may in a measure testify.

Susanna (Parker) Lawrence died at Groton, May 2, 1845, aged 89 years.

The following letter was written to Mrs. Lawrence at Groton, by Miss Cornelia Wells Walter (afterwards Mrs. William Boardman Richards), who was in charge of the Post Office Department of the great Fair held in Boston in 1840, under the auspices of the Bunker Hill Monument Association.

QUINCY HALL, POST OFFICE DEPARTMENT,
BOSTON, September 12th, 1840.

MRS. SUSANNA LAWRENCE, Groton.

Beloved and respected Madam, — Amidst an extensive correspondence sustained during the great Fair for the completion of the Bunker Hill Monument, with people from every part of our favored country, and with half of the Whig Delegates from New England — your venerated name has frequently occurred to my recollection, and I cannot resist the inclination to add it to my list. Language, however, would fail me, to express my admiration for those fine traits of character, which, brought into high relief in your domestic life for a period of eighty-five years, has made you the venerable matron, and the idolized parent. Such admiration cannot be otherwise than unqualified. You have been the "nursing mother" of sons loved and honored by their friends; and, as fellow-citizens of a commercial and literary metropolis, held in high respect as upright merchants and honorable men. The memory of their father being intimately connected with the glorious war of our country's Revolution, has served to incite them to exert their influence and pecuniary aid largely in behalf of the final attempt made by the ladies of our city, to place the capstone on the " Battle Monument," which has been so long a dishonor to the consecrated spot on which it stands, and a reproach to *us* especially as citizens of a proud Republic — proud of our *free rights*, and proud, above all, of the memory of our heroic ancestry, who fought in perilous times, but in a cause so glorious, believing that,

> " Their lives were given
> To die for home, and leant on Heaven
> Their hand."

The object of our Fair, dear Madam, I know you will appreciate; and, most happy am I that the task is mine to assure you that it will be successful. The Monument *will* be finished; and, could it "rise like a pyramid and o'ertop the skies," it would be like the memory of the "loved and lost" in that memorable battle which has "blossomed as the rose, and smelt to Heaven." — You have wrought, my dear Madam, for this Fair, with your own hands, evincing thereby an ardent interest in its success, and verifying, also, the benevolent actions of former days, and the proverbs of the " Book of Books " —

"She layeth her hands to the spindle, and her hands hold the distaff."

"She maketh fine linen and selleth it, and delivereth girdles unto the merchant."

"Her children arise up and call her blessed; her husband also, and he praiseth her."

Would that the young people of the present day would imitate so virtuous an exemplar!

I could write much more, but the demands upon my time are so exceedingly pressing, that I am obliged to close my letter very unwillingly, with the assurance of the profound respect and unfeigned regard of your sincere friend,

CORNELIA.[1]

SIXTH GENERATION

FAMILY NO. 2

2. **Luther,** m. at Worcester, Mass., June 19, 1805, Lucy, fifth and youngest child of Colonel Timothy Bigelow of Worcester (1739–1790) and Anna (Andrews) Bigelow. She was born May 13, 1774; d. at Boston, Oct. 6, 1856.

Their children were:

11. I. **Anna Maria,** b. at Groton, March 25, 1806. Family No. 9. Rutland, Vt.

12. II. **Emily,** b. at Groton, June 24, 1807; d. May 3, 1808, at Groton.

---

[1] Mr. William Reuben Richards makes the following statement: "This letter was written on the occasion of the Fair, which was held for the purpose of raising funds to put the capstone on Bunker Hill Monument. My mother at the time had charge of the post-office, which meant that she wrote most of the letters. She has told me the story of how the son (Amos Lawrence) asked to have the letter written, and was so pleased with it that he came back with a twenty-dollar gold-piece."

13. III. **Elizabeth Andrews,** b. at Groton, June 29, 1809; d. Aug. 19, 1830, at Groton.

14. IV. **Catharine,** b. at Groton, April 26, 1811; m. Charles Tilden Appleton. Family No. 10. Lowell.

15. V. **Rufus Bigelow,** b. at Groton, July 13, 1814.

Rufus Bigelow Lawrence received instruction at Groton and Stow academies, and under a private tutor. Entering Harvard, Aug. 24, 1829, he remained two years with the Class of 1833, but graduated with the Class of 1834. He then began the study of law in his father's office at Lowell, and became a member of the Middlesex bar in Dec., 1837. Two years later he started to practise his profession in Boston, but his health failing, he went abroad and spent many months in travel. He died at Pau, Basses Pyrénées, France, Jan. 13, 1841, much regretted.

The Hon. Luther Lawrence prepared for college at Groton Academy, which he entered in 1794, when the institution was first opened for the reception of students. He received the degree of A. B. from Harvard in 1801, and then studied law in the office of Hon. Timothy Bigelow, being admitted to the bar in June, 1804, after which he engaged in successful practice in Groton, where he had a large clientage. In 1812 he was elected representative from Groton to the Massachusetts General Court, serving for twelve years in that capacity, and as speaker in 1822. Mr. Lawrence was a trustee of Groton Academy for twenty-eight years. He was also active in the militia, being captain of the south military company of Groton. In 1831 he removed his residence to Lowell, where his brothers were prominent among the originators of several important manufacturing enterprises. Here he built a house on Lawrence Street, and continued the practice of law in partnership with Elisha Glidden, Esq. At a town meeting held at Lowell, Feb. 3, 1836, Mr. Lawrence was appointed chairman of a committee of twenty-five citizens, who were instructed "to consider if any alterations or modifications in the municipal regulations of said town were necessary, and also the expediency of establishing a city government." At a later meeting, Feb. 17, 1836, Mr. Lawrence, as chairman of the above-named committee, made a report, recommending that the legislature be petitioned to grant a charter to make the town a city. He was elected the second mayor of the new city of Lowell, March 6, 1838, and served in that office with ability, being reëlected the ensuing year. On April 17, 1839, while inspecting some new buildings of the Middlesex Mills in company with his friend and classmate, Tyler Bigelow, Esq., he made a misstep, and falling into an open wheel-pit, was almost instantly killed. Luther Lawrence was held in much esteem in the community, and was one of Lowell's most honored citizens. The City Council passed appropriate resolutions "bearing testimony to his high-minded and honorable character, his judicious administration of the city government, his lively interest in the various public institutions with which he had been connected, his unselfishness and liberality, his efforts to promote

the moral and religious interests of the place, his
amenity of behavior and kindliness of feeling for all
around him."

Colonel Timothy Bigelow (fifth son of Daniel and
Elizabeth (Whitney) Bigelow), whose youngest child,
Lucy, became the wife of Hon. Luther Lawrence, was
born at Worcester, Mass., Aug. 2, 1739. He was of
the fourth generation from John Biglo or Bigelow, the
emigrant ancestor. Colonel Bigelow married, July 1,
1762, Anna, daughter of Samuel and Anna (Rankin)
Andrews When a young man he learned the trade
of a blacksmith, and carried on that business. On
the Lexington alarm, April 19, 1775, he marched to
Cambridge as captain of a company in Colonel Artemas Ward's regiment, and was on duty during the
early part of the siege of Boston. In Sept., 1775, he
accompanied Benedict Arnold in the expedition sent
to attempt the capture of Quebec, and was taken
prisoner in the assault on that city, Dec. 31, and de-
tained until August following, when he was ex-
changed, and returned home. He became colonel of
the Fifteenth Massachusetts Regiment, Feb. 8, 1777,
and was present at the surrender of General Burgoyne
to General Gates at Saratoga in October following.
Colonel Bigelow took part in other campaigns of the
Revolution, and was at Valley Forge, West Point,
Monmouth, and Yorktown. When the war was over
he returned to his home, having earned an excellent
reputation as an efficient officer, but with health impaired by the privations and hardships which he had
experienced, and with diminished means, owing to a
depreciated currency and scant remuneration for his

military services. "With a resolute spirit he set to work to repair his shattered fortune, and resumed his old occupation of a blacksmith. With others he obtained a grant of land in Vermont, consisting of a township of 23,040 acres, upon which was founded the town of Montpelier, but he never went to live upon the grant. Through the machinations of false friends, who owed much to his patriotism of former days, he found himself tangled in debt, unable to extricate himself or to satisfy their Shylock demands; and to their shame and disgrace he was thrown into jail, where, overwhelmed by adverse circumstances, he died, March 31, 1790. His widow d. at Groton, Mass., July 9, 1809."[1]

On April 19, 1861, the eighty-sixth anniversary of the battle of Lexington, and also memorable for the attack on the Sixth Massachusetts Regiment in the streets of Baltimore, the so-called "Bigelow Monument" was dedicated at Worcester, Mass. It was erected in memory of the Revolutionary services of the distinguished patriot, Colonel Timothy Bigelow, by his great-grandson, Colonel Timothy Bigelow Lawrence.

FAMILY NO. 3

4. **William,** m. May 20, 1813, Susan Ruggles Bordman, only child of William and Elizabeth (Davis) Bordman of Boston. She was b. April 29, 1787; d. at Boston, Aug. 7, 1858.

[1] *The Bigelow Family*, by Gilman Bigelow Howe, p. 76.

Their children :

16. I. **William Bordman**, b. Feb. 18, 1814; d. Sept. 7, 1840. He entered Groton Academy in 1822, and later attended Chauncy Hall School.

17. II. **Samuel Abbott**, b. at Boston, July 28, 1815; m., Nov. 24, 1845, Sallie Cresson Bunker, daughter of Nathan Bunker, Esq., of Philadelphia. She was b. Feb. 12, 1823; d. at Newport, R. I., Jan. 29, 1886.

Samuel Abbott Lawrence received early instruction at Groton Academy and Chauncy Hall School in Boston. In his youth he was much interested in military affairs, and held commissions in the militia. In 1837 he engaged in business with the firm of Macgregor, Tucker & Lawrence, afterwards Tucker, Lawrence & Co., in Boston. After a ten years' residence abroad, he made his home at Newport, R. I., in 1858, and was active in the promotion of the interests of musical science in that city. His death occurred there, Sept. 8, 1863. The following obituary notice, prepared by Henry Austin Whitney, appeared in the " Boston Daily Advertiser," Sept. 9, 1863:

" We regret to learn of the death of Samuel Abbott Lawrence, which occurred at Newport, Rhode Island, yesterday morning. He married in Philadelphia, Sallie Bunker, a sister of the late Mrs. Dahlgren, whose surviving husband is now in command of our fleet before Charleston. A few weeks ago Mr. Lawrence visited Washington to care for the welfare of Captain Ulric Dahlgren, whose serious wounds and gallantry have been the subject of much general remark. While in Washington, during the extreme heat of

summer, his exertions brought on an attack of faint-
ing, to which he was subject, and since his return
to his own house, bringing with him the young hero,
he has been gradually failing. . . . Of late years he
had devoted himself to the interests of his adopted
home, and has taken an earnest interest in the Episcopal Church, of which he was a member. He was
in the forty-ninth year of his age."

At a regular meeting of the Union League of
Newport, R. I., holden Monday evening, Sept. 14,
1863, the following preamble and resolutions were
unanimously adopted:

"Whereas, by the death of Samuel Abbott Lawrence, Esq., of this city, this organization has sustained a loss in its loyal ranks, of which it seems
most proper and becoming that we should publicly
express our appreciation, Therefore, Resolved, That
we hold in highest honor and respect the memory of
one to whose many estimable qualities, to whose private worth, to whose gifts of fortune, wealth, and
social station was superadded the crowning virtue (in
these times of national jeopardy) of a steadfast faith
in the triumph of the principles of the national unity,
republican integrity, and universal liberty; and who
was ever ready to employ his influence and his wealth
in the furtherance of his conviction; whose loyalty
to his country, its government, and its institutions
was worthy of Bayard's motto (being "without fear
and without reproach"), unblemished by a selfish
motive, and evincing a generous singleness of purpose, and a fixed devotion to a principle in every
word and act, worthy of all emulation."

18. III. **Lydia Elizabeth,** b. June 15, 1818; d. June 29, 1818.

19. IV. **Sarah,** b. Aug. 20, 1819; d. Aug. 24, 1819.

20. V. **George Henry,** b. Jan. 9, 1821; d. Jan. 5, 1823.

21. VI. **Susan Elizabeth,** b. Oct. 5, 1822. Family No. 11. Boston.

22. VII. **Mary Bordman,** b. Feb. 21, 1824; d. Aug. 24, 1824.

23. VIII. **Harriet Bordman,** b. Jan. 8, 1826. Family No. 12. Boston.

24. IX. **Fanny** (christened Mary Francis), b. Aug. 19, 1828. Family No. 13. Boston.

Mrs. Susan Ruggles Bordman Lawrence died Aug. 7, 1858.

William Lawrence was born at Groton, Sept. 7, 1783, and there passed his boyhood and youth, receiving his education at Groton Academy, which he entered in 1794. As a young man he devoted himself to agricultural pursuits, having the management of his father's farm. His health becoming impaired by overwork, he gave up this care, and passed the winter of 1809–10 in Boston with his brother Amos, establishing himself in business the following spring in a small store near that of his brother. Mr. Lawrence's name first appears in the Boston Directory for 1810, as a shopkeeper at No. 32 Cornhill. In 1820 he was in the dry goods business at No. 7 Market Street. His mercantile career, thus simply begun, was eminently successful. In 1822 he formed a partnership with his brother Samuel, under the firm name of W. & S. Lawrence, and soon became actively interested in manufacturing enterprises at Lowell, Mass.

In 1826 the style of the firm was changed to W. & S. Lawrence & Stone, and Mr. William W. Stone was admitted as a partner, their place of business being at 85 State Street. Mr. Lawrence retired in 1842, having then acquired a considerable fortune. He was an original director of the Suffolk Bank, which was chartered Feb. 10, 1818, and, together with his brothers Luther, Amos, and Abbott, was a subscriber to its capital stock. His name is identified with the introduction of the " Suffolk Bank System," a chief feature whereof was the redemption of banknotes issued by institutions outside of Boston, a system " which has made New England banking famous for all time."

William Lawrence served nine years as a representative from Boston to the Massachusetts General Court, from 1829 to 1833 inclusive, 1835–36, and 1840–41. He was elected a director of the Western Rail-Road Corporation at the time of its organization, Jan. 4, 1836.

During the earlier years of his married life he lived in a house on Southac Court, now Howard Street, but about the year 1822 he removed his residence to No. 3 Bulfinch Street, where he remained for twenty-five years, until 1847 or thereabouts, when he occupied a house on Tremont Street adjoining that of his brother Amos on Colonnade Row, which was afterwards called by the residents Fayette Place, in honor of the visit of General Lafayette in 1824. The latter name failed, however, to receive official sanction. Mr. Lawrence made liberal donations to Groton Academy, whereby it was placed upon a permanent foundation, and its sphere of influence greatly enlarged. He also made generous bequests to the institution in his will.

At a special meeting of the trustees of Groton Academy, held April 17, 1844, the following resolution was unanimously adopted:

"Whereas William Lawrence, Esq., of Boston, by a donation of ten thousand dollars to this Academy, has laid us, and the community in which we live, under deep and lasting obligations to him; and whereas the responsibility of this Board is greatly increased by this munificent act, therefore — Resolved, that the thanks of this Board be presented to Mr. Lawrence for this noble charity, and for the truly liberal conditions on which he has presented it to this institution, and that we pledge ourselves to him and the public, that we will use our best endeavors to appropriate the income of this fund in such manner as to secure the object of the donor in the cause of education."

At the same meeting, the trustees appointed a committee to petition the General Court to change the name of the corporation to " the Lawrence Academy at Groton," and this petition was granted at the next session of the legislature. Mr. Lawrence died at Boston, Oct. 14, 1848.

THE BORDMAN FAMILY [1]

William Bordman, the emigrant, b. about 1614, came to this country in 1638, with his mother and her husband, Stephen Daye, his stepfather. He was a tailor, and served as steward and cook of Harvard College. He resigned the former position in 1668, but retained the latter until his death, March 25, 1685. Lieutenant Aaron Bordman, a son of the emigrant, b. in 1649, was steward of the College from 1687 to 1703, succeeding his brother Andrew, who served in a like capacity from 1682 to 1687. He was a locksmith and m. Mary —— about 1673. He d. Jan. 15, 1702–3. Andrew Bordman, a son of Lieutenant Aaron, b. at Cambridge about 1692, m. Sarah Goddard at Roxbury, Oct. 20, 1715. He was a shopkeeper and dealt in various kinds of cloths, handkerchiefs, gloves, pins, and other articles of haberdashery. He d. at Boston, May 31, 1751. (Granary Epitaph.)

William Bordman, a son of Andrew and Sarah (Goddard) Bordman, was b. at Roxbury, Nov. 6, 1724. He m., Nov. 9, 1749, Susanna, daughter of Captain Thomas Stoddard. Mr. Bordman was a deacon of the Second Church in Boston, and his house was on Ann Street. He d. Feb. 9 (?), 1806. The "Massachusetts Centinel" announced that his funeral would be on Feb. 12, "if weather fair; if not, the first fair day." William Bordman, the fifth child of William,

---

[1] The early American lineage of the Bordmans, hitherto obscure, has been satisfactorily determined by the researches of Mr. Joseph Cutler Whitney, who has furnished the information here given, regarding the first three generations of the family.

senior, was born at Boston, May 1, 1760. He m., June 2, 1785, (1) Elizabeth, daughter of Hon. Caleb and Hannah (Ruggles) Davis, and their only child was Susan Ruggles Bordman (b. at Boston, April 29, 1787), who m., May 20, 1813, William Lawrence (Family No. 3). Mrs. Elizabeth Bordman d. Dec. 14, 1790, and her husband was afterwards twice married. Mr. Bordman was a highly respected merchant of Boston. He d. May 1, 1842.

The Hon. Caleb Davis, a son of Joshua and Sarah (Pierpont) Davis, was b. at Woodstock, Conn., Oct. 25, 1738. He was a prominent attorney in Boston and an active promoter of the rights of the people. He was a member of the order of the " Sons of Liberty," and was one of those who dined at the Liberty Tree, in Dorchester, Aug. 14, 1769. Mr. Davis was a member of the first General Court under the Constitution, in 1780, and was elected speaker of the same. He was also a member of the committee from Boston under the Confiscation Act of 1779, and of the Constitutional Convention of 1788. He was a brother of General Amasa Davis and of Major Robert Davis. Hon. Caleb Davis d. at Boston, July 6, 1797. The following brief obituary notice appeared in the " Independent Chronicle " and " Columbian Centinel ": " It may be said with strict truth that he was a good man, exemplified the Christian character in the numerous stations which he sustained, served his generation according to the will of God, and rests from his labors."

Samuel Ruggles (whose daughter Hannah married Mr. Davis, Sept. 30, 1760) was b. on Christmas

Day, 1706, and was descended from George Ruggles, the emigrant, through his son Samuel and wife Sarah, grandson John and wife Tabitha. He was a master-builder and the constructor of Faneuil Hall in 1742. His wife's name was Hannah Lowden.

FAMILY NO. 4

5. **Amos,** m. (first), June 6, 1811, at Boston, Sarah, the eldest of ten children of Giles and Sarah (Adams) Richards of Dedham. She was b. at Boston, July 25, 1790, and her mother was a daughter of Rev. Amos Adams of Roxbury.

Their children, born at Boston, were as follows:

25. I. **William Richards,** b. May 3, 1812. Family No. 14. Boston and Brookline.

26. II. **Amos Adams,** b. July 31, 1814. Family No. 15. Boston and Brookline.

27. III. **Susanna,** b. May 23, 1817. Family No. 16. Salem and Boston.

Mrs. Sarah Richards Lawrence d. at Boston, Jan. 14, 1819, aged 28.

Amos Lawrence, m. (second), April 16, 1821, at Amherst, N. H., Nancy (Means) Ellis, daughter of Robert and Mary (McGregor) Means, and widow of Hon. Caleb Ellis, Associate Justice of the Supreme Court of New Hampshire (d. May 9, 1816). She d. at Boston, Nov. 27, 1866. They had:

28. IV. **Mary Means,** b. April 15, 1823; d. at Boston, Dec. 8, 1828.

29. V. **Robert Means,** b. Sept. 17, 1826; d. at Boston, Nov. 1, 1845.

He entered the Boston Latin School in 1837. A member of the Class of 1847, of Harvard College, and a youth of much promise. According to the college records, he was admitted Aug. 25, 1843, and "offered" by Robert Harlow. At a Class meeting held Nov. 3, 1845, it was "Resolved, that the memory of our classmate Lawrence shall ever be sacred and dear to us; that we never can forget the virtues which he displayed, the social qualities which endeared him to us, and to all with whom he was acquainted; and that kindness to all around him, and constant regard for the feelings of others, which ever distinguished him."

Amos Lawrence, the fourth son of Major Samuel and Susanna (Parker) Lawrence, was born at Groton, Mass., April 22, 1786. He received elementary training in the district schools of his native town, and was for a short time a student at Groton Academy. Not having a robust physique, he did not work on the farm, but in the autumn of 1799, when thirteen years of age, he took a position as clerk in a country store in the town of Dunstable. Here he remained for a few months only, and then began an apprenticeship of seven years in the large variety store of James Brazer in Groton. By faithfulness in the discharge of his multifarious duties, and by the scrupulous honesty and exactness of his business methods, he rapidly acquired the confidence of his employer and established a reputation for integrity and fair dealing. Hence, naturally, greater responsibilities devolved upon him, and he soon became the virtual manager of the store, while yet of an age when most boys of to-day devote their leisure time to out-door sports. It was at this period that the youthful clerk gave evidence of that decision of character which thereafter was so marked a trait with him. At the age of fourteen, he became a total abstainer from stimulating beverages, although it was one of his duties to prepare daily gallons of rum, duly spiced and sweetened, which was partaken of freely by clerks and customers alike as a matter of course, according to the usage of those times.

Soon after attaining his majority, in the month of April, 1807, Amos Lawrence went to Boston on a prospecting business trip. His worldly property consisted of twenty dollars, and of this amount he gave two dollars to a neighbor for driving him to town. After serving as clerk for a few months in a respectable mercantile house, he began business for himself in a modest way, Dec. 17, 1807, in a small dry goods store at No. 31 Cornhill (now Washington Street) "on the corner which makes the turn into Dock Square," shortly afterwards removing to No. 46, on the opposite side of the street. The follow-ing year he was joined by his brother Abbott, who became his apprentice, and in Oct., 1809, his elder brother William, whose health had become impaired by overwork on the farm, also came to Boston and assisted Amos for a few months, later taking a small store near by. Mr. Lawrence married, at Boston, June 6, 1811, Sarah, the eldest of ten children of Giles and Sarah (Adams) Richards of Boston, afterwards of Dedham, Mass.

After Abbott Lawrence came of age, the two brothers formed a partnership, Jan. 1, 1814, under the firm name of A. & A. Lawrence. They occupied a store at No. 15 Market Street (the Cornhill of to-day), "on the north side, near the alley leading down the steps to Brattle Street Church." Afterwards they removed to No. 11 Liberty Square, and still later to "Lawrence Block," Milk Street. The business of the firm of A. & A. Lawrence rapidly developed, until it became second in importance to no other mercantile house in New England. Mrs. Sarah (Richards) Lawrence d. at Boston, Jan. 14, 1819, and Mr. Lawrence m. at Amherst, N. H., April 16, 1821, Mrs. Nancy (Means) Ellis. The same year he served as a member of the Massachusetts House of Representatives.

During the ten years ensuing, Mr. Lawrence was engrossed in the cares of business, his firm having become largely interested in domestic manufactures, and especially in the cotton mills of Lowell and Lawrence. He found time, however, for other matters, and was especially active as a member of the building committee of the Board of Directors of the Bunker Hill Monument Association. He would have been glad to have had the whole battlefield preserved for posterity as a "legacy of patriotism," and he himself contributed largely to the building fund. The completion of the monument in 1843 was therefore to him a source of unmixed gratification. On the first day of June, 1831, Mr. Lawrence was seized with an acute gastric affection, apparently caused by drinking cold water, the weather at the time being very warm. Thenceforth he was obliged to retire from active business, and to adopt the life of an invalid. For many years he did not take a meal with his family, and his food, which was extremely simple, was regularly weighed on scales which always stood upon his desk.

His life was now more than ever devoted to charities and philanthropic objects. It was his great pleasure to be his own almoner, and besides this, in his daily drives he carried along a supply of books and tracts which he dispensed to passers-by. Among the educational institutions liberally aided by Mr. Lawrence were Williams College (whose library was called " Lawrence Hall " in his honor), Wabash and Kenyon colleges, the academy at Groton, and Bangor Theological School. During the early days of his married life his home was on Sudbury Street, but about the year 1820 he removed his residence to Colonnade Row, his house being on the corner of Tremont and West streets, with a garden extending back to Mason Street. His brother William occupied the adjoining house. Amos Lawrence died at Boston, Dec. 31, 1852.

THE RICHARDS FAMILY

Giles Richards, who was born at Waterbury, Conn., Feb. 17, 1754, was the second son of Abijah (1718–1773) and Hulda (Hopkins) Richards of Waterbury; grandson of Thomas (1685–1726) and Hannah (Upson) Richards; great-grandson of Thomas Richards (b. about 1600; d. before 1639), an original settler of Hartford, Conn. Giles Richards married at Pepperell, Oct. 6, 1789, Sarah, daughter of Rev. Amos and Elizabeth (Prentiss) Adams of Roxbury, and took up his residence in Cambridge, removing to Boston in 1801.[1] He was a man of enterprise and superior mechanical skill, and was highly respected in the community. In 1788 he formed a partnership with his brother Mark and Amos Whittemore, for the manufacture of cotton and wool cards by newly invented machinery. Their factory was situated on the north side of Hanover Street, Boston, close to the Mill-Bridge, so called, and about midway between the present Union and Cross streets. The lot extended back to Link Alley. (See Drake's "Old Landmarks of Boston," pp. 151–153.) The establishment of Giles Richards & Co. furnished employment at one time to more than a thousand persons, and was regarded with pride by the people of Boston, as one of their chief industrial enterprises. "The necessity of obtaining improved machinery for use in the manufacture of woollens, led to measures on the part of the legislatures of several States in favor of the makers of this sort of machinery. By the year 1789 there were three quite extensive manufactories of cotton and wool cards in the town, making sixty-three thousand pairs of cards per year, and underselling those of foreign manufacture. Concerning one of these General Washington says (in his Diary, Mount Vernon Papers, No. 12), referring to his visit to Boston in the year above mentioned: 'I went to

[1] At a meeting of the selectmen of Boston, Aug. 16, 1786, "Gyles Richards, near Mill-Bridge, was approbated for a License as a Retailer."

a card manufactory where, I was informed, there were about nine hundred hands. . . . All kinds of cards were made, and there are machines for executing every part of the work in a new and expeditious manner, especially in cutting and bending the teeth, which is done at one stroke.' "[1]

Mr. Richards was a member of the first Board of Trustees of the Massachusetts Charitable Mechanic Association (founded in 1795), of which organization Paul Revere was the first president. He retired from business in 1816 and removed his residence to Dedham, where he occupied a house in the Upper Village, facing the southwesterly corner of the Common, on the high road formerly known as the Hartford Turnpike. This house was built in 1768 by Josiah Fisher, and was bought by Amos Lawrence in Nov., 1816, for the occupancy of his father-in-law, Giles Richards, by whom it was enlarged. Mr. Lawrence sold the estate, March 1, 1830, to John Ellis, and the latter conveyed it to John Baker, 2d, the sheriff of Norfolk County, whose daughter was living in the house in 1902. Mr. Richards was admitted a member of the First Church in Dedham, April 16, 1820, and died at Dedham, June 3, 1829, at the age of 75. His widow, Mrs. Sarah (Adams) Richards, went to Ohio to live with her sons, who had settled there. After several years, her health failing, she returned to Massachusetts, and on the invitation of the Misses Porter, nieces of Rev. Eliphalet Porter, her father's successor as minister of the First Parish in

[1] *The Memorial History of Boston*, edited by Justin Winsor, 1881, vol. iv. p. 78.

Roxbury, she made her home with them in the old parsonage which was her birthplace, and there she remained until her death, April 12, 1836. Sarah, the eldest child of Giles Richards, b. at Boston, July 25, 1790, became the wife of Amos Lawrence, June 6, 1811.

George Thomas Richards (eighth child of Giles and younger brother of Sarah Richards Lawrence), b. at New York, April 28, 1806, went abroad as a young man in 1828, and took up his residence in Paris, France. After a number of years' experience in financial affairs, he there began a banking business on his own account, April 1, 1843, and became a partner in the firm of John Munroe & Co., May 1, 1846. Mr. George Lawrence Richards writes from Washington, D. C., under date of April 12, 1903, as follows: "Where my father obtained his schooling is a point on which I am ignorant. His studies were probably not carried very far, for he became clerk in a country grocery store at an early age. But he read much, and was a very well-informed man, not only on current questions, but on general history and literature. His technical knowledge could not have been extended, but that he took an interest in the arts and sciences was evinced by a visit which he made with me to the Paris Exposition of 1867, where we strolled through the galleries devoted to the exhibit of machinery. The machines, their details, devices, and mode of working seemed to interest him much. . . . My father witnessed the fall of Charles X. as a result of the famous '*trois journées*' of July, 1830. My impression is that your father and my cousin

Amos, then students at Versailles, were with him on that occasion. I have a recollection of your father [William Richards Lawrence] recounting to me his experiences at that time, and telling of his having witnessed the Royal Guard fire on the mob, as it advanced on the Tuileries. . . . My father also saw the Revolution of 1848, and the fall of Louis Philippe."

George Thomas Richards m. at Boston, Oct. 17, 1853, Lucy Ellen Kelleran.

Their children:

1. George Lawrence, b. Sept. 16, 1854. He is a civil engineer by profession, and resides at Washington, D. C.

2. Anna, b. Nov. 15, 1855; d. in infancy.

3. Marian, b. April 19, 1857; resides in Paris.

4. Arthur Waldo, d. in infancy.

5. William Stell, b. July 23, 1860; d. Aug. 15, 1887.

6. Elise, b. July 26, 1862. She m. at Paris, Oct. 15, 1895, M. Jean Jules Jusserand, who in 1902 was appointed Ambassador of France to the United States.

Mrs. Richards has continued to reside in Paris since her marriage. Her husband d. May 8, 1871.

Hon. Edward Kelleran, great-grandfather of Mrs. George Thomas Richards, b. in 1751, was a resident of Thomaston, Me. His home in that town was situated on the shore of St. George's River (a deep, narrow inlet of the sea), and was there to be seen as late as 1884. He was at one time a sea-captain, and represented the town of Cushing in the Maine legislature. He d. May 23, 1828.

Captain Edward Kelleran, the second of eleven children of Hon. Edward, was born about the year 1777. He settled in Portland, and married Lucy, daughter of Colonel John and Rachel (Thorn) Reed of Bath, Me. During the war of 1812 he commanded the brig *Dash*, which was the most efficient and successful of the private armed fleet owned in Portland.

Captain Kelleran was an interesting character, a fine type of the American merchantman "skipper" in the palmy days of our merchant marine. After the war he became a large landowner, and acquired what was considered a handsome fortune at that time. " Those who recollect the presidential campaign of 1840, will recall Captain Kelleran's jolly face and figure, which would rival Hackett's personification of Falstaff. He was then well along in years, and an enthusiastic Harrison man." [1]

Captain Kelleran was extravagantly fond of reading history and of memorizing poetry, and could repeat at length from the writings of Burns, Scott, and Byron.

He had six daughters, five of whom lived to mature age and were married. They were all handsome and gifted by nature, and were known in Portland as the " Graces," although they exceeded in number their prototypes of classical mythology. Of these daughters, the eldest, Eliza, born at Portland in 1800, was the mother of Mrs. George Thomas Richards of Paris, France.[2]

[1] See *Portland in the Past*, by William Goold, 1886, pp. 450–455.
[2] Eliza Kelleran became the wife of Luther Richardson, a young

Of the ten children of Giles Richards, three sons, Giles, Jr., Amos Adams, and Charles, removed to Ohio, and became permanent residents of that State. The youngest child, Mary Elizabeth, m., about 1835, John Richardson Adan, a lawyer of Boston (H. U. 1813; adm. Suffolk bar, 1816; d. 1849). She d. Jan. 15, 1845.

A daughter of Charles, Mrs. Mary Garrison, resides with one of her married children at Buffalo, N. Y., and her daughter Charlotte is living in 1903 at Dedham, Mass.

From the Massachusetts Centinel, Oct., 1789

" Married at Pepperell, [Oct. 6,] Mr. Giles Richards of Boston, to the amiable Miss Sally Adams, youngest daughter of the late Rev. Mr. Adams of Roxbury."

Extracts from a letter written by Amos Adams Richards to his brother, Giles Richards:

CHICAGO, Feb. 21, 1870.

DR. BRO. GILES, — My earliest dream of life was in Charlestown, in the Kimball house in 1798, where our first sister Mary was born, our sister Sarah then being about eight years of age ; in 1799 we lived in the Foxcroft house in Cambridge, where our sister Mary died, July 26, and in the same year our grandmother Adams, whose maiden name was Chauncy, — the same year General Washington died, — the death of both I distinctly remember. The next year we

lawyer of Portland. The marriage was not a happy one. They soon separated, and she resumed her maiden name.

lived in the Holmes house, owned by Rev. Abiel
Holmes, who was an inmate of our family, and a
great favorite with us children, Sarah then being
ten, you eight, and myself six years of age. One day
he invited us into his study, and placed Sarah on a
stool, which I suppose he had selected for declama-
tion, when she recited Pope's " Messiah " in a very
approving manner ; our attempt, I think, was not so
happy, but sufficiently so to elicit from him a book
each, mine being " The Life of Sir Charles Grandi-
son." I think the above Rev. A. Holmes was father of
the renowned O. W. Holmes. While we lived in Cambridge, our sister spent much of her time with Mrs.
Caleb Gannett, who had two daughters, Catherine
and Eliza, and two sons, Thomas and Ezra Stiles,
now I think in Boston. Mrs. Gannett, I think, was
sister to President Stiles of Yale College, after whom
her son was named. President Willard was the
President of Harvard College. The next year we
moved to the Cunningham house, —— Street, near
Dr. Lathrop's meeting-house, Boston. The next
move was to Eliot Street, at the South End, near
West Street. Here Charles was born, July 3, 1802,
when we moved to Groton, and lived in the family
of Rev. Daniel Chaplin, and we children attended
Groton Academy, Mr. Butler, principal. We (you
and I) for some reason boarded with a Mr. Tarbell,
who lived about midway between Mr. Chaplin's and
the academy. Mr. Tarbell had a son Thomas and a
daughter Martha. The next house was that of Hon.
Timothy Bigelow, who had two sons, Andrew and
John, and a daughter Catherine, whom I well remem-

ber as honoring me, speaking dialogues in the academy hall, and, I think, once at an exhibition in the meeting-house. I have not seen her since. At this place and time our sister Sarah being twelve years of age, she was a great favorite with us all, though her general deportment was considered rather pensive and demure; but the more attractive and engaging from a graceful dignity of manners. . . . I was with her much of the time in 1812–13, and the Lawrence family, from the good deacon to the youngest, were much endeared to me by the kind and affectionate regard they always expressed. . . . It was in August or September, 1802, I first saw Mr. Amos Lawrence in Groton in company with a young man by the name of Jonas Brown, then both apprentices to Mr. James Brazer. They, and a few other young gentlemen, one of whom was a young Rufus Langly, were very kind and attentive, and the latter was very marked in his attentions to our sister, whose extreme coyness was quite a foil to his ardency to become better acquainted. . . . About 1812 we (you and I), moved to Rhode Island and established ourselves there during the war, when our father, in Boston, and a Mr. More, were engaged in making cabinet mountings, etc.; commodes of lion-head patterns, etc.

Affec. yours,

A. A. RICHARDS.

REV. AMOS ADAMS

The Rev. Amos Adams, whose daughter Sarah married Giles Richards, was the eldest of eleven children of Henry and Jemima (Morse) Adams, and was born at Medfield, Mass., Sept. 1, 1728. His great-grandfather, Henry Adams, born in England in 1604, came to this country with his eight sons, and settled at Medfield, where he served as the first town clerk, chief military officer, selectman, and representative to the General Court. He was slain by the Indians at his own doorway during King Philip's war, Feb. 21, 1676. His wife, Elizabeth (Paine) Adams, who had taken refuge in the minister's house at Medfield, was mortally wounded a few hours after, by the accidental discharge of a gun in the hands of a soldier.

Rev. Amos Adams was a graduate of Harvard in 1752, and was ordained minister of the First Church in Roxbury, Sept. 12, 1753. He m. (first), Oct. 18, 1753, Elizabeth Prentiss (b. Oct. 17, 1727), fifth child of Deacon Henry and Elizabeth (Rand) Prentiss of Cambridge, Mass. Sarah, the youngest of their eight children (b. at Roxbury, March 26, 1769), m. Giles Richards. Mrs. Elizabeth (Prentiss) Adams d. Aug. 10, 1769. Mr. Adams m. (second), Feb. 15, 1770, Mrs. Abigail Mears. She d. and he m. (third), July 16, 1771, Sarah, the third and youngest child of Rev. Charles Chauncy, D. D. (1705–1787), pastor of the First Church in Boston, and a descendant and namesake of the second president of Harvard College, and Elizabeth (Hirst) Chauncy. They had no children. Mrs. Sarah (Chauncy) Adams d. at Cambridge in July, 1799.

Mr. Adams is described as " an energetic preacher, having an extremely sonorous and plaintive voice, and notwithstanding the length of his sermons and his plainness of speech, he was popular in the pulpit, and had great influence over the people. He was an ardent patriot, and secretary of the convention of ministers at Watertown which recommended to the people to take up arms." He was chaplain of Colonel David Brewer's Ninth Continental Regiment. His death occurred Oct. 5, 1775, and was due to a fever, occasioned by over-exertion and exposure during the performance of his official duties.

An obituary notice of Rev. Amos Adams, which appeared in the " Boston Gazette," reads as follows : " He spent his time and strength with pleasure, in the service of a grateful people, till by the distress of the times they were dispersed, and he himself was obliged to leave his habitation and pulpit ; from which time his labors were increased, but through an affection for the people of his charge, he performed them with cheerfulness, attending the small remainder of his flock every Sunday, though his family was removed to a distance, among his friends."

The old parsonage occupied by Mr. Adams at Roxbury is still standing, on the north side of Eliot Square, fronting the church. It is placed well back from the street, and is shaded by some fine old trees. The house was built by Rev. Oliver Peabody, who died in 1752.

At the beginning of the siege of Boston, in 1775, the right wing of the American army was at Roxbury, with its main post on Meeting-House Hill, while the commander, General John Thomas, made the parsonage his headquarters. For this purpose it was admirably adapted, as its rear windows commanded a view of the British works on the Neck, and of the heights of Charlestown. From these windows General Thomas and his officers witnessed the battle of Bunker Hill.[1] Of late years the house has been the residence of Charles K. Dillaway, Esq. It is earnestly hoped that this historic mansion may long be preserved as a memorial of Revolutionary days.

From the Boston Gazette, Oct. 16, 1775

" Died, last Thursday night, after a short illness, in Dorchester; Rev. Amos Adams, pastor of the 1st Church of Christ in Roxbury; aged 48, and in the 23d of his Ministry. His family, as well as his church and people, now driven into various parts of the country, refuse to be comforted."

From the Columbian Centinel, July 10, 1799

" On Monday last was entombed the remains of that truly pious and amiable lady, Miss [Mrs.] Sarah Adams, relict of the late Rev. Mr. Adams of Roxbury, and daughter of that great Divine, the late Rev. Dr. Chauncy."

From the same, July 6, 1799

" Died, July, 1799, Mrs. Sarah (Chauncy) Adams, relict of the late Rev. Mr. Adams of Roxbury. Funeral from the house of Giles Richards, at Cambridge."

FAMILY NO. 5

7. **Mary**, m., July 28, 1818, Rev. Samuel Woodbury (b. at Salem, N. H., Dec. 21, 1784; A. B., Dart-

---

[1] Francis S. Drake, *The Town of Roxbury*, 1878, p. 310.

mouth College, 1811; ordained pastor of the Congregational Church, North Yarmouth, Me., Nov. 5, 1817; d. at Groton, July 6, 1819).

They had one daughter,

30. **Sarah Lawrence,** b. Sept. 20, 1819, who m., March 10, 1841, at the Lawrence Mansion, Farmer's Row, in Groton, Rev. David Fosdick, Jr., and had the following:

31. I. **Samuel Woodbury,** b. at Sterling, Mass., Dec. 10, 1841; m., Feb. 8, 1865, at Groton, Christina Dakin Caryl, daughter of Alexander Hamilton and Elizabeth (Kip) Caryl. She was born at Buffalo, N. Y., July 22, 1840; and was postmistress at Groton from July 2, 1880. She d. at Groton, Aug. 21, 1902.

Samuel Woodbury Fosdick received early instruction from his father, and did not attend any school or college. His brother Charles wrote as follows regarding him: " My brother Samuel had an exceedingly bright mind in the line of mathematics and was also a good linguist. He could read easily and could talk fairly in the French, Spanish, Italian, and German tongues, and he had an excellent knowledge of Greek, Hebrew, and Latin. In mechanics he would have made, I think, a leading mind in invention, but his early death by typhoid fever cut this short. He had a remarkable memory, and had memorized almost the entire contents of one or more of the mechanical handbooks that were then in existence, could repeat whole tables of logarithms and other dry figures, in fact had a fondness for memorizing that sort of thing which might be useful to him in his chosen line. Minds like his were less common in those days than nowadays, when there are so many technical schools, where the information which he picked out and assimilated by himself, is taught so readily to the students of to-day." He was a one third owner of the J. B. Parker Machine Company of Clinton, Mass. His death occurred in that town, April 3, 1865.

32. II. **Mary,** b. at Sterling, Feb. 19, 1844; resides at Groton, where she has of late been engaged in literary work.

33. III. **George,** b. at Sterling, Jan. 14, 1845; d. at Groton, Oct. 4, 1848.

34. IV. **Charles,** b. at Groton, March 9, 1848; m., at Fitchburg, Mass., Oct. 1, 1874, Mary Louise Snow, daughter of William and Adaline (Willis) Snow.

They have these, born at Fitchburg:

35. 1. **Margaret Willis,** b. Aug. 1, 1875.

36. 2. **Charles Mussey,** b. Nov. 15, 1877; graduate of the Fitchburg High School and of the Massachusetts Institute of Technology; assistant instructor in the latter.

37. 3. **Elsie Woodbury,** b. Aug. 26, 1882.

38. 4. **Marion Lawrence,** b. July 31, 1888.

Charles Fosdick was born in the Lawrence Mansion at Groton, now the residence of James Lawrence, Esq. This was also the birthplace of his mother, and of his grandmother, Mary (Lawrence) Woodbury. He spent his boyhood and early youth in Groton, and was taught by his father at home. In early manhood he went to Fitchburg, and became superintendent of the Fitchburg Steam Engine Company, a position which he has held for thirty years. He has been president of the Common Council and of the Merchants' Association of that city, and a trustee of the Fitchburg Savings Bank. He has been much interested in the Fosdick genealogy, and has traced his descent, in the ninth generation, from Stephen Fosdick, who settled in Charlestown, Mass.; also from Elder William Brewster of the Mayflower, Rev. Samuel Skelton of Salem, and from John Lawrence of Watertown and Groton.

39. V. **Frederick**, b. at Groton, April 24, 1850; m., at Groton, April 24, 1873, Lucy Maria, daughter of Henry and Abigail (Coffin) Hill of Groton.

They have these, born in Fitchburg:

40. 1. **Frederick Woodbury**, b. April 28, 1875. He received his education in the Fitchburg schools, Amherst College, and Harvard Law School. Practises law at 28 State Street, Boston.

41. 2. **Nellie**, b. Nov. 5, 1878.

42. 3. **Richard Coffin**, b. April 20, 1883.

43. 4. **Miriam Eddy**, b. Dec. 26, 1890.

Frederick Fosdick was instructed by his father at home in Groton. He is by election an honorary alumnus of Middlebury College, Vermont. Coming to Fitchburg in 1870, he was for a year in the office of the Burleigh Drill Company, and was afterwards draughtsman for the Haskins Machine Company. When the Fitchburg Steam Engine Company was formed he was appointed treasurer and general manager, and is now its president. He served on the School Committee of Fitchburg for ten years, was president of the Common Council for two years, and mayor of the city in 1887–88. He has held other official positions, as follows: trustee of the Fitchburg Savings Bank, a deacon of the Congregational Church, and president of the Young Men's Christian Association in Fitchburg. Member of the Pan-American Commission for Massachusetts. He has made occasional contributions to mechanical and engineering journals.

44. VI. **David**, b. Dec. 14, 1852; d. at Groton, Dec. 21, 1854.

45. VII. **Rose**, b. July 24, 1855; d. July 15, 1870, at Groton.

46. VIII. **Lucy**, b. at Groton, Nov. 21, 1858; m., at Longwood, June 1, 1889, Charles Sedgwick Minot of Boston.

Charles Sedgwick Minot, son of William and Katharine (Sedgwick) Minot, was born at West Roxbury, Mass., Dec. 23, 1852. He graduated in the chemical course at the Massachusetts Institute of Technology in 1872, and then made special studies in biology at Leipzig, Paris, and Würzburg, receiving the degree of S. D. from Harvard in 1878, and LL. D. from Yale in 1898. He is president of the American Association for the Advancement of Science, and a corresponding member of the British society of like name. He is also president of the Boston Society of Natural History, a member of the National Academy of Science, of the American Academy of Arts and Sciences, and of the American Philosophical Society. He is professor of Histology and Human Embryology in Harvard Medical College. Author of "A Bibliography of Vertebrate Embryology" (Bos. Soc. of Nat. Hist. Memoirs, vol. iv. Boston, 1886–1893); "Human Embryology," New York, Wood & Co., 1892, Macmillan, 1897.

47. IX. **Sarah Woodbury**, b. at Groton, Nov. 4, 1860. Residence at Ware, Mass.

THE FOSDICK FAMILY

David Fosdick, Jr., was a descendant in the eighth generation from Stephen Fosdick, the first settler of the name in this country. He came from the east coast of England, near the estuary known as "the Wash," to the north of London, where he was born in 1583. Arriving in this country about the year 1635, he settled in Charlestown, Mass.; and was admitted a member of the church there in 1638. He had eight children and was apparently a man of prominence in the town. Stephen Fosdick died in 1664. By his will, which is remarkable for its quaint wording, he left his wife " 3 pounds every year, 6 cords of wood yearly, and cow and cow common to keep the cow on," which cow, it was directed, should " be divided after his widow's decease, with the movables." He also gave to his grandson Samuel real estate, " to him and his heirs male or female, and so to run in the generations of the Fosdicks forever; " but so far as known this real estate did not run far in the line. To another grandson he gave " half a cow and hay lot, house and land in Malden and a wood lot." His estate inventory was £500, which made him a rich man for those days. His seventh son, John, was born in 1626 and died at the age of 90 in 1716. His gravestone can still be seen in the old burying-ground at Charlestown. He was twice married and had ten children. His will left "12½ acres in Malden between Fosdick's Gate and Charlestown below land," also "eleven acres and 100 poles at the head of Fosdick's plain," "1¼ acres in the first Division Stinted Pasture in Charlestown, and 7 acres wood lots in Charlestown on Mistic side," beside much other real estate. His son Samuel Fosdick, born Dec. 15, 1655, was a captain in King Philip's war, and married Mercy Pickett, who was the great-granddaughter of Elder William Brewster of Mayflower fame, her mother being Ruth Brewster, her grandfather Jonathan Brewster, son of Elder William Brewster. He removed to New London, Conn., where he lived many years, finally returning to Charlestown. His name appears frequently in the New London records. Captain Samuel Fosdick received a tract of land in the town of Westminster, Mass., in return for military service during King Philip's war.

Samuel, a son of the preceding, was a native of New London. He was twice married and was the father of nine children. His will was proven in 1784, and he probably died in that year at the ripe old age of 100 years.

James, his sixth son, was born in 1716; and was baptized at New London in 1717. There is a queer old advertisement in a newspaper of Dec. 28, 1758, which says that his son, James, Jr., was the victim of burglars. It is as follows:

Stolen out of the House of the Subscriber living at the South end of Boston on Monday evening last, a blue Damask Sack Gown with close Cuffs, lined with White Stuff most to the top, a flowered Silk Capuchin, with a Pink colour'd Lining, a Garlick Shift with Holland sleeves, a white Fustian Jacket without sleeves; also 15 dollars and a 50s. piece. Whoever will discover the Person or Persons that took the above things, so that they may be brought to justice and convicted shall receive **Ten Dollars** as a Reward. If any of the above Apparel be offered to Sale, it is desired they may be stopped, and notice given to the Printer hereof.

JAMES FOSDICK, JUN'R.

James married, at Boston, Elizabeth Darling, and died in 1784, aged 68; his widow died in 1799 at the age of 80 years. They had twelve children, one of whom, James, served in the Revolutionary war as a drummer and fifer, and also in the artillery. His daughter Sarah married James Frothingham, of the well-known family of that name in Charlestown. The son William was in the army, serving three years. The eleventh son, David, of the sixth generation, lived in Charlestown and also married into the Frothingham family, his wife's name being Mary; she was a granddaughter of William Frothingham, the first settler of the name in Charlestown. David died in 1812, the father of twelve children, of whom his son David, born in 1786 at Charlestown, died at Groton in 1872, being nearly 86 years of age. He was three times married. His first wife, Joanna Skelton of Billerica, was a direct descendant, six generations, from Rev. Samuel Skelton, born in England, a man of great prominence in Salem, Mass., and one of the King's Councillors.

David Fosdick, Jr., second son of Deacon David and Joanna (Skelton) Fosdick, was born at Charlestown, Mass., Nov. 9, 1813. He attended private schools in Charlestown, and Bradford Academy, graduated at Amherst College in 1831, and entered the Andover Theological Seminary. After several years' residence in Andover, Brookline, and Groton, during which time he was engaged in teaching and literary work, he was ordained pastor of the Unitarian Church at Sterling, Mass., March 3, 1841, and retained that position several years. He was installed as pastor of the Hollis Street Church in Boston, March 3, 1846, succeeding Rev. John Pierpont. Here he remained for some eighteen months, his farewell sermon being preached Sept. 19, 1847. He then took up his residence in Groton, where he devoted himself to the education of his children. In 1854 he organized a Unitarian church at Groton Junction, which was called "the South Groton Christian Union," of which he retained the charge for six years. He served also on the Groton School Committee, and was a linguist of superior attainments, being able, it was said, to read fluently in thirteen languages. Mr. Fosdick compiled French and German grammars, a German and English dictionary, and was a diligent translator of foreign works, among which may be mentioned "Proofs of the Genuineness of the Writings of the New Testament, from the German of Hermann Olshausen (1796–1839). Andover: Gould & Newman, 1838."

Mrs. Sarah Lawrence (Woodbury) Fosdick died at Groton, Nov. 25, 1860, and he married (second) Mrs. Jane Applin of Groton, who died June 13, 1879.

His death occurred at Groton, Jan. 28, 1892.

FAMILY NO. 6

8. **Abbott,** m., June 28, 1819, Katharine, eldest daughter of Hon. Timothy Bigelow of Medford, Mass., and Lucy (Prescott) Bigelow.

Their children :

48. I. **Annie Bigelow,** b. April 28, 1820. Family No. 17. Boston.

49. II. **James,** b. at Boston, Dec. 6, 1821. Family No. 18. Boston.

50. III. **George,** b. at Boston, April 16, 1824; d. Aug. 7, 1824.

51. IV. **John Abbott,** b. at Boston, June 11, 1825; d. June 22, 1826.

52. V. **Timothy Bigelow,** b. at Boston, Nov. 22, 1826.

Timothy Bigelow Lawrence received instruction from Messrs. Thayer and Cushing at Chauncy Hall School in Boston, and was admitted to Harvard College, Aug. 27, 1842, at the age of fifteen, graduating Aug. 26, 1846. Served as aide-de-camp on the staff of Governor George Nixon Briggs. He married (first), Dec. 5, 1848, Sallie Ward of Louisville, Ky. (daughter of Robert F. Ward, Esq.), who was noted for her personal charms and beauty. A legal separation followed not long after. He married (second), March 16, 1854, Elizabeth Chapman, eldest daughter of Judge Henry and Elizabeth Stewart Chapman of Bucks County, Pennsylvania, who survived him.

In 1849 he accompanied his father to England, and served efficiently as an *attaché* of the American Legation in London, continuing in service under the Hon. James Buchanan, afterwards President of the United States, and until his father's death in 1855, when he returned home. During the ensuing years he travelled abroad extensively.

At the outbreak of the Rebellion, he offered his services to Governor Andrew, and was also active in the organization of the famous Nims Battery. He was for a time on the staff of Gen. Erasmus D. Keyes, and participated in the campaign of 1861, under Gen. George B. McClellan, but was soon obliged to withdraw from active service in the army on account of his deafness.

In 1862 he was appointed consul-general of the United States in Italy, having his residence at Florence. This position he filled with marked ability and success, being well qualified therefor by his native courtesy, tact, and hospitality, as well as by his diplomatic experience and knowledge of the world, gained by travel. His death occurred at Washington, D. C., during a visit on official business, March 21, 1869.

The following extract from the " Boston Atlas " of Nov. 4, 1852, may be appropriately given here. It was written soon after the return of Hon. Abbott Lawrence from England:

" Nor can we withhold our expression of regard

for, and our cordial welcome to, Colonel Bigelow Lawrence, whose connection with the embassy has given opportunity for the display of his many excellent qualities of head and heart. We were hoping that he would have continued abroad as secretary to the new Minister, however much we should have missed him at home. The experience which he has had, and the popularity he has gained among Americans who have visited London during his sojourn there, would have made his appointment most acceptable."

Mr. Lawrence, during his long residence abroad, was greatly interested in forming his fine collection of armor and weapons, which was to be seen at his house in Beacon Street, and is referred to by Arthur Dexter in the following extract from a chapter on "The Fine Arts in Boston," in The Memorial History of Boston, vol. iv. pp. 404, 405 :

" The foundation of the Museum of Fine Arts was the most important step ever taken in Boston for the promotion of art. In 1869, when Colonel T. B. Lawrence bequeathed his valuable collection of arms and armor to the Athenæum, it was plain that the time had come when a new building was necessary for the Art Gallery. Mrs. Lawrence at once offered to contribute twenty-five thousand dollars ; Harvard College agreed to place temporarily in it the Gray collection of engravings ; and the trustees of the Public Library, the Institute of Technology, and the Lowell Institute offered assistance. An act of incorporation was procured, and trustees appointed early in 1870. A lot of land had some years before been

given by the Water Power Company to the city for a
Fine Arts Institute or Public Square, which the city
now presented to the trustees, with the condition
that the building should be open to all on four days
in each month."

A plan submitted by Sturgis & Brigham having
been selected, the centre and one wing, being a sixth
part of the whole design, were built, and the Art
Museum was formally opened to the public, July 3,
1876. Meantime the Lawrence armor had been destroyed in the great fire of Nov., 1872, but with the
insurance money a collection of carvings and em-
broideries was bought. Mrs. Lawrence, besides her
donation of money, contributed "a room of rare old
English panelling."

53. VI. **Abbott,** b. Sept. 9, 1828. Family No.
19. Boston.

54. VII. **Katharine Bigelow,** b. Feb. 21, 1832.
Family No. 20. Boston.

Mrs. Katharine (Bigelow) Lawrence was born May
20, 1793. The date of her death was Aug. 21, 1860.

The Hon. Abbott Lawrence, seventh child of
Samuel and Susanna (Parker) Lawrence, was born at
Groton, Dec. 16, 1792. He received early instruction at the district school and at Groton Academy,
which he entered in 1805, when twelve years of age.
Thus the educational advantages which he had were
but meagre. Meanwhile in the summer seasons he
worked on his father's farm. In 1808, at the age of
fifteen, he was sent to Boston, and became an apprentice in the store of his brother Amos, who was

already established in business on what was then Cornhill, now a part of Washington Street. After several years' service as apprentice and chief clerk, upon his coming of age, he was admitted to partnership with his brother; and the firm of A. & A. Lawrence was formed Jan. 1, 1814. Their business was the importation and sale of foreign manufactures.

At the outbreak of the war with England, Abbott Lawrence assisted in the organization of the New England Guards, one of the foremost military companies of the day in Massachusetts, and in return for services rendered during the war, at the Charlestown Navy Yard and elsewhere, he received a grant of land from the United States government. At this time he seriously contemplated entering the army, and applied to the War Department for a commission, but before a reply was received came the news of peace. Being intrusted with the negotiation of an important purchase of goods at Manchester, England, he embarked in March, 1815, on the fine ship *Milo*, which was the first vessel sailing for the mother country from the port of Boston after the termination of hostilities.

Through his energetic dispatch of the business in hand Mr. Lawrence was enabled to ship his purchases by the packet *Milo* on her return voyage, and they reached Boston and were sold at a large profit within three months from the time of his sailing. Before returning home he visited the Continent, and saw the allied armies immediately after their victory at Waterloo. In the early years of his business career he made several other successful trips to England. The firm of A. & A. Lawrence later became interested in the Lowell cotton mills, and were large owners in the Suffolk, Lawrence, and Tremont companies. Mr. Lawrence married, June 28, 1819, Katharine, eldest daughter of Hon. Timothy Bigelow of Medford.

He was preëminently a public-spirited citizen and became actively interested in various matters affecting the welfare of the community. He was a member of the Boston Common Council in 1831, and three years later was elected as representative to the twenty-sixth Congress, serving two years as an influential member of the Committee of Ways and Means. Declining a reëlection, he returned to Boston and again engaged in business. Two years later he was reëlected and took his seat in the House, but soon after his arrival in Washington he was taken ill of typhus fever, and was obliged to resign in Sept., 1840. Mr. Lawrence was appointed a commissioner, in the year 1842, by the State of Massachusetts, to determine the so-called "northeastern boundary" of the State, the present dividing line between Maine and Canada. Lord Ashburton was the representative of Great Britain, and as a result of their conference this difficult question was settled in a manner satisfactory to both governments. On July 1, 1843, Mr. Lawrence, accompanied by his wife and eldest daughter, sailed for Europe on the Cunard steamship *Columbia*, which was wrecked on Black Ledge, near Seal Island, off the western coast of Nova Scotia. The passengers were landed safely on the island and after several days were taken to Halifax by the steamer *Margaret*, thence proceeding by the Cunarder *Hibernia* to England. The party spent the summer in Great Britain and returned to Boston in October following.

Mr. Lawrence was energetic in advocating the introduction of an adequate supply of pure water for the city of Boston. His views on this subject at length prevailed, and " on the twenty-fifth of October, 1848, under the mayoralty of the younger Quincy, the Cochituate water was brought to Boston."

In the year 1847 he gave the sum of fifty thousand dollars to Harvard, to found the Scientific School which bears his name, as a separate department of the University, and by his will he bequeathed a like sum to the same institution. He also made a bequest of fifty thousand dollars for the erection of model lodging houses for the poor on East Canton Street, Boston, and one of ten thousand dollars to the Boston Public Library. He likewise established the " Lawrence prizes " for meritorious students of the Public Latin and High Schools of Boston.

The honorary degree of Doctor of Laws was conferred upon him by Williams College in 1852, and by Harvard two years later. Soon after the inauguration of President Zachary Taylor, in 1849, Mr. Lawrence was offered the position of Secretary of the Navy, and later that of Secretary of the Interior, both of which he declined. Afterwards he accepted the post of Minister to England, the highest in the diplomatic service, and sailed from Boston Sept. 26, with Mrs. Lawrence and their daughter Katharine. The duties of this most important station were performed by

him with consummate tact and ability, thereby promoting and strengthening the friendly relations between the two countries.   After three years' service,
he resigned his charge and returned home in Oct.,
1852.   In the autumn of 1854 Mr. Lawrence had a
recurrence of the malady which he had contracted at
Washington many years before, and which was the
cause of his death in Boston, Aug. 18, 1855.

At a public meeting of citizens, held in Faneuil
Hall, Aug. 20, speeches were made by Hon. Robert
C. Winthrop, Hon. Edward Everett, and others,
highly eulogistic of the character and services of
Abbott Lawrence.   Mr. Winthrop, in the course of
his address, said: " His name was a tower of strength
to every good cause, and was never given to a bad
one.   His noble bearing and genial presence seemed
the very embodiment of an enlarged and enlightened
public spirit."   Mr. Everett said: " Such he was, —
so kind, so noble, so complete in all that makes a
man ; and the ultimate source of all this goodness,
its vital principle, that which brought all his qualities
into harmonious relation, was religious principle —
the faith, the hope of the gospel."   The daily press
of New England and of other portions of the country devoted much space to laudatory notices of Mr.
Lawrence, whose nobility of character, integrity,
public spirit, and genial disposition bound him with
the strong ties of affection to his fellow-citizens.

The Hon. Timothy Bigelow, whose eldest daughter, Katharine, married Hon. Abbott Lawrence, was
the second child of Colonel Timothy Bigelow and
Anna (Andrews) Bigelow.   He was born at Worces-

ter, Mass., April 30, 1767, and graduated in 1786 at Harvard. Being admitted to the bar three years after, he entered upon the practice of law in Groton, and soon attained eminence in his profession. Mr. Bigelow was also active in politics as a member of the Federalist party, and was a representative from Groton to the General Court from 1793 to 1806, with the exception of one year, and from Medford, whither he removed in 1806, during twelve years. He held the office of speaker for eleven years.

Hon. Timothy Bigelow married, Sept. 3, 1791, Lucy, sixth child of Dr. Oliver and Lydia (Baldwin) Prescott of Groton. He was one of the founders of Groton Academy, and an original member of its board of trustees. His death occurred at Medford, May 18, 1821. (A fuller account of Mr. Bigelow may be found in Groton Historical Series, vol. iii. pp. 208–211, by Samuel Abbott Green, M. D.)

FAMILY NO. 7

9. **Eliza**, m., at Groton, Jan. 5, 1824, Dr. Joshua Green.

Their children:

55. I. **William Lawrence**, b. at Sunderland, Mass., Oct. 28, 1824; d. at Groton, Aug. 28, 1825.

56. II. **William Lawrence**, b. at Groton, Aug. 22, 1826; d. at Groton, Oct. 21, 1847. He was of the firm of Jewett, Tebbetts & Green of Boston, and one of the most interesting and promising young men in the community. " He had endeared himself to a large circle of friends, and possessed such qualities

of mind and heart as had made him the stay and hope of his parents in their declining years."

57. III. **Henry Atkinson,** b. at Groton, April 29, 1828; m., at Fishkill Landing, N. Y., Nov. 25, 1857, Emily, daughter of Dr. John and Lydia Maria (Brett) Wagner of Charleston, S. C. She d. Jan. 4, 1885.

They had:

58. 1. **Caroline Sargent,** b. Dec. 18, 1859, who m., at Boston, Sept. 15, 1885, William Appleton Meredith, M. D.

Their children:

59. i. **Frances Amory,** b. at London, Sept. 26, 1886.

60. ii. **Gertrude Emily,** b. at London, July 13, 1888.

61. iii. **William Morris,** b. at London, June 21, 1891.

William Appleton Meredith, son of Samuel Ogden and Frances Maria (Amory) Meredith, was born at New York, N. Y., March 3, 1848. He received instruction from a private tutor, and at college in Boulogne-sur-Mer, France. Later he attended University College, London, Eng., and the University of Edinburgh. He is senior surgeon to the Samaritan Hospital for Women, London, and Fellow of the Royal College of Surgeons, London, and of several medical societies. M. B., C. M., University of Edinburgh. Dr. Meredith is the author of various publications on abdominal surgery. Residence, London, Eng.

62. 2. **William Lawrence,** b. at Boston, Dec. 7, 1861, who m., at Albany, N. Y., Jan. 9, 1889, Har-

riet Lloyd, daughter of A. Bleecker Banks, Esq., of Albany, and Phœbe (Wells) Banks.

William Lawrence Green was educated at Boston schools, and under a private tutor, and was for a time a member of the Harvard Class of 1884. He made a trip around the world in 1886–87. Since his marriage he has been in the publishing business in Albany, N. Y.

Henry Atkinson Green spent his boyhood in Groton, and was a student in Lawrence Academy from 1833 to 1842. After leaving that institution, he passed a year in a country store. In 1846 he came to Boston, and began business with Messrs. Wilkinson, Stetson & Co., dry goods commission merchants, and afterwards became a partner in the house of Mackintosh, Green & Co., remaining with the same concern, under its various titles, for thirty-five years. He was also a director of the Washington National Bank of Boston. Of commanding stature and striking personality, his kindly disposition and agreeable manners made him a general favorite, while his strict business integrity gained for him the esteem of the community. He died at Boston, Jan. 8, 1891.

63. IV. **Samuel Abbott,** b. at Groton, March 16, 1830.

The Hon. Samuel Abbott Green is a descendant of Percival and Ellen Green, who came to America in 1635, and were living in Cambridge the following year. He received instruction at Lawrence Academy, Groton, and was admitted to Harvard, Aug. 24, 1847, and graduated with the Class of 1851. Soon after leaving college he began the study of medicine under the tuition of Dr. J. Mason Warren, and the ensuing winter he attended lectures at the Jefferson Medical College in Philadelphia. He then entered the Harvard Medical School, graduating in 1854, after which he continued his studies in Paris. After four years abroad, he returned home and began the practice of medicine in Boston, serving meanwhile as a district physician of the Boston Dispensary. He was appointed surgeon of the Second Regiment, M. V. M., by Gov. N. P. Banks, May 19, 1858, and at the beginning of the Rebellion he was commissioned assistant surgeon of the First Regiment, M. V. M., and was promoted, Sept. 2, 1861, surgeon of the Twenty-fourth Regiment, Massachusetts Volunteers, retaining the latter position for more than three years. In Jan., 1862, he had charge of the hospital ship *Recruit*, which was attached to the Burnside expedition to Roanoke Island, and was also in charge of the hospital ship *Cosmopolitan*, off the South Carolina coast. He served also as chief medical officer on Morris Island, during the siege of Fort Wagner. In Oct., 1863, Dr. Green was stationed at St. Augustine and Jacksonville, Fla., as post-surgeon, and later he was sent to Virginia, being with the army at the capture of Bermuda Hundred. After the fall of Richmond he served as staff surgeon in that city for three months. Dr. Green was brevetted lieutenant-colonel of Volunteers "for gallant and distinguished services in the field during the campaign of 1864." He resigned from the army, July 9, 1865, and after the war served for seven years as superintendent of the Boston Dispensary, and for nine years as a member of the Boston School Committee. He was also a trustee of the Public Library from 1868 to 1878, and acting librarian for one year. From 1871 till 1880 he was city physician, mayor of Boston in 1882, and an overseer of Harvard College from 1869 to 1880, and again from 1882 to 1900. He has been the librarian of the Massachusetts Historical Society since 1868, and its vice-president since 1895. Dr. Green was appointed a trustee of the Peabody Educational Fund, and secretary of the board, in 1883, and has continued to hold these positions. He has also been a member of the State Board of Health, Lunacy, and Charity, and one of the Massachusetts commissioners appointed under chapter 60 of the Resolves of 1884, "to investigate the condition of the records, files, papers, and documents in the State Department."

Dr. Green is the author of a large number of publications relating to his native town. Among the more important of these are the following: "Epitaphs from the Old Burying Ground in Groton, Mass.," 1878; "The Early Records of Groton, Mass. (1662–1707)," 1880; "Groton during the Indian Wars," 1883; "Groton Historical Series," 4 volumes, 1887–1899; "Groton during the Revolution," 1900. He also prepared an account of the History of Medicine in Massachusetts, for the "Memorial History of Boston," published in 1881.

63a. V. **Elizabeth Lawrence,** b. at Groton, June 5, 1832; m., Oct. 5, 1854, John Kendall (b. April 17, 1833; graduate Dartmouth College, 1853; son of the Hon. Amos and Jane (Kyle) Kendall of

Washington, D. C.   He d. Dec. 7, 1861, at Washington).   She m. (second), Sept. 8, 1862, Dr. Charles Young Swan of New York (b. at Belfast Ireland, June 25, 1833, a son of William and Mary (Lyttle) Swan; graduate N. Y. College of Physicians and Surgeons, 1856; d. Oct. 7, 1900).   Mrs. Elizabeth Lawrence (Green) Swan d. at Morristown, N. J., March 29, 1882.

63b. VI. **Joshua,** b. at Groton, May 7, 1834; d. Feb. 13, 1846.

Dr. Joshua Green, a son of Joshua and Mary (Mosley) Green, was born at Wendell, Franklin County, Mass., Oct. 8, 1797.   He was a student at New Salem, Westfield, and Milton academies, and a graduate of Harvard College, Class of 1818, and of the Medical School in 1821.   In the autumn of the latter year he assumed the duties of apothecary at the Massachusetts General Hospital, then newly opened, serving also as a house-physician and house-surgeon for one year.   He first practised medicine at Sunderland, a village near Wendell, but removed to Groton in the spring of 1825, about a year after his marriage to Eliza Lawrence, which took place at Groton, Jan. 5, 1824.   Here he continued in the practice of his profession until the year 1832, when he was obliged to relinquish it, owing to impaired health.   In 1836 and 1837 he represented Groton in the legislature, and was for thirty-six years a trustee of Lawrence Academy, serving often as secretary or president of the board.   Dr. Green was much interested in antiquarian and genealogical subjects, and was chosen a corresponding member of the New England Historic Genealogical Society, Aug. 18, 1849. He died at the home of his daughter, in Morristown, N. J., June 5, 1875. Mrs. Eliza (Lawrence) Green died at Groton, Aug. 20, 1874. (See Groton Historical Series, by Samuel Abbott Green, M. D., vol. ii. p. 140, and vol. iii. pp. 20–22.)

FAMILY NO. 8

10. **Samuel**, m., April 2, 1833, at Baltimore, Md., Alison, daughter of William and Mary (Nisbet) Turnbull of Philadelphia.

Their children :

64. I. **Charles**, b. at Boston, May 27, 1835 ; d. at Lowell, Mass., April 15, 1842.

65. II. **Henry**, b. at Boston, April 28, 1837; m., at New York, June 26, 1871, Marie Therese, daughter of Dr. Joseph and Sophie Russell (Sterry) Mauran of Providence, R. I.

Henry Lawrence attended school in Lowell and Boston, and in Paris, France. He was for a time a member of the Harvard Class of 1858, being admitted Aug. 31, 1854, but left college during the second term of the Freshman year, and went abroad for his health. Returning home, he was with the firm of Jewett, Tebbetts & Co., Boston, until the late spring of 1857, when he sailed from Boston on the American ship *Amazon*, loaded with lumber, bound for Melbourne, Australia. Everything went well until the morning of the sixtieth day, off Cape

Saint Roque, the easternmost point of Brazil, when the vessel was found to be leaking. The ship's company consisted of the captain, two mates, ten seamen before the mast, the cook, and the subject of this sketch. All hands had to take their turn at the pumps. On the second day after the leak was discovered, four of the sailors refused to work, using threatening language to the captain and others, but after considerable resistance they were put in irons; a consultation was held, and it was determined to make for Rio Janeiro. Early on the morning of the fourth day thereafter, the "Sugar Loaf" rock at the entrance of the harbor of Rio was sighted. The ship's signals of distress were seen from the shore, and powerful tugs towed her up to the city, where she was condemned as unseaworthy. After the lapse of four months, the Swedish barque *Hoppet* was chartered, the cargo reshipped, and after a voyage of sixty days, Melbourne was reached. While in Rio Janeiro, Mr. Lawrence stayed for a while at the house of the American consul, who lived at Botafogo, one of the city's attractive suburbs, and with him many pleasant trips were taken. Among the more notable places visited was Petropolis, which was reached by railway over the Pedro Segundo road, so called in honor of the Emperor of Brazil, Dom Pedro II. It was Mr. Lawrence's privilege to meet the Emperor and Empress frequently, both being most hospitable and kind-hearted.

On arrival at Melbourne, letters and advices from Boston announced the great financial crisis of the summer of 1857, in which disaster, among many large mercantile firms crippled thereby, was the house of Lawrence, Stone & Co. Therefore, instead of being provided with plenty of funds, Mr. Lawrence found himself without a dollar. He obtained a copy of the Melbourne " Argus," at that time the most important journal of the Australian colonies, and there read an advertisement wherein the services of a young and active man were desired as groom, the wages being fixed at two pounds sterling a week. This position he obtained, and worked for three months in that capacity, sleeping in the stable.

An American firm, doing a trucking business from Melbourne to the several diggings, made him an offer to drive one of their six-horse teams on the Bendigo road, to take provisions up and bring back wool, hides, and leather. This offer was accepted, at ten pounds sterling a week, and he continued this work for six months, in the mean time making the acquaintance of the drivers, who were also owners, of the American line of mail coaches over the same route from Melbourne to Sandhurst or Bendigo, about one hundred miles. Mr. Lawrence applied for a situation as driver, contributing his share to the partnership fund, and received as wages twenty pounds weekly, taking the royal mail, with six horses, every other afternoon from Melbourne, returning the following afternoon from Sandhurst. The trip occupied eleven hours, changing horses every ten miles.

He continued this business for four months, when he fell in with a very energetic young American from Natchez, Miss., who was engaged in the live stock business, buying horses, cattle, and sheep, driving them overland from the stations, and selling them on the hoof at the various diggings. The life of a drover, so called, or rancher, is of necessity one of great exposure to weather and all sorts of perils. Mr. Lawrence had several encounters with the natives, once being wounded quite seriously, and for eleven months in the year he did not sleep in a house, camping nearly all the time. The distance travelled on the several trips varied, the longest one being eight hundred miles from the northern part of Queensland, through New South Wales to the river Murray at Moama, on the borders of Victoria. Sometimes there would be three droves on the route at once, separated by a few miles. The settlers or squatters, who lease from the government large tracts of land for the raising and grazing of their herds, are principally English and Scotch, some of them native born, but it was not considered *comme il faut* to ask who so-and-so's father was, or when and why he came to Australia. Some of the most respected and respectable station-holders were sent out from England for greater or less offences against the Crown. After several years of bush life, the longing for home became irresistible, and in the early part of 1863 Mr. Lawrence left Melbourne for London, in the Black Ball liner *Donald Mackay*, sailing eastward through the South Pacific, around Cape Horn and thence to England, sighting the Lizard lighthouses after a voyage of one hundred and twenty days. He spent a few days in London, and then embarked for New York, where he arrived safe and sound, after an absence of six years.

Mr. Lawrence was for a time in business with his father, and also with Messrs. D. Appleton & Co., in New York. Since 1871 he has devoted himself largely to sketching and drawing. He resided in Brooklyn, L. I., for some twenty years, but since 1895 Mr. and Mrs. Lawrence have made their home in Newport, R. I., where he d. March 7, 1904.

66. III. **George,** b. at Lowell, Jan. 22, 1839.

George Lawrence prepared for college at the school of Mr. T. G. Bradford in Boston, and graduated at Harvard in 1859. He engaged in business in Baltimore and New York. From Aug., 1861, until Oct., 1864, he served as assistant paymaster and paymaster in the United States Navy. Afterwards he went into business with his father in Boston, but retired after a year or two, and made his home at Stockbridge, Mass. He died at Nahant, Oct. 1, 1884.

67. IV. **Mary Nisbet,** b. at Lowell, Oct. 26, 1841. Family No. 21. Staten Island, N. Y., and Brookline.

68. V. **Alison Turnbull,** b. at Lowell, May 24, 1843. Family No. 22. Stockbridge.

69. VI. **Nisbet,** b. at Lowell, Nov. 29, 1844; d. at Boston, March 24, 1868.

Nisbet Lawrence was a student at Lawrence Academy, Groton, Mass., in 1858–59, and during that time lived at the old homestead on Farmer's Row, with his aunt, Mrs. Mary Woodbury. He then went to Staten Island, where his parents had taken up their residence in 1860, and later continued his preparatory studies under Mr. Albert Stickney at Cam-

bridge. He was admitted to Harvard, July 15, 1862,
and remained one year as a member of the Class of
1866, but left college at the beginning of the first
Sophomore term, in the autumn of 1863, and entered
business with Messrs. Lawrence, Wright & Co., wool
commission merchants at 115 Federal Street, Boston, representatives of the New York firm of Samuel
Lawrence & Sons. He was one of the resident partners in Boston, being associated with John G. Wright,
who had been a bookkeeper for Samuel Lawrence
in New York. Nisbet Lawrence had a remarkable
aptitude for business, but met with some reverses.
His manly qualities and affectionate disposition endeared him to a large circle of relatives and friends,
who greatly deplored his untimely death, which occurred March 24, 1868.

70. VII. **Samuel**, b. at Lowell, Sept. 27, 1846;
d. June 19, 1885.

71. VIII. **Caroline Turnbull**, b. at Boston, Sept.
14, 1850. Resides at Stockbridge.

Mrs. Alison (Turnbull) Lawrence was born Oct. 2,
1811, and died at Stockbridge, Sept. 20, 1892.

Samuel Lawrence, the youngest child of Major
Samuel, was born in Groton, Mass., Jan. 15, 1801.
He entered Groton Academy in 1812. At the age
of fourteen he went to live at the house of his brother
William, in Boston, and there remained during his
minority. In 1822 the two brothers formed a partnership under the firm name of W. & S. Lawrence,
and during the next few years Samuel Lawrence
made many business trips to Europe, whereby he

gained much valuable knowledge of mercantile affairs. He married, April 2, 1833, at Baltimore, Md., Alison Turnbull, youngest daughter of William Turnbull, Esq., of Philadelphia, and Mary, daughter of Rev. Charles Nisbet, D. D.

Mr. Lawrence continued to reside in Boston for several years after his marriage. In 1838 he removed to Lowell, where his firm had become largely interested in manufacturing enterprises. Here he was active in the establishment of the Middlesex Company, besides being closely connected with other industries of that young and thriving city. His own words may be appropriately quoted in this connection: "When the Middlesex Company started, most of the woollen goods consumed here were from England, imported by men from Yorkshire, who for many years evaded paying the full amount of duties by undervaluation. One of the difficulties in the early production of woollens here was a defect in dyeing. This company was most fortunate in early discovering that this evil arose from the simplest cause, the imperfect cleansing of the wool. Mr. Compton of Taunton, Mass., became employed by the Middlesex Company, to adapt his principle to their looms, in order to produce a fabric like the Sedan, and was entirely successful. Thus commenced in this country the manufacture of fancy cassimeres. The shawl manufacture was commenced by the Middlesex Company in 1847. Up to that time the fringes were twisted by hand, and success depended upon its being done by machinery. At that time Mr. Milton D. Whipple was in the company's employ, perfecting a felting machine, and he was engaged to produce a mechanism for twisting fringes, in which he succeeded perfectly."

Mr. Lawrence was chosen president and treasurer of the Merrimac Water Power Association (formed in 1843, incorporated March 20, 1845), and was prominent as one of the founders of the city of Lawrence. With his brothers he was influential in the establishment of this new and important manufacturing centre, which bears the family name in grateful and fitting recognition of their services. Some account of the inception of this successful enterprise may therefore be properly given here:

"At Mr. Lawrence's suggestion Mr. George Baldwin made an examination of the Merrimac River below Hunter Falls, and his report being favorable, Bodwell's Falls, at Andover Bridge, was fixed upon as the place for a dam. On speaking to certain friends of the matter, he was told that Mr. Daniel Saunders of North Andover had contemplated the same project. An interview having been obtained with that gentleman, Mr. Lawrence found him well informed about the lands bordering on the Merrimac in Andover and Methuen, and Messrs. John Nesmith, J. G. Abbott, and Thomas Hopkinson were invited to consider with them the question how to get control of the lands, so as to make it an object to build a dam on a solid and expensive plan, and an association was formed for the purpose of establishing a water power at Andover. Mr. Daniel Saunders, Jr., was engaged to give his time to bargaining for the lands, getting bonds for deeds, etc., a work which he performed with entire success. In Feb., 1845, the time had come to petition the legislature for a charter giving the right to dam the river below Lowell. An understanding with those to be affected by the measures proposed in Lowell was obtained without difficulty, and the petition for a charter of the Essex Company, with a capital of one million dollars, was signed by John Nesmith, Edwin Bartlett, Daniel Saunders, and Samuel Lawrence. Mr. Lawrence had not as yet acquainted his brothers in Boston with the proposed operations, and on doing so, called on other men of business, whom he invited to meet at Andover, where the party was taken in carriages to the Methuen side of the river to examine the rocks and banks on which the dam was to be located. The names of the gentlemen invited were as follows: Patrick T. Jackson, Thomas H. Perkins, Francis C. Lowell, George W. Lyman, Nathan Appleton, William Sturgis, Abbott Lawrence, John A. Lowell, William Appleton, William Lawrence, Eben Chadwick, Ignatius Sargent, Theodore Lyman, John Nesmith, Jonathan Tyler, James B. Francis, Charles S. Storrow."

After dinner at the Merrimac House in Lowell, in the late afternoon of March 20, 1845, the very day on which the act incorporating the Essex Company had been approved by Governor Briggs, were taken the first steps toward the permanent organization of the company and the commencement of manufacturing operations. The successful inauguration of this important enterprise was largely due to the energy, foresight, and business sagacity of Samuel Lawrence.

Mr. Lawrence was the first treasurer and general manager of the Bay State Mills at Lawrence, which began the manufacture of woollen goods in 1848. He returned to Boston in 1850, and occupied the house 11 Beacon Street, which was the family residence for several years, after which he lived for a time in Andover. He was the first president of the Boston Board of Trade, in 1854. After the disastrous financial panic of 1857, which swamped many of the leading mercantile houses (including his own, which then bore the firm name of Lawrence, Stone & Co., commission merchants), Mr. Lawrence spent two years abroad, his family living meanwhile in Baltimore. In 1860 he removed to Staten Island, N. Y., which was his residence for eleven years, during which time he had business interests in New York, N. Y. In 1873 he made his home at Stockbridge, Mass., where he remained until his death, which occurred there, March 18, 1880.

From a letter written by William R. Lawrence to Amos Lawrence

BALTIMORE, April 3, 1833.

MY DEAR FATHER,—I was interrupted at Washington by Captain Turnbull, who came to see us, and therefore could not finish my letter. He is a captain of Engineers, and is superintending some work on this station. Last evening Samuel Lawrence, Esq., led to the altar Miss Alison Turnbull. There were about sixty people present, and among them Mr. and Mrs. Abbott Lawrence and two children, the younger of whom fell asleep just after the ceremony was completed. The ceremony lasted three minutes, fifteen seconds, and passed off very pleasantly. Alison was dressed in plain white, with a sprig of white in her hair. There were neither bridesmaids nor grooms-men. The company was brilliant, and there were some fine specimens of female beauty. To-day we are going to dine with them, and in the evening they will receive company. On Monday they will leave for Philadelphia. . . . Uncle Abbott is holding a levee in his parlor this morning, and has already received half Baltimore, not counting people from other cities. Uncle Sam says he is the happiest man in the country, and I think he speaks the truth. The people here are very polite and hospitable, and by no means treat us badly. Our acquaintance is now very much extended, both in Baltimore and Philadelphia, so that any member of the family will find no difficulty in visiting as much as he likes in either city. Mrs. Turnbull is rather better, but does not leave her apartment. I hope to have a chance to send my mother some of the wedding cake *to dream upon*, and distribute about the city. I hope we shall persuade Uncle Abbott to remain in the South at least a month, and if you can make him think his presence is not required in Boston, he may be contented here and in Philadelphia.

We are all very well, and I hope you can say the same in Boston. Give my love to all. I would be glad to hear from you when I arrive at Bunker's in New York.

From your ever affectionate son,

WILLIAM R. LAWRENCE.

Rev. Charles Nisbet, D. D., third son of William and Alison Nisbet, and maternal grandfather of Mrs. Alison (Turnbull) Lawrence, was born at Haddington, a town of Scotland, on the river Tyne, Jan. 21, 1736. He entered the University of Edinburgh in 1752, at the age of sixteen, and graduated in 1754. He then spent six years as a student in the Divinity Hall, Edinburgh, and was licensed as a preacher of the gospel, Sept. 24, 1760. During the ensuing two years he supplied the pulpit of a church at Gorbals, a suburb of Glasgow. He then removed to Montrose, an important seaport town on the east coast of Scotland, where he became assistant pastor, and in 1773 sole pastor of a large church. About 1765 he married Anne, daughter of Thomas Tweedie, Esq., of the town of Quarter, near Hamilton. The degree of D. D. was conferred upon him in 1783 by Princeton College, New Jersey, and the following year he was chosen the first president of Dickinson College, Carlisle, Pa. After long consideration he decided to accept the position, and sailing from Greenock, he reached Philadelphia, June 9, 1785, after a voyage of forty-six days. Dr. Nisbet was a man of great integrity of character, and was, moreover, an eminent scholar and linguist. He continued ably to perform his duties as president of Dickinson College until his death, Jan. 18, 1804.

Mary, eldest daughter of Dr. Nisbet and Anne (Tweedie) Nisbet, married William Turnbull, Esq., of Philadelphia, and their daughter Alison married Samuel Lawrence.

SEVENTH GENERATION

FAMILY NO. 9

11. **Anna Maria,** m., at Groton, Dec. 1, 1829, Norman Seaver of Boston.

Their children:

72. I. **Edward Lowell,** b. at Boston, Jan. 11, 1831 ; d. Feb. 28, 1886, at Rutland, Vt.

73. II. **Norman,** b. at Boston, April 23, 1834 ; m., at Rutland, Dec. 10, 1863, Caroline Keith Daniels, daughter of Luther and Caroline (Keith) Daniels of Rutland.

Rev. Norman Seaver is an alumnus of Williams College, Class of 1854. He studied theology at Andover Theological Seminary, graduating therefrom in 1860, and was ordained colleague pastor of the First Congregational Church in Rutland, Vt., Aug. 29, 1860. Three years later, upon the resignation of Rev. Dr. Silas Aiken, he became sole pastor, and continued in charge until his dismissal, at his own request, in Sept., 1868. On Dec. 30, following, he was installed as pastor of the First Presbyterian Church in Brooklyn, N. Y.

He received the honorary degree of D. D. from Middlebury College in 1866. Of recent years he has again been engaged in ministerial work in Rutland and its neighborhood.

74. III. **Emily,** b. at Charlestown, Nov. 5, 1835.

Miss Emily Seaver lived in Boston and vicinity until 1860, when she went to Rutland, Vt., with her mother, to reside with her brother, Rev. Dr. Norman

Seaver. She had marked literary ability, and was the authoress of a volume of poems, which was published by A. Williams & Co., Boston, 1878. She died at Rutland, Dec. 3, 1896.

Mrs. Anna Maria Seaver died at Rutland, Jan. 25, 1895, at the age of 88.

Norman Seaver, Sr., son of Heman and Elizabeth (Weeks) Seaver, was born at Groton, April 7, 1802. His early schooling was obtained at Montreal, Canada. After a year at Middlebury College, Vermont, he took the full course at Harvard, graduating in 1822. He then studied law in the office of the Hon. Luther Lawrence at Groton, and was admitted to the Middlesex bar in Oct., 1827. He practised his profession in Boston for several years, and in 1828 served as a member of the Common Council, but ill-health was the cause of his abandonment of the law in 1834 or thereabouts. He then engaged in business as a member of the firm of Stone, Seaver & Bush. His death occurred at St. Louis, Mo., May 12, 1838. (See Groton Historical Series, vol. iii. No. vi., 1892, " The Lawyers of Groton.")

FAMILY NO. 10

14. **Catharine,** m., at Lowell, Oct. 1, 1839, Charles Tilden Appleton, who was b. at Baltimore, Md., Jan. 11, 1809, and d. at Roxbury, Mass., March 16, 1859. He held the office of treasurer of the Lowell Bleachery. Mrs. Catharine (Lawrence) Appleton d. at Lowell, April 18, 1846.

Their children:

75. I. **Catharine Lawrence**, b. at Lowell, July 4, 1841; d. at Boston, May 29, 1887.

76. II. **Elizabeth Lawrence**, b. at Lowell, March 6, 1843; m., at Roxbury, Sept. 1, 1870, Charles Pickard Ware, the youngest child of Henry Ware, Jr., and Mary Lovell (Pickard) Ware.

They have these:

77. 1. **Henry Ware**, b. at Brookline, Dec. 26, 1871, who m., June 8, 1898, Louisa Fuller Wilson, daughter of Charles Lush and Caroline Fuller (Farrar) Wilson.

They have a daughter,

78. **Caroline Farrar**, b. Aug. 14, 1899.

Henry Ware attended private schools in Boston, and Roxbury Latin School. Graduated at Harvard in 1893, receiving the degree of A. M. in 1894 and LL. B. *cum laude* in 1896. He was assistant in Forensics in 1893–94. Admitted to the Suffolk bar in Dec., 1895, in July following he entered the law office of Storey & Thorndike, Boston. Mr. Ware is treasurer of the First Parish of Brookline.

79. 2. **Mary Appleton Ware**, b. at Brookline, May 17, 1877.

Charles Pickard Ware is a descendant of Robert Ware, who came from England about the year 1642 and settled in Dedham. He attended Milton Academy and the private school of Epes Sargent Dixwell, Esq., in Boston. He is a graduate of Harvard, Class of 1862. After leaving college, he was for three years superintendent of plantations at St. Helena Island, S. C. He taught school in Boston from 1867 to 1872, and was instructor in English at Harvard University from 1877 to 1880. Since 1890 he has been with the American Bell Telephone Company in Boston. He was one of the compilers (with William Francis Allen and Lucy McKim Garrison) of "Slave Songs of the United States," published in 1867 by A. Simpson & Co., New York. His residence is on Allerton Street, Brookline.

80. III. **Helen Lawrence,** b. at Lowell, March 29, 1846; m., Jan. 1, 1873, Francis Tucker Washburn of Boston:

They had a daughter,

81. **Frances Tucker Washburn,** who was born at Milton, March 26, 1874, and died at Roxbury, Jan., 1880.

Francis Tucker Washburn, son of William Rounseville Peirce and Susan Ellen (Tucker) Washburn, was born at Boston, Sept. 24, 1844. He received his early education at the Boston Latin School, and graduated at Harvard in 1864. After less than a year at the Divinity School in Cambridge, he went abroad, and spent three years in travel and residence in the south of Europe. Returning home in 1869, he resumed his theological studies, and on March 2, 1871, was ordained as associate pastor of the First Congregational (Unitarian) Church in Milton, Mass. He died of typhoid fever at Milton, Dec. 29, 1873.

Helen Lawrence (Appleton) Washburn m. (second), at Roxbury, Mass., June 1, 1880, John Graham Brooks.

They had:

82. 1. **Lawrence Graham,** b. at Roxbury, Feb.

21, 1881.   He attended schools in Berlin, Freiburg in Baden, and Cambridge, Mass.   A member of the Harvard Class of 1902.

83. 2. **Charles Appleton**, b. at Freiburg, Baden, July 13, 1884; d. June 17, 1889.

84. 3. **Guy**, b. at Brockton, Mass., Nov. 30, 1886; d. Feb. 2, 1900.

John Graham Brooks, son of Chapin Kidder and Pamelia (Graham) Brooks, was born at Acworth, Sullivan County, N. H., July 19, 1846.   He attended school at Meriden, N. H.; after which he spent one year as a student in the Law School of the University of Michigan, at Ann Arbor, three years at Oberlin College, Ohio, and a like period at the Harvard Divinity School, graduating in 1875.   He was pastor of the First Religious Society of Roxbury from 1875 until 1882, when he went abroad and pursued his studies in Economics and Ethics at the universities of Berlin, Jena, and Freiburg, Baden.   Returning home, he was settled at Brockton, Mass., from 1885 to 1891.   His present residence is at Cambridge.   Mr. Brooks was for two years instructor in Economics at Harvard, and is a lecturer and writer upon economic and social subjects.   He is president of the National Consumers' League.

He is also the author of the Government Report on Compulsory Insurance in Germany, and of several articles in the Dictionary of Political Economy.   He has furnished numerous contributions to English and American Reviews.

FAMILY NO. 11

21. **Susan Elizabeth**, m., March 30, 1843, William Warren Tucker of Boston, son of Alanson and Eliza (Thom) Tucker of Derry, N. H.

Their children:

85. I. **Lawrence**, b. at Boston, Nov. 4, 1844.

Lawrence Tucker attended schools in Boston and at Vevay, Switzerland. At the outbreak of the civil war he enlisted, at the age of seventeen; but his father, thinking him too young to enter the army, procured his discharge. Mr. Tucker graduated at Harvard in 1865. Immediately afterwards he went to Europe, where he remained for seven years, with the exception of a few weeks passed in this country. During the siege of Paris he lived in various small towns of France, returning to Paris some time before the outbreak of the Commune and the so-called second siege, during which time he remained in the capital. He was forced by the Communists to aid in the construction of barricades, and upon the entry of the Versailles troops, and while the fighting was still going on in the streets, he was arrested, charged with being a Communist, and tried before a drumhead court-martial at the Luxembourg Palace. Although the evidence was strong against him, and he had no witnesses in his own behalf, he was acquitted. In 1872 he entered the Harvard Law School, graduating in 1875, and was admitted to the Suffolk bar, Jan. 30, 1876. That same year he visited Europe, where he passed two years. After an interval he went to Kansas, where he lived on a ranch for three years. Returning to Boston, he was foremost in organizing the Boston Athletic Association in 1887, and served as one of its officers for a long period. During the last few years he has travelled considerably in the United States and Mexico. He resides in Boston, and usually spends his summer months in the State of Maine.

86. II. **Alanson,** b. at Boston, April 20, 1848; m., at Boston, Nov. 25, 1899, Katharine Sawin Davis, daughter of William H. and Elizabeth H. (Basset) Davis of Milton.

Alanson Tucker received his early education at Mr. Dixwell's school in Boston, and graduated at Harvard in 1872. For about a year after leaving college he was connected with the Ocean Cotton Mills at Newburyport, Mass. He then became associated with the firm of Upham, Tucker & Co., afterwards Dana, Tucker & Co., commission merchants, at 48 Franklin Street, Boston. Retiring from active business some years ago, he has since travelled extensively in Europe, India, China, Japan, Java, Burmah, Australia, North and South America, and in the West Indies.

William Warren Tucker was born at Boston, March 18, 1817. His parents were Alanson Tucker (b. at Middleborough, Mass., Jan. 25, 1777) and Eliza (Thom) Tucker (b. at Londonderry, N. H., April 19, 1790), who were married May 9, 1809. Alanson Tucker was a representative to the General Court of New Hampshire from the town of Derry in 1828–29, and 1831. The paternal grandfather of

William Warren Tucker was Nathaniel (b. at
Middleborough, Oct. 15, 1744), and his great-grandfather was Benjamin Tucker, who was born in the
same town about the year 1705.   The subject of this
sketch graduated from Dartmouth College in the
Class of 1835, and received the degree of A. M. from
that institution in 1838, and from Harvard in 1861.
He was a trustee of Lawrence Academy, Groton,
from 1844 to 1852, and in 1878 he served as a member of the Executive Council under Gov. Alexander
H. Rice.   Mr. Tucker was a partner in the firm of
Upham, Tucker & Co., commission merchants, of
Boston.   His death occurred at Paris, France, Nov.
26, 1885.   Mrs. Susan Elizabeth (Lawrence) Tucker
died at Paris, Jan. 8, 1891.   The surname Tucker
is believed to be derived from the old English
word *tucker*, now mostly obsolete, signifying a trade,
and the latter in turn from *tuck*, a piece of cloth.
In modern dictionaries, *tucker* is synonymous with
fuller.

FAMILY NO. 12

23. **Harriet Bordman**, m., at Boston, Sept. 11,
1848, Seth Edward Sprague, and had these:

87. I. **William Lawrence**, b. July 20, 1849.

William Lawrence Sprague fitted for Harvard
College at Mr. Dixwell's school, Boston, and graduated with the Class of 1871.   In Jan., 1873, he went
to San Francisco in search of health, and soon after
entered the business house of E. E. Morgan's Sons
in that city.   In the autumn following, with the assistance of others, he established the Harvard Club

of San Francisco, which has proved to be a very successful institution. After returning home he entered the Harvard Medical School, and received the degree of M. D. in June, 1880. He died June 22, 1884. At the annual business meeting of the Class of 1871, held on Commencement Day, 1884, it was voted "that we recall with tender recollection the many good qualities of our friend and classmate, William Lawrence Sprague, his kindly, affectionate disposition, and his loyal attachment to his friends."

88. II. **Fanny Bordman,** b. Sept. 29, 1851; d. July 16, 1856.

89. III. **Charles Franklin,** b. at Boston, June 10, 1857; m., at Boston, Nov. 25, 1891, Mary Bryant Pratt, daughter of George Langdon and Sarah (Weld) Pratt.

They had:

90. 1. **Marion,** b. at Beverly, Mass., June 20, 1893.

91. 2. **Elinor,** b. at Washington, D. C., March 26, 1898.

Charles Franklin Sprague obtained his early education at the school of Mr. John Prentiss Hopkinson in Boston, and at Phillips Exeter Academy. He then entered Harvard College, taking the regular undergraduate course, and receiving the degree of A. B. (as of the Class of 1879) at Commencement, 1880, after which he studied three years at the Harvard Law School, and began the practice of law in Boston. He soon became interested in politics, and was elected a member of the Common Council in 1888 and 1889, and of the lower branch of the legislature of Massachusetts in 1891 and 1892. He also

served as park commissioner from 1893 to 1895.   In
the latter year he became a state senator from the
Ninth Suffolk district, and served on the committees
on   Metropolitan   Affairs,   Federal   Relations   and
Constitutional Amendments, Education and Libraries.   In the autumn of 1896 he was elected to the
fifty-fifth Congress from the eleventh Massachusetts
district, and was reëlected the ensuing year.   During
his residence at Washington the development of a
nervous affection obliged him to retire from public
life.   His death occurred at Providence, R. I., Jan.
30, 1902.

Previous to his removal to Washington, Mr.
Sprague resided on his fine Brookline estate, noted
for its beautiful park and Italian garden.

92. IV. **Richard,** b. at Brookline, June 16, 1859.

Richard Sprague attended the schools of Messrs.
Kidder and Hopkinson in Boston.   He graduated
at Harvard in 1881, and entered the Medical School
in Sept., 1883, taking the three years' course.   He
was for two years a surgical house-officer at the
Massachusetts General Hospital, and received the
degree of M. D. at Commencement, 1887.   The
following spring he went abroad, and spent two
years and a half in studying medicine at Vienna and
in travel.   Returning to Boston, he began practice
in the autumn of 1890.   He died June 28, 1902.

93. V. **Elizabeth Lejée,** b. April 25, 1863; d.
Sept. 7, 1864.

Seth Edward Sprague was a son of the Hon.
Peleg Sprague (H. U. 1812), U. S. senator from

Maine, 1829–35; judge of the U. S. District Court for Massachusetts, 1840–65) and Sarah (Deming) Sprague, and was born at Hallowell, Me., April 12, 1821. He attended the public schools in that city, and later the private school of the Hon. Stephen Minot Weld in Jamaica Plain. Graduate of Harvard College, Class of 1841, and of the Law School. Admitted to the bar, Sept. 3, 1844. He received an appointment as clerk of the United States District Court in 1842, and retained this office for twenty-seven years, until he was obliged to resign by reason of failing health. Mr. Sprague visited Europe twice, and made a trip to California in 1852. He died at Boston, June 22, 1869.

FAMILY NO. 13

24. **Fanny,** m., March 3, 1852, Henry Austin Whitney, son of Joseph and Elizabeth (Pratt) Whitney.

Their children:

94. I. **Henry Lawrence,** b. Oct. 27, 1853; d. Oct. 23, 1866.

95. II. **Joseph Cutler,** b. Dec. 7, 1856; m., Nov. 9, 1882, at King's Chapel, Boston, Georgiana Hayward, daughter of Dr. George (Harvard, 1839) and Annie (Upton) Hayward.

Their children, born at Boston, are:

96. 1. **Henry Lawrence,** b. Jan. 13, 1886.

97. 2. **George Hayward,** b. Jan. 31, 1892.

98. 3. **Robert Upton,** b. Nov. 6, 1895.

Joseph Cutler Whitney fitted for college at Mr.

Dixwell's school, and studied for a year under Professor George M. Lane as tutor. He graduated at Harvard in 1878, and is the secretary of his Class. He has made various mercantile and financial ventures. For more than eight years previous to Nov. 1, 1886, he was engaged in a wool commission business in Boston, but of late years the care of real estate and trust property has occupied much of his time. His office is at 53 Mason Building, Boston. Mr. Whitney has been a trustee of the Milton Public Library since 1884, and served as a selectman of Milton in 1894 and 1895. He is the author of a Memoir of his father, Henry Austin Whitney, which first appeared in the " New England Historical and Genealogical Register," April, 1889, and was later revised and reprinted with additions, in pamphlet form. He has also prepared four Reports of the Class of 1878 (H. U.). In the summer of 1879 he made a journey of four hundred miles on horseback, from Helena, Mont., through the Yellowstone National Park, which at that time was without shelter or other accommodation for tourists. In numerous business trips he has come to know intimately the States traversed by the Rocky Mountains, as well as many other Western States.

99. III. **Ellerton Pratt,** b. Aug. 21, 1858 ; m., at Magnolia, Mass., June 5, 1901, Ellen Cushman Sargent, daughter of Joseph and Ellen Louise (McClure) Sargent.

They have a daughter,

99a. **Ellen Louise,** b. Dec. 12, 1902.

Ellerton Pratt Whitney obtained his early education at Mr. Hopkinson's school and elsewhere. He did not go to college. Mr. Whitney is vice-president of the Merchants' and Miners' Transportation Company, a trustee for several large estates, and a member of the Massachusetts Metropolitan Park Commission. His residence is in Milton, where he passes the entire year. He has always taken an interest in the affairs of his town and has held various town offices, and was president of the local water company from the date of its origin until it was sold to the town. Arboriculture is one of his many interests.

100. IV. **Elizabeth**, b. March 23, 1860; m., at Milton, Oct. 30, 1884, James Jackson Minot, M. D., son of George Richards and Harriet (Jackson) Minot.

Their children, all born at Boston, are:

101. 1. **George Richards**, b. Dec. 2, 1885.

102. 2. **James Jackson**, b. Nov. 17, 1891.

103. 3. **Henry Whitney**, b. Feb. 6, 1896.

Mrs. Elizabeth (Whitney) Minot d. at Boston, Feb. 19, 1903.

James Jackson Minot was born at West Roxbury, Oct. 11, 1852. He attended the private schools of Miss Lane in Jamaica Plain, and of Mr. Dixwell in Boston. A. B., 1874, M. D., 1878, Harvard. He served a year as medical house-officer in the Massachusetts General Hospital, and in the summer of 1878 he went to Europe and continued his studies at the Universities of Vienna, Berlin, and Strasburg. Returning home in Aug., 1880, he began practice in Boston, serving on the medical staff of the Boston Dispensary from 1880 to 1889, and also as visiting physician to the Carney Hospital, and as physician to the Out-patient Department of the Massachusetts General Hospital. He became a Fellow of the Massachusetts Medical Society in 1877, and is a member of other medical and scientific organizations.

104. V. **Constance,** b. May 11, 1865; m., at Milton, Sept. 11, 1890, Franz Edouard Zerrahn, and has these:

105. 1. **Constance,** b. at Brush Hill, Milton, June 21, 1891.

106. 2. **Elizabeth,** b. at Brush Hill, Milton, March 21, 1899.

Franz Edouard Zerrahn was born in Massachusetts, March 17, 1858. He is a son of Carl Zerrahn of Rostock, Mecklenburg-Schwerin, Germany, and was educated in the Boston public schools and at the Massachusetts Institute of Technology. He is an architect.

107. VI. **Hugh,** b. at Brush Hill, Milton, Sept. 7, 1870; m., at Beverly, Mass., Oct. 20, 1897, Eleanor Amalia Cecilia Marguerite Shattuck, daughter of Dr. George Brune and Amalia Schutte (Lavalle) Shattuck.

They have:

108. I. A son, b. at Beverly, July 20, 1898; d. the next day.

109. II. **Eleanor,** b. at Brush Hill, Milton, Sept. 2, 1899.

Henry Austin Whitney, the only son of Joseph and Elizabeth (Pratt) Whitney, was born at Boston, Oct. 6, 1826. He was christened Henry Augustus Whitney, but his middle name was changed as above by decree of Probate Court, in Feb., 1857. His Puritan ancestor, John Whitney of Isleworth, County of Middlesex, England, emigrated with his family to New England in the year 1635, and settled at Watertown, Mass., where he became a prominent citizen and land proprietor, serving as selectman seventeen years, and continuing a resident of that town until his death in 1673. His son Thomas, who was born in England, lived successively in Watertown, Stow, and in that portion of Lancaster township which is now called Bolton. Benjamin Whitney (1687–1737), a son of Thomas, was a resident of Marlborough, and was active in the defence of the frontier settlements against the Indians. His son Samuel (1734–1808) was engaged in business for some years in Boston, but removed to Concord in 1767, where he became an earnest patriot during the Revolutionary period, and took part in the Concord fight. Joseph Whitney (1771–1812), a son of the preceding, engaged in mercantile affairs in Boston, and his only son Joseph (1796–1869) was left an orphan at the age of sixteen. While still a youth, Joseph Whitney, Jr., became a partner in a business firm in Boston, and by industry, ability, and strict integrity he met with ample success, and that too during times of financial depression. He married, in 1822, Elizabeth, the second daughter of John and Mary (Tewksbury) Pratt. Their son, Henry Austin Whitney, obtained his early training chiefly at Asa Wing's boarding-school at Sandwich, Mass., and at Chauncy Hall School, Boston. He took the four years' course at Harvard, graduating with the famous Class of 1846.

Upon leaving college, Mr. Whitney was for two years a clerk in a dry goods house, and in 1849 he was admitted a partner in the firm of Joseph Whitney & Co., manufacturers of men's boots and brogans. His father retired at the close of the year 1866, and Mr. Whitney continued in business with the remaining partners until 1872, when the firm was dissolved. He was for many years a director and later vice-president of the Merchants' and Miners' Transportation Company, and was also a director of the New England Trust Company and of the Shoe and Leather Dealers' National Bank, a trustee of the Provident Institution for Savings, and a director of the Boston and Providence Railroad Company from 1871 and its president for thirteen years. He held many other official positions at different times, serving as a trustee of the Massachusetts General Hospital, and vice-president of the Humane Society of Massachusetts.

Mr. Whitney had marked literary tastes, and was especially interested in antiquarian and genealogical researches. He prepared a number of articles relating to the Whitney family which were privately printed. A list of these, together with the titles of some of his other literary contributions, is contained in a Memoir prepared by his son, Joseph Cutler Whitney, and reprinted in pamphlet form, with additions, from the " New England Historical and Genealogical Register." From this Memoir chiefly, the compiler has derived the information contained in this sketch. Mr. Whitney's death occurred at Boston, Feb. 21, 1889.

FAMILY NO. 14

25. **William Richards,** m., at St. Paul's Church, in Boston, Dec. 6, 1838, Susan Coombs Dana (b. July 16, 1817), sixth child of Rev. Samuel Dana of Marblehead and Henrietta (Bridge) Dana.

THE DANA FAMILY

All persons in the United States who bear the name of Dana are believed to trace their lineage from Richard Dana, who emigrated from England in the year 1640, and settled on the south side of the Charles River, in Cambridge, Mass., within the present limits of Brighton. According to tradition, his father was a French Huguenot, who sought refuge in England on account of religious persecution, during the reign of Louis XIII. In the early Cambridge records the name is sometimes spelled *Dany*, and is so pronounced not infrequently at the present time in the rural districts of New England. Richard Dana married Ann Bullard of Cambridge about 1648. He died April 2, 1690.

Benjamin Dana (1660–1738), the seventh child of Richard, m. Mary Buckminster, May 24, 1688. They had ten children, of whom the fifth, Joseph (1700–1778), m. (first), March 2, 1726, Rebecca Hamblet. She d. Dec. 28, 1730, and he m. (second), about 1733, Mrs. Mary Fulham Moore.

Their third and youngest child was Joseph Dana, who was born at Pomfret, Conn., Nov. 2, 1742. He saw, in his boyhood, the wolf which was killed by Israel Putnam. Mr. Dana graduated from Yale in

1760, and studied divinity with Rev. Dr. Hart of Preston, Conn., being licensed to preach before he had attained his majority. He was ordained pastor of the Second Church in Ipswich, Mass., Nov. 7, 1765, and retained the position for more than sixty years. He m. (first) Mary, daughter of Daniel and Mary (Burnham) Staniford. She d. May 14, 1772, and he m. (second) Mary, daughter of Samuel Turner of Boston. He received the degree of S. T. D. from Harvard in 1801. Died Nov. 16, 1827.

Samuel, the only son of Joseph and Mary (Turner) Dana, was born May 7, 1778; grad. Harvard, 1796; ordained pastor of the First Congregational Church in Marblehead, Oct. 7, 1801. He m. (first) Susan Coombs, who d. Sept. 13, 1805, aged 26. Rev. Mr. Dana m. (second) Henrietta Bridge, daughter of Richard Perkins Bridge, M. D., of Petersham, Mass., and Anna (Harrington) Bridge. She was born Aug. 20, 1781, and died at Marblehead, April 1, 1863. Rev. Samuel Dana d. Aug. 16, 1864, aged 86 years.

From a letter of Richard H. Dana to Samuel T. Dana of Boston, June 9, 1842

The genealogical letter I send you begins with Richard Dana, our common ancestor, who came to this country about the middle of the seventeenth century. He was the lineal descendant, and, as far as we can learn, the only one living at the time of his emigration, of William Dana, Esq., who was sheriff of Middlesex during the reign of Elizabeth. To William Dana was given the coat of arms (a copy of which I send you) used by him and his descendants, and now to be found in the Heralds' College, London. A relative of ours made inquiries for it there a few years ago, and gave us a minute description of it, by which we rectified an error in the color of the fox at the top: the coat of arms has this motto, "Cavendo tutus," and is dated 1569. We have not the line of descent from William to Richard. The latter was a Puritan, and took little pains to preserve his genealogy, thinking it savored of the pride of life. He, however, kept this coat of arms and left it to his descendants, with the tradition of his descent. The accompanying letter is from John Jay Dana, clergyman of Canaan, N. Y. dated Aug. 19, 1841: "Richard Dana, who died at Cambridge, Mass., April 2, 1690, was the first and only one of our ancestors who emigrated to America, and from him, it is supposed, are descended all the branches of the family. The year of his arrival is unknown. The first act of Richard's which appears on record is a deed of fifty-eight acres of land, sold by him to Edward Jackson, April 20, 1656, situated on the south side of Charles River, on the road from Newton Four Corners to Boston, known now as the 'Hunnewell Farm.' He married Ann Bullard of Cambridge. He died suddenly, left no will, and his estate was settled by the mutual consent of his children. The agreement was signed April 15, 1695, by his widow Ann and his sons Jacob, Joseph, Benjamin and Daniel, and by his sons-in-law, Samuel Oldham, Daniel Woodard, and Samuel Hyde. (Middlesex Probate Records, vol. 8, p. 331.) Richard and his wife were members of Cambridge Church as early as 1660."

Children of William Richards and Susan Coombs (Dana) Lawrence:

110. I. **Francis William**, b. at Brookline, Nov. 20, 1839; m., at Framingham, Mass., Jan. 27, 1863, Lucilla Train (b. at Framingham, Aug. 8, 1842), elder daughter of Hon. Charles Russell and Martha Ann (Jackson) Train, who was born at Hopkinton, now Ashland, Mass., Nov. 13, 1819; d. Nov. 14, 1867.

THE TRAIN FAMILY [1]

John Train, born in England about 1610, came to this country on the ship *Susan and Ellen* in 1635, and settled at Watertown, Mass. His first wife was Margaret Dix, who d. Dec. 18, 1660. He m. (second) Abigail Bent, Oct. 12, 1675. He d. at Watertown, Jan. 29, 1681.

John, the sixth of eight children of John and Margaret Train, was born May 25, 1651. He removed from Watertown to Weston. He m., March 24, 1674-5, Mary, daughter of Joshua Stubbs; d. at Weston in 1718.

John Train, third of the name, fourth child of John and Mary, was born Oct. 31, 1682. He m., May 5, 1705, Lydia, daughter of Samuel Jennison. They had nine children.

Samuel, third child of John and Lydia, was born Dec. 22, 1711. He m. (first) Mary Holden of Con-

[1] Formerly sometimes written Trayne or Traine.

cord. (The bans were published April 2, 1738.) She d. and he m. for his second wife, Dec. 31, 1741, Rachel Allen. He d. at Weston in 1806, at the age of 95.

Deacon Samuel Train, second child of the preceding, was born Aug. 11, 1745. He m. Feb. 21, 1771, Deborah Brown, daughter of Arthur Savage (Weston church records), who d. in 1828. He served as constable in 1786, selectman in 1797, and held other offices at Weston. He d. in 1839, aged 93.

Rev. Charles Train, third child of Deacon Samuel and Deborah, was born at Weston, Jan. 7, 1783. He graduated at Harvard in 1805, and was preceptor of the Framingham Academy in 1808. Ordained pastor of the Baptist church in Framingham, Jan. 30, 1811. He was a representative to the General Court for six years, and state senator. He m. (first), Aug. 15, 1810, Elizabeth, third daughter of Abraham Harrington of Weston. She d. Sept. 14, 1814, and he m. (second), Oct. 10, 1815, Hepzibah Harrington, younger sister of his first wife. Rev. Charles Train d. at Framingham, Sept. 17, 1849.

The Hon. Charles Russell Train, second son of Rev. Charles and Hepzibah (Harrington) Train, was born Oct. 18, 1817. He attended Framingham Academy, graduated at Brown University in 1837, and then studied law, spending a year at the Harvard Law School. In 1841 he was admitted to the bar, and practised law in Framingham, until 1863, when he removed to Boston. Mr. Train represented Framingham in the Massachusetts General Court in 1847–48, and Boston in 1868 and in 1870–71. He was district attorney for the Northern District, 1848–51 ; and representative from the eighth Massachusetts district in the thirty-sixth and thirty-seventh Congresses. Mr. Train served in the War of the Rebellion as assistant adjutant-general on the staff of Brigadier-General George H. Gordon. He was attorney-general of Massachusetts for seven years from 1871. During the latter part of this period, William Caleb Loring, now a justice of the Supreme Court of Massachusetts, held the office of assistant adjutant-general. Mr. Train m. (first), Oct. 27, 1841, Martha Ann Jackson, who d. Nov. 14, 1867. He m. (second), June 14, 1869, Sarah Maria Cheney. His eldest child, Lucilla, m., at Framingham, Jan. 27, 1863, Francis William Lawrence. The Hon. Charles Russell Train d. at Conway, N. H., July 29, 1885.

Francis William Lawrence received his early education at Lawrence Academy, Groton, Phillips Academy, Andover, and at private schools in Boston and Paris, France. He was for three years a member of the Class of 1861, Harvard College, and afterwards studied medicine at the Portland Medical School and at the Harvard Medical School. Soon after the breaking out of the civil war, in 1862, while a medical student, he went to Port Royal, S. C., as one of the surgeons of the Massachusetts Educational Commission, and after holding that position a few months, received an appointment as acting assistant surgeon U. S. A., and was stationed on St. Helena Island, S. C. While there he purchased a large cotton plantation, and was quite successful in raising the celebrated sea island cotton. At the close of the war in 1865 he sold his plantation and returned to Boston, and in the following year he settled in Longwood, Brookline. Mr. Lawrence served for eleven years as a selectman of Brookline, being chairman of the board a part of the time, and was for twelve years chairman of the Brookline Park Commission. He served for six years on the staff of the Second Brigade, M. V. M., as provost-marshal with the rank of captain, and as assistant adjutant-general with the rank of lieutenant-colonel. In 1881 he was appointed by President Garfield one of the Board of Visitors to the U. S. Naval Academy at Annapolis, Md. He has served continuously as vestryman, treasurer, and warden of the Church of Our Saviour, Longwood, since 1868. He was for many years a director of the Brookline Gas-Light Company, and for some time its clerk and treasurer.

Mr. Lawrence was president of the Brookline National Bank, and of the Globe Gas-Light Company of Boston ; a director of the Ipswich Mills and of the Merrimac Chemical Company, and a trustee of various private trusts. He was also president of the Boston Dispensary, vice-president of the New England Conservatory of Music, and a trustee of St. Luke's Home for Convalescents in Roxbury, of the Trustees of Donations, and of the Boston Episcopal Charitable Society.

In 1882 he built a cottage at Bar Harbor, Me., which was destroyed by lightning in June, 1901. Mr. Lawrence was an active worker in the parish of St. Saviour at Bar Harbor, and served on its financial committee. He was an original member of the Kebo Valley Club and of the Mount Desert Reading Room.

He died at Longwood, March 10, 1903.

Resolutions on the death of Francis William Lawrence adopted by the Trustees of the New England Conservatory of Music:

"The executive committee of the board of trustees of the New England Conservatory of Music met on Wednesday afternoon, March 18, 1903, to take action on the death of Mr. Francis W. Lawrence, a valued member of the board. Mr. Lawrence became a trustee of the Conservatory on Jan. 16, 1896, and was elected a vice-president of the board on May 18, 1898. His deep interest in the work of the institution and the esteem in which he was held by his associates on the board of trustees are set forth in the following resolutions which were presented at the meeting:

"*Resolved*, That the government of the New England Conservatory of Music has received with the keenest sorrow the announcement of the death of Francis William Lawrence, one of its most esteemed and beloved members.

"His musical taste and knowledge, fostered by natural ability, by long experience in musical bodies, and by delightful practice in the domestic circle, gave especial value to his interest in our objects; and his business capacity, exercised in so many other public functions, was of the greatest importance in our practical and financial concerns.

"His devotion to our welfare and progress, shown not only by attendance and wise counsels at our meetings, but also by frequent visits to our house and constant presence at our private and public performances, was of the greatest encouragement to his associates as well as to teachers and pupils.

"*Resolved*, That these resolutions be entered upon our records, in remembrance of all that we have lost, and that they be communicated to his family in token of heartfelt sympathy."

At a meeting of the Vestry of the Church of Our Saviour, Longwood, holden March 19, 1903, it was *resolved* that "*Whereas*, by the will of Almighty God, the parish and Church of Our Saviour has been deprived by death of its Senior Warden, Francis William Lawrence; we, the Vestry of said Church of Our Saviour, desire to record our deep sense of grief in the loss of a faithful Christian worker in the church, a beloved friend, and a valued counsellor. Mr. Lawrence has been a constant worshipper here ever since this church was built and presented to the corporation by his father and uncle in 1868. After being a vestryman for several years, he became treasurer of the church corporation in 1878, serving for two years in that capacity. He was junior warden from 1885 to 1893, and senior warden for the ten succeeding years till his death. The Church owes much to his faithful work and wise counsel. As a token of our sense of bereavement, we direct that this resolution be inscribed in the records of the corporation, and that a copy be sent to his afflicted family."

At a meeting of the directors of the Brookline National Bank, March 24, 1903, the following vote was placed on record: "The Brookline National Bank, in the death of Francis W. Lawrence, has been greatly bereaved. He was one of its incorporators, had been a director continuously since its organization, serving the last seven years as president. A Christian gentleman, bearing a name which has been identified for generations with the religious, social, and business development of New England, he brought to the conduct of the bank's affairs rare tact, sound judgment, and a degree of financial ability worthy of his distinguished ancestry. To whatever of success as a conservative and safe institution the bank has attained, the counsels of Mr. Lawrence contributed generously. To us, the surviving original directors, his loss has come as a personal sorrow, for he was to each a faithful friend, whose memory will possess an abiding charm. We place this tribute of affectionate appreciation upon the records of the bank, and send a copy thereof to his family with sincere sympathy.

> C. H. W. FOSTER,
> M. W. QUINLAN,
> THOS. B. GRIGGS,   } Directors."
> REUBEN S. SWAN,
> GEO. W. WORTHLEY,

Appropriate resolutions were also adopted by the Board of Managers of the Boston Dispensary, and by other organizations with which Mr. Lawrence was connected.

111. II. Arthur, b. at Brookline, Aug. 22, 1842. Family No. 22. Stockbridge.

112. III. **Robert Means**, b. at Boston, May 14, 1847. Family No. 23. Boston.

William Richards Lawrence passed his early childhood in Boston. When his mother died, in 1819, he and his brother Amos were sent to Groton, where they remained two years in the care of their grandparents and aunts, and during this time William attended school at Groton Academy, afterwards called " Lawrence Academy." Upon their father's second marriage, in 1821, the two boys returned to Boston, and William entered the Public Latin School. In 1824 he was sent to Dummer Academy, Byfield, Mass., of which institution Nehemiah Cleaveland, LL. D., was the principal, and here the succeeding three years were passed, after which he entered the Lyceum at Gardiner, Me., remaining there a year. In the autumn of 1828, when sixteen years of age, he was sent to Europe to obtain the liberal education afforded by travel and residence abroad, and by the study of foreign languages and customs. He proceeded at once to Paris, and devoted himself chiefly to the study of French and Spanish, living at the capital during the first winter, and afterwards with a private family at Versailles.

Mr. Lawrence, then a youth of eighteen, was an eye-witness of many exciting scenes in Paris during the Revolution of 1830, when Charles X. was dethroned and Louis Philippe became king. He frequently saw General Lafayette, who at that time commanded the National Guard, and was afterwards introduced to the aged hero at a military reception at the latter's house.

In Feb., 1831, accompanied by Mr. Stephen Salisbury of Worcester, Mass., he proceeded to Spain, reaching Madrid after a three weeks' journey over the snowy Pyrenees and through the provinces of Barcelona and Valencia. He then made a tour in Andalusia and Granada, travelling with post-horses, and thence on horseback through a bandit-infested region, to Malaga, and from there sailed in a small schooner to Gibraltar. Continuing, he embarked in a coast-wise vessel for Cadiz, and proceeded by diligence to Seville and Madrid. Mr. Lawrence now established himself in the latter city, living at the house of a Spanish lady, Dona Florentia Gonsalez, where the poet Longfellow had previously stayed. And here he rapidly acquired a good knowledge of the language and familiarized himself with the mode of life of the people. He left Madrid in Sept., 1831, and after a month's tour in Switzerland he again visited Paris, where the winter was passed.

The following spring, after travelling in Great Britain, he embarked for home. His frequent letters to relatives during four years' residence abroad contain many shrewd observations on the political situation in the countries where he sojourned, and he returned to Boston in July, 1832, with increased loyalty and affection for his native land. That same autumn he entered the counting-room of Messrs. A. & A. Lawrence, and soon after formed a business partnership with the late Samuel Frothingham, which continued for several years.

Owing to a delicacy of constitution, Mr. Lawrence was obliged to spend several successive winters in climates more genial than that of his native city. In Dec., 1834, he made an extended Southern tour with his friend, Francis Boott, spending some ten weeks in Cuba. In the following year he became a member of the recently formed " French Club," composed chiefly of young men who had travelled abroad. This was the nucleus of the present Somerset Club.

In Feb., 1838, he became engaged to Miss Susan Coombs Dana, daughter of Rev. Samuel Dana of Marblehead, Mass. Miss Dana was living at that time in Beverly with her aunt, Mrs. Israel Thorndike, in the fine old mansion which has been for many years the Town Hall building. The wedding took place at St. Paul's Church, Boston, on Dec. 6, following. After his marriage, Mr. Lawrence resided for several years in Brookline, which was the birthplace of his two elder sons.

In 1841 he began the study of medicine, attending lectures at the Harvard Medical School, and graduating therefrom in 1844. In November of that year he sailed with his family for Havre, and thence went to Paris, where the ensuing sixteen months were devoted to visiting the hospitals and attending clinics. After his return home, with his father's aid he fitted up a large building on " Boston Neck," and there instituted a Children's Infirmary.

Dr. Lawrence was an original member of the Warren Club, afterwards called the " Thursday Evening

Club," which was founded in 1847. In that year he left Brookline and occupied a house on Colonnade Row, Tremont Street, in Boston, and in the autumn of 1851 he purchased a house on Beacon Street, nearly opposite Arlington Street. This house was at that time the most westward of inhabited dwellings on the so-called Mill-dam. After 1866 he made his home at Longwood.

Dr. Lawrence was a member of the New England Emigrant Aid Society, which was formed with a view to the prevention of slavery in Kansas and Nebraska, an enterprise wherein his brother Amos was especially prominent as a trustee and treasurer of the society, devoting thereto much time, energy, and material aid. Dr. Lawrence was interested in many philanthropic undertakings, and was a life member of the Boston Dispensary and for many years chairman of its Board of Managers. He was also a trustee of the Boston City Hospital, of the Church Home for Orphan and Destitute Children, and of St. Luke's Home for Convalescents in Roxbury.

In 1855 he published " The Diary and Correspondence of Amos Lawrence," a work which had a wide circulation. He was also the author of a " History of the Boston Dispensary," and of a volume entitled " The Charities of France."

Dr. Lawrence was an active worker for the interests of the Episcopal Church, and was instrumental in founding three parishes: St. John's, Jamaica Plain; Emmanuel, in Boston; and, with the coöperation of his brother, the Church of Our Saviour in Longwood, a memorial to their father. After his marriage he attended St. Paul's Church, Boston, and had a class in its Sunday-school. Among his scholars were Arthur J. C. Sowdon, Charles H. Appleton, Dr. Hasket Derby, and Bishop Phillips Brooks.

During the later years of his residence at Longwood, symptoms of a spinal affection appeared, which developed slowly, but made it necessary for him to have an attendant. In the ensuing season of weakness and dependence upon others, he displayed constant patience and resignation, fully appreciative of the loving ministrations of those about him. His death occurred at Swampscott, Sept. 20, 1885.[1]

Mrs. Susan Coombs (Dana) Lawrence died at Magnolia, Mass., Aug. 14, 1900.

As a memorial to William Richards Lawrence and Susan Coombs (Dana) Lawrence, their three sons built and gave to St. Luke's Home for Convalescents in Roxbury a chapel, to be known as St. Luke's Chapel. The corner-stone was laid Nov. 21, 1901, by Bishop William Lawrence, assisted by Rev. Arthur Lawrence, D. D., Rev. Reginald Heber Howe, D. D., and Rev. Charles Henry Brent, Bishop-elect of the Philippines. The first service in the new chapel was held on Sunday, June 22, 1902, and the building was consecrated by Bishop Lawrence, assisted by several of the clergy, Nov. 8, 1902. St. Luke's Chapel is constructed of brick and stone, and its entrance faces the Convalescent Home, with which it is connected by a covered gallery, which

[1] No memoir of Dr. Lawrence having been published, the compiler has given the more space to this sketch, which is condensed from a fuller account, intended for separate publication.

also serves as a sun-parlor. The chapel is of the perpendicular Gothic style of architecture, and is well proportioned, having a seating capacity for seventy persons.

FAMILY NO. 15

26. **Amos Adams**, m., at her father's house, 54 Beacon Street, Boston, March 31, 1842, Sarah Elizabeth, the second daughter of Hon. William and Mary Anne (Cutler) Appleton. She was born at Boston, Feb. 9, 1822; d. at Longwood, May 27, 1891.

Their children:

113. I. **Marianne Appleton**, b. at Boston, May 12, 1843; m. Dr. Robert Amory. Family No. 24. Brookline.

114. II. **Sarah**, b. at Brookline, July 5, 1845; m. Peter Chardon Brooks. Family No. 25. Boston and West Medford.

115. III. **Amory Appleton**, b. at Boston, April 22, 1848. Family No. 26. Boston.

116. IV. **William**, b. at Boston, May 30, 1850. Family No. 27. Boston.

117. V. **Susan Mason**, b. at Longwood, Feb. 4, 1852; m., at Longwood, Sept. 25, 1883, William Caleb Loring.

THE LORING FAMILY

William Caleb Loring is of the eighth generation in descent from Thomas Loring of Axminster, Devonshire, England, whose wife was Jane Newton, also of Axminster. They crossed the sea to New England in 1634, with their sons Thomas and John, and made their home at Dorchester, Mass., for a short time, afterwards removing to Hingham, where he became one of the first deacons of the church established there in 1635. He was made a freeman at about the same time. In 1641 he settled at Hull, where he was elected constable in March, 1646. Deacon Thomas Loring is described as a " godly and religious man, who was a sufferer for his religion in his native land," and his wife was "a woman of a lively, active spirit, whose skill in the practice of physic brought her into an acquaintance with some of the principal persons in the country."

John Loring, second son of Deacon Thomas, was born at Axminster, England, Dec. 22, 1630, and was but four years old when he accompanied his parents to America. In an old manuscript, a copy of which is to be found in the " Chronicles or Ancestral Records of the Loring Family of Massachusetts Bay," it is stated (p. 29) that " before he had attained the age of five years, he began to be religious. Going abroad to play, upon the Lord's Day, he fell down upon a stone and hurt his knee; this had a deep impression upon his young and tender soul." John Loring's first wife was Mary, only child of Nathaniel and Sarah (Lane) Baker of Hingham, and their marriage took place Dec. 16, 1657. They had eight sons and three daughters. She d. July 13, 1679, and he m. for his second wife, Sept. 22, 1679, Rachel (Wheatly) Buckland, widow of Benjamin Buckland of Rehoboth. They had four children, of whom the youngest was Caleb. She d. Sept. 20, 1713, and her husband d. at Hingham, Sept. 19, 1714.

Caleb Loring, first of the name, was born at Hull, Jan. 2, 1689. He m. (first) Elizabeth Baker, June 24, 1714. She d. Sept. 9, 1715, and he m. (second), Feb. 15, 1719, Susanna Coxe, who d. April 8, 1723. Caleb Loring m. for his third wife, Feb. 6, 1732, Rebecca Lobdell. He was a justice of the peace, and a selectman of Hull. He d. Sept. 15, 1756.

Caleb Loring, " second," son of the preceding, was born at Hull, March 29, 1736. He settled first at Hingham, and was "engaged in navigation." His first wife was Sarah Bradford, whom he m. in 1760. She d. July 11, 1769, and he m. (second). in 1770, Margaret (Tidmarsh) Loring, widow of his brother Joshua, and took up his residence in Boston, where he died in 1787.

Caleb Loring, " third," son of Caleb and Sarah (Bradford) Loring, was born Jan. 13, 1764. He was a resident of Boston, and a member of the firm of Loring & Curtis, merchants. He m., Feb. 22, 1789, Ann, daughter of Captain Jonathan Greely. Caleb Loring was a member of the Massachusetts Humane Society, and senator from Suffolk County in 1828. He d. in Boston, Oct. 31, 1850.

Charles Greely Loring, third child of Caleb and Ann (Greely) Loring, was born at Boston, May 2, 1794. His mother was a daughter of Captain Jonathan Greely, who was killed in an engagement with a British frigate off Marblehead, during the Revolutionary war. He was a medal scholar at the Boston Public Latin School, and entered the Sophomore Class at Harvard in 1809, graduating in 1812. After studying law at Litchfield, Conn., and in the office of

Judge Charles Jackson, in Boston, he began practice
in 1815, and in the following year formed a partnership with Franklin Dexter. Mr. Loring was married
three times, first in 1816, to Anna Pierce Brace of
Litchfield, Conn., who d. in 1836. She was the
mother of Caleb William Loring. In 1840 he m.
(second), Mary Ann, daughter of Judge Samuel
Putnam. She d. in 1845, and he m. for his third
wife, July 3, 1850, the widow Cornelia Goddard, whose
maiden name was Amory. Mr. Loring continued to
practise law in Boston for many years, and rose to
eminence in his profession. From 1835 to 1857 he
was a Fellow of Harvard College; LL. D. 1850. In
1854 he became the actuary of the Massachusetts
Hospital Life Insurance Company, and was elected
to the State Senate in 1862. He d. at Beverly, Mass.,
Oct. 8, 1867.

Caleb William Loring, eldest child of Charles
Greely and Anna Pierce (Brace) Loring, was born at
Dorchester, Mass., July 31, 1819. At the age of ten
he entered the Public Latin School in Boston, graduated at Harvard in 1839, and at the Law School two
years after. He was admitted to the Suffolk bar,
July 6, 1842, and entered into partnership with his
father and William Dehon. Mr. Loring m., Jan.
15, 1846, at Boston, Elizabeth Smith, daughter of
Joseph Augustus and Louisa (Putnam) Peabody of
Salem. He was at one time president of the Plymouth Cordage Company. He d. at Camden, S. C.,
Jan. 29, 1897. Mrs. Elizabeth Smith (Peabody) Loring d. at Boston, Dec. 13, 1869.

William Caleb Loring, a son of Caleb William and

Elizabeth Smith (Peabody) Loring, was born at Beverly, Mass., Aug. 24, 1851. He attended the private schools of Messrs. Fettee and Dixwell in Boston, and took the regular course at Harvard (A. B. 1872, A. M. 1875). After leaving college, he entered the Law School, from which he was graduated, receiving the degree of LL. B. *cum laude*, at Commencement, 1874, and was admitted to the Suffolk bar, June 21 of that year. In Aug. and Sept., 1875, he held the position of secretary to Chief Justice Horace Gray, and in December following was appointed assistant attorney-general of Massachusetts under Hon. Charles Russell Train, which office he held until July, 1878, when he resigned and entered the firm of Ropes, Gray & Loring. Mr. Loring continued to practise law for twenty-one years, and from May, 1882, to June, 1884, he held the position of general solicitor and general manager of the New York and New England Railroad Company. His marriage to Susan Mason Lawrence occurred Sept. 25, 1883. He was appointed an associate justice of the Supreme Court of Massachusetts, Sept. 7, 1899, and at Commencement, 1901, Harvard University conferred upon him the degree of Doctor of Laws.

Justice Loring and Mrs. Loring have made many trips abroad and have travelled extensively in Europe. Among his publications is an article on " The Effect of the Seventeenth Section of the Statute of Frauds," in the " American Law Review," Jan., 1875.

118. VI. **Hetty Sullivan,** b. at Longwood, Nov. 21, 1855; m. Frederick Cunningham. Family No. 28. Longwood.

119. VII. **Harriett Dexter,** b. at Longwood, June 8, 1858; m. Augustus Hemenway. Family No. 29. Boston and Readville.

Mrs. Sarah Elizabeth (Appleton) Lawrence died at Longwood, May 27, 1891.

Amos Adams Lawrence, the second son of Amos and Sarah (Richards) Lawrence, was born at Boston, July 31, 1814. His mother died when he was but four years old, and he and his brother William were then sent to Groton, where they passed two years at the old homestead. After his father's second marriage, April 16, 1821, he received instruction at private schools in Boston for several years, and in 1827 he was sent to Franklin Academy, a boarding-school situated in the North Parish, Andover, Mass. The master of this institution, Simeon Putnam, Esq., was a strict disciplinarian. Amos spent four years at Franklin Academy, and during that period were already noticeable those sterling traits of character which later rendered his name synonymous with the strictest integrity.

He was admitted to Harvard, Aug. 31, 1831, and in the following spring occurred a so-called " gunpowder plot," in which some of his classmates were involved. Although not directly implicated in the affair, it was thought advisable that he should leave college for a time, in view of the excited state of feeling prevalent among the students, and this course was advocated by President Quincy.

Accordingly he continued his studies during the ensuing eighteen months under the instruction of

Hon. John F. Stearns as tutor, taking up his abode at first in the town of Bedford. Here "the study of the village characters and his interest in the town meetings, with their lively Orthodox and Liberal discussions, gave him that experience in affairs and that tact in meeting men of all classes, which he felt was a part of the education of every American boy, and which served him well in later years."[1]

After leaving Bedford, he spent some months at Andover, and rejoined his class at Harvard, April 26, 1833.

During the following spring vacation Amos made a journey to Washington, where he visited the Houses of Congress and was introduced to President Andrew Jackson by Hon. Franklin Pierce, who in 1853 himself succeeded to the presidency.

Graduating in 1835, he was for a short time with the firm of Almy, Patterson & Co., dry goods commission merchants in Boston; and then made an extended trip in the Western and Southern States, whereby he acquired much practical knowledge of business methods, which was of value in his subsequent mercantile career. After his return home, Mr. Lawrence was for three years engaged in business on his own account as a commission merchant. Owing to the unsettled conditions following the financial crisis of the year 1837, he decided to close up his affairs, and in Nov., 1839, he visited Europe with his brother-in-law, Rev. Charles Mason (H. U. 1832).

---

[1] *Life of Amos A. Lawrence*, by his son, William Lawrence, 1888, p. 15. The compiler is indebted chiefly to the above-mentioned volume for the facts contained in this account.

He remained abroad for about two years, travelling chiefly in Great Britain and Italy, and during this period maintained a frequent and voluminous correspondence with his father, his brother William, and other relatives. Soon after his return home, he married, March 31, 1842, Sarah Elizabeth Appleton, and took up his residence in Pemberton Square, Boston. In May, 1843, he formed a business partnership with Robert M. Mason, under the style of Mason & Lawrence. After three years Mr. Mason retired, other partners were admitted, and the business was continued under the firm name of Lawrence & Co. For more than forty years they were selling agents for the Cocheco and Salmon Falls Manufacturing Companies. Of the former Mr. Lawrence was president, and of the latter treasurer for a long period. He also served as a director of the Suffolk Bank, Massachusetts General Hospital, American Insurance Office, Boston Water Power Corporation, Amesbury Company, Middlesex Canal, Massachusetts Bible Society, Massachusetts Board of Domestic Missions, and Groton Academy.

But his manifold and engrossing business cares did not prevent him from devoting much time and attention to philanthropic and church work. Freely of his abundance he dispensed to the poor, and to his ready sympathy was joined a wise discrimination in giving.

About the year 1846 he became the owner of a large tract of land in eastern Wisconsin, and here, on the banks of the Fox River, was founded the town of Appleton, which is now a thriving city and the capital of Outagamie County. Here in 1849 was established "Lawrence University," a Methodist educational institution, named after Mr. Lawrence, its founder and principal benefactor.

In the autumn of 1851 he removed his residence from Pemberton Square, Boston, to Cottage Farm, afterward included in "Longwood," where he and his brother had bought many acres of land.

When in 1854 the new Territory of Kansas was involved in a struggle between the pro-slavery party and the free-soilers, Mr. Lawrence became actively interested in promoting the cause of the latter, and served as treasurer and as one of three trustees of the New England Emigrant Aid Company, whose chief object was to prevent the establishment of slavery in Kansas and Nebraska. In furtherance of this aim he gave liberally of his means, and devoted to it much time and thought. Indeed it may truly be said that chiefly through his efforts and those of Mr. Eli Thayer of Worcester, Kansas became a free State. It was therefore most fitting that one of its principal cities should bear the name of Lawrence.

In 1857 he was appointed treasurer of Harvard College, which position he held for about five years.

In the fall of 1860 he was chosen by the so-called "Union Party" as their candidate for governor of Massachusetts. Previous to the outbreak of the civil war, and for some time after, Mr. Lawrence, always intensely patriotic, was very active in furthering the Union cause by every means in his power. In spite of numerous official and business cares, he devoted a portion of each day to military drill and to the instruction of college students and his fellow-townsmen in the manual of arms. In the autumn of 1862 he was foremost in recruiting the Second Regiment, Massachusetts Volunteer Cavalry, commanded by Colonel Charles R. Lowell, and in the following year he served as a member of the committee appointed by Governor Andrew to organize and recruit the Fifty-fourth Mass. Regiment (colored), of which Robert G. Shaw was the colonel.

In the summer of 1865 steps were taken for the erection of a Memorial Hall at Cambridge in honor of those sons of Harvard who had given their lives for the preservation of the Union, and Mr. Lawrence was appointed chairman of the Finance Committee, whose task it was to raise funds for this object.

In 1867 he and his brother erected the Church of Our Saviour, Longwood (in memory of their father), a handsome edifice, built of Roxbury stone, with granite trimmings. The church was consecrated by Bishop Eastburn, Sept. 29, 1868. In 1885 the stone rectory was built by Mrs. Amos A. Lawrence and presented to the parish; and in 1893 the beautiful transept of the church was finished by their children as a memorial to her.

When the Episcopal Theological School at Cambridge was founded, Mr. Lawrence was chosen its treasurer, and held the position fifteen years. In 1873 he built and presented to the school one half of a stone dormitory, known as " Lawrence Hall," which he finished seven years later. From 1879 to 1885 he was an overseer of Harvard College. He was the first president of the New England Trust Company, and a director of the Massachusetts Hospital Life Insurance Company. He was also for a time president of the National Association of Cotton Manufacturers and Planters, and of the Association of Knit-Goods Manufacturers. Mr. Lawrence died at Nahant, Aug. 22, 1886.

From the Boston Daily Advertiser, Aug. 31, 1886

To the Editor of the Advertiser : Many notices have appeared in the public prints of the death of Amos A. Lawrence, but I have seen none which, to my mind, gave any adequate idea of his simple and unassuming but uncommon character. His most striking qualities were, perhaps, religion, benevolence, and public spirit. He was diligent in acquiring wealth, but his only object in doing so seemed to be to bestow it on others. His own tastes and requirements were most simple. Entirely without ostentation, thoroughly imbued with the democratic spirit of our institutions, he was a man of whom Bostonians should be proud as a simple, true American gentleman, a natural product of the soil, whose purse and aid could always be counted upon for the furtherance of any good object, and who was equally prompt to speak out against and set his foot upon whatever seemed to him wrong. I know of no man whose relations to his fellow-men are more nearly expressed by Goldsmith's lines:

" His ready smile a parent's warmth expressed,
  Their welfare pleased him and their cares distressed;
  To them his heart, his love, his griefs were given,
  But all his serious thoughts had rest in heaven."

He never knowingly spoke an unkind word or did an unkind action, and this, not from forethought, but because it would have been contrary to his kindly nature.

His religious feeling manifested itself not only by the churches and religious schools which he built and endowed, but by his every-day conversation and writings, and though perhaps a little intolerant of the materialistic tendencies and unbelief of the present day, he was never a bigoted sectarian; in fact, quite the contrary, and always took great satisfaction in the church which he attended in summer at Nahant, from the fact that its pulpit was filled by ministers of every persuasion, and that its congregation was equally varied, and it was a source of peculiar pleasure to him that Christians of all sects could thus worship together.

His home was an ideal one. Though endowed with " all that beauty, all that wealth e'er gave," it took its example from its head and was not spoiled by luxury.

In Amos A. Lawrence the nation has lost one of its most patriotic citizens, his town one of its most liberal and public-spirited men, and his family its honored head and loving protector. But kind words can never die, nor a character like his be forgotten, and his memory will be cherished by a host of loving friends and be green in the hearts of his townsmen for many a day to come.

BROOKLINE.

The lineage of the Appleton family of New England has been authentically traced from John Appulton, or Appleton, of Great Waldingfield, Suffolk, England, where he was living at the beginning of the fifteenth century; and it is probable that he was a descendant of William de Appleton of Suffolk, who died in 1326.

Samuel Appleton, the emigrant ancestor, of the seventh generation from John, was born at Little Waldingfield in 1586. He m. (first), Jan. 24, 1616, Judith Everard, at Preston, Lancashire. She d. and he m. (second) Martha —— about 1633. Samuel Appleton came to America in 1635, and settled at Ipswich, Mass. He was made a freeman, May 25, 1636, and was a deputy to the General Court in 1637. He d. at Rowley in June, 1670.

Colonel Samuel Appleton, second child of Samuel, the emigrant, and Judith (Everard) Appleton, was born in Waldingfield in 1624, and came to this country with his father when eleven years old. He m. (first), April 2, 1651, Hannah, daughter of William Paine of Ipswich. They had three children. She d. and he m. for his second wife, Dec. 8, 1656, Mary, daughter of John Oliver of Newbury. He was a deputy to the General Court in 1668, and served several years. A commission as captain of a foot company of one hundred men was issued to him, Sept. 24, 1675. In this capacity he rendered valuable service during the early part of King Philip's war, and was promoted major and commander-in-chief of the New England

forces on the Connecticut River. He was an assistant under the Massachusetts colonial government
from 1682 to 1686, and a member of the first Provincial Council under Sir William Phipps. In 1687
he was imprisoned by the governor, Sir Edmund
Andros, "as a person disaffected to his Majesty's
Government," by reason of his resistance to the arbi-
trary usurpation of power by the governor. Colonel Samuel Appleton was a judge of the Inferior
Court of Common Pleas from 1692 until his death
at Ipswich, May 15, 1696.

Major Isaac Appleton, son of Colonel Samuel
and Mary (Oliver) Appleton, was born at Ipswich in
1664. His wife was Priscilla, daughter of Thomas
Baker of Topsfield, and granddaughter of Lieuten-
ant-Governor Symonds. He d. at Ipswich, May 22,
1747.

Isaac, son of Major Isaac and Priscilla (Baker)
Appleton, was born at Ipswich, May 30, 1704. He
m. (first) Elizabeth, daughter of Francis Sawyer of
Wells, Me. (The bans were published April 25,
1730.) She d. April 29, 1785, and he m. (second),
Dec. 11, 1785, Hephzibah, widow of Joseph Appleton.
She d. at Ipswich, July 7, 1788. Isaac Appleton removed, about the year 1752, to New Ipswich, N. H.,
where he became a deacon of the church and a respected citizen. " He was a true patriot, and on the
news of the Concord fight reaching town, he exerted
himself to arouse the people to hasten to repel the
enemy, and went himself with them." He d. Dec.
18, 1794, at the age of 90 years.

Rev. Joseph Appleton, tenth and youngest child of

Isaac and Elizabeth (Sawyer) Appleton, was born at Ipswich, Mass., June 9, 1751. He graduated at Brown University, Providence, R. I., in 1772, and was ordained minister of the church in the Second Precinct of Brookfield (now North Brookfield), Mass., Oct. 30, 1776. His wife was Mary, daughter of Jacob Hook, a "gentleman farmer" of Kingston, N. H. He d. July 25, 1795.

William Appleton, fourth child of Rev. Joseph and Mary (Hook) Appleton, was born at North Brookfield, Nov. 16, 1786. He attended schools at New Ipswich and Francestown, N. H., and Tyngsborough, Mass., and began business as a clerk in a country store kept by Artemas Wheeler at Temple, N. H. In 1807 he went to Boston and was there engaged for several years in trading in West India products, afterwards becoming an importer of English goods. Mr. Appleton was highly successful as a merchant, and having acquired a handsome fortune he retired from active business about the year 1825. He was deservedly held in high esteem in the community, by reason of his integrity and liberal donations to philanthropic objects. From 1832 to 1836 he was president of the United States Branch Bank in Boston and of the Provident Institution for Savings, the pioneer savings bank in this country. He was also president of the Board of Trustees of the Massachusetts General Hospital. In Nov., 1850, Mr. Appleton was elected a representative to the thirty-second Congress from the Suffolk District of Massachusetts, and served with ability during the sessions of the Congresses of 1851–52 and 1853. He was re-

elected in 1860, and represented his constituents at
the special session of the thirty-seventh Congress,
which was called in July, 1861, but he was obliged to
return home on account of ill-health before the con-
clusion of the session. Mr. Appleton was a prominent layman of the Episcopal Church. In 1819,
together with Daniel Webster and several others, he
was appointed a member of the Building Committee
of St. Paul's Church, Boston, and was also one of
its first Board of Vestrymen in 1820. He built and
conveyed to the Episcopal City Mission, in 1847,
St. Stephen's Church, which stood on Purchase
Street in Boston. This building was destroyed by
the great fire of Nov., 1872. Mr. Appleton married, at
Boston, Jan. 8, 1815, Mary Anne, daughter of James
Cutler of Boston. Their fourth child, Sarah Elizabeth, married Amos Adams Lawrence of Boston,
March 31, 1842. The Hon. William Appleton died
at Longwood, Feb. 15, 1862.

FAMILY NO. 16

27. **Susanna,** m., June 11, 1838, at Boston, Rev.
Charles Mason of Salem, Mass. She d. at Salem,
Dec. 2, 1844.

Their children are:

120. I. **Susan Lawrence,** b. at Salem, Aug. 25,
1839; m., at Emmanuel Church, Boston, July 17,
1866, Fitch Edward Oliver, M. D.

They had the following, all born at Boston:

121. 1. **Charles Edward,** b. Aug. 29, 1868.

Charles Edward Oliver attended the schools of

Henry S. Mackintosh and G. W. C. Noble in Boston.
In 1885 he took a special course at the Massachusetts
Institute of Technology, and the following autumn
entered Harvard with the Class of 1890, remaining
one year. He then spent three years in the service
of the Boston and Albany Railroad Company at
East Boston, and has since been interested in building construction, having served for seven years as a
draughtsman in the office of Winslow & Wetherell,
architects. He is now assistant New England agent
of the Columbia Fireproofing Company of Pittsburg,
Pa. In 1894, upon the reorganization of Battery
A (Light Artillery), M. V. M., Mr. Oliver enlisted
for three years. At the close of his term of service,
the Spanish war having begun, he reënlisted for one
year. Battery A was assigned to coast defence duty
in Massachusetts, their headquarters being the estate
of the late William R. Lawrence, M. D., at Galloupe's
Point, Swampscott.

122. 2. **Andrew,** b. Nov. 1, 1869.

Andrew Oliver had his preparatory training at
Noble's school, Boston; graduated at Harvard in
1891, and adopted classical teaching as his profession.
After leaving college he was for a year instructor in
Greek and Latin at the College of St. James, Mary-
land; and for two years held a similar position at
Selwyn Hall Military Academy, Reading, Pa. While
here he was offered the position of classical tutor at
St. Mark's School, Southborough, which he declined.
Returning to Harvard, he pursued his studies there
for a year, receiving the degree of A. M. in 1895.
During the ensuing two years he was associated with

the late William E. Peck as head classical master at Pomfret School, Connecticut; after which he spent a second year of graduate study at Columbia and New York universities, receiving the degree of Ph. D. from the latter in 1898. He then assumed charge of the Latin department at St. Matthew's School, San Mateo, Cal.; where he has since remained. Mr. Oliver has been very successful as a teacher, and has many testimonials from the authorities of the several institutions with which he has been connected, as to his efficiency and good work in his chosen profession. He is a member of the American Dialect Society, the Harvard Classical Club, and the American Philological Association, and has written various articles on educational subjects and on matters of outdoor sport, besides occasional contributions to the classical and philological journals.

In the summer of 1898 he journeyed through Canada, travelling by sea from Victoria, British Columbia, to San Francisco. The following season he made a voyage to the Hawaiian Islands, and passed the summer of 1900 in visiting the Yosemite Valley and other points of interest in California. The vacation of 1901 was spent in Europe.

DEPARTMENT OF LATIN AND GREEK.

ST. MATTHEW'S SCHOOL, founded A. D. 1866 by the late Rev. Alfred Lee Brewer, D. D.

SAN MATEO, CAL., April 13, 1903.

DR. R. M. LAWRENCE:

Dear Sir, — I received from you a few weeks ago a notice concerning "The Descendants of Major Samuel Lawrence." The only "additional items," in my case, of any possible interest to the family may be, first, my election last year to membership in the Sierra Club, an organization whose objects are "to explore, enjoy, and render accessible the mountain regions of the Pacific coast; to publish authentic information concerning them; to enlist the support and coöperation of the people and the government in preserving the forests and other natural features of the Sierra Nevada Mountains."

The second item that may possibly be of interest is the fact that I have recently declined a call to the headmastership of the Ohio Military Institute in Cincinnati.

Wishing you all success in the completion of the Lawrence genealogy and biography,

I am, very sincerely yours,

ANDREW OLIVER.

123. 3. **Mary Mason**, b. March 28, 1871; m., Aug. 15, 1894, Theophilus Parsons.

Their daughter,

124. **Susan Lawrence Parsons,** was born July 28, 1895.

Mary Mason (Oliver) Parsons d. at Boston, Oct. 23, 1895.

Theophilus Parsons, son of Thomas and Martha (Franklin) Parsons, and great-grandson of the eminent jurist, Theophilus Parsons, chief justice of the Supreme Court of Massachusetts (1750–1813), was born at Brookline, Mass., July 1, 1849. His emigrant ancestor, Jeffrey Parsons, came from England to Barbadoes Island, West Indies, about the year 1645, and settled in Gloucester, Mass., some nine years later. Theophilus Parsons, the subject of this sketch, had his early training at the preparatory schools of his native town, and at the Brookline High School. Entering Harvard in the autumn of 1866, he was graduated with the Class of 1870. While in college he was a member of the University Crew. In Oct., 1870, he went to Holyoke, Mass., to study the manufacture of cotton cloth at the Lyman Mills, remaining there until Nov., 1872, after which he went abroad, visiting many European manufactories. He was appointed agent of the Pocasset Manufacturing Company, Fall River, Mass., Jan. 1, 1880, and of the Lyman Mills in the following September. Since Oct. 1, 1884, he has been treasurer of the Lyman Mills. Mr. Parsons is senior warden of St. Paul's Church, Brookline.

125. 4. **Edward Pulling,** b. Oct. 3, 1873.

Edward Pulling Oliver studied at the private schools of Messrs. Hopkinson and Albert Hale in Boston. After leaving the latter, he took a course of two and a half years at the Bussey Institution, and in 1893 he worked as a farm-hand for some six months on a large dairy farm at North Williston, Chittenden County, Vt. In Oct., 1894, he entered the employ of the Lyman Mills at Holyoke, Mass. (cotton spinning and weaving), working in the various departments of the mills until June, 1897, in order to become conversant with the practical manufacturing operations. He then entered the Boston office of the same company, where he has since remained.

126. 5. **Everard Lawrence**, b. Jan. 11, 1876.

Everard Lawrence Oliver pursued his early studies at Mr. Hopkinson's school in Boston, and entered Harvard with the Class of 1899, but left college in the middle of the Senior year on account of illness. He was a member of Light Battery A, M. V. M., from 1896 to 1900. In Dec., 1899, he went abroad with a friend and classmate, Mr. Jordan Dumaresq, and spent eight very interesting months travelling in England, France, Switzerland, Italy, Greece, Turkey, the Holy Land, and Egypt. He also saw the Passion Play at Ober-Ammergau. Mr. Oliver is now a student at the Harvard Medical School, Class of 1904.

127. 6. **Susan Lawrence**, b. Feb. 15, 1881.

THE OLIVER FAMILY

Fitch Edward Oliver, the youngest son of Dr. Daniel and Mary Robinson (Pulling) Oliver, was born at Cambridge, Mass., Nov. 25, 1819. He traced his ancestry from Dr. Thomas Oliver of London, England, who came to this country in the *William and Francis* in the year 1632, and became a resident of Boston. Many of the descendants of this emigrant ancestor had a collegiate education, and became prominent as merchants and in political life, or as men of letters. Dr. Daniel Oliver, of the seventh generation, the father of Fitch Edward Oliver, was professor of Intellectual Philosophy at Dartmouth College, and lecturer on Chemistry and Materia Medica in the Medical School of that institution.

Fitch Edward Oliver pursued his early studies at the Franklin Academy in North Andover, Mass., at the Moors school, Hanover, N. H., and at Kimball Union Academy, Meriden, N. H. He took the regular course at Dartmouth College, graduating in 1839. After a brief period spent in the law office of the Hon. Ira Perley of Concord, N. H., he decided to begin the study of medicine, and during the next two years he attended courses of lectures at the Harvard and Dartmouth Medical Schools, and at the Medical College of Ohio, in Cincinnati. He continued his studies in Boston until the spring of 1843, receiving the degree of M. D. (Harvard) in that year. He then devoted more than a year to study and travel in Europe, and returning home in the autumn of 1844, he began the practice of medicine in Boston. For three years he served as one of the Boston Dispensary physicians.

In 1849 Dr. Oliver was elected a corresponding member of the Glasgow Medico-Chirurgical Society in Scotland. From 1856 to 1860 he was recording secretary of the Boston Society for Medical Improvement, and for eight years an editor of the "Boston Medical and Surgical Journal." When, in 1864, the Boston City Hospital was opened for the reception of patients, he was appointed one of the visiting physicians, and retained the office until 1872, when he resigned, and was then appointed a consulting physician. He also served as one of the physicians of St. Luke's Home for Convalescents, and of the House of the Good Samaritan, and from 1860 to 1870 he was an instructor of Materia Medica in the Harvard Medical School.

In addition to his professional work Dr. Oliver devoted considerable time to literary pursuits. In 1848, together with Dr. William W. Morland, he translated from the French a learned treatise entitled "The Elements of General Pathology," by Dr. A. F. Chomel. In 1872 he contributed for the annual report of the Massachusetts State Board of Health an important article on "The Use and Abuse of Opium," and in 1875 he wrote a valuable paper on "The Health of Boston," which appeared in the seventh annual report of the same board. In 1880 he edited and caused to be printed the manuscript Diaries of two of his ancestors, Benjamin Lynde and Benjamin Lynde, Jr., both of whom held the office of chief justice of Massachusetts Bay. These Diaries cover the period from 1690 to 1780. He also edited and published in 1890, "The Diary of William Pynchon," a distinguished lawyer of Salem, Mass., at the time of the Revolution. Dr. Oliver also prepared manuscript memoirs of fourteen persons bearing the name of Oliver. In 1852 he published a small Book of Chants, which has passed through seven editions, and in 1856, jointly with Bishop Horatio Southgate, he edited the Psalter with appropriate chants, the first volume of the kind published in this country.

In 1876 he was elected a member of the Massachusetts Historical Society, and afterwards rendered valuable service as its cabinet-keeper. He was a member of the corporation of the Church of the Advent for forty-five years, and was its senior warden at the time of his death. The degree of Master of Arts was conferred upon him by Trinity College, Hartford, Conn., in 1860. Dr. Oliver died in Boston, Dec. 8, 1892.[1]

128. II. **Amos Lawrence**, b. at Salem, Mass., April 20, 1842; m., at Boston, Sept. 30, 1874, Louisa Blake Steedman, daughter of Rear Admiral Charles Steedman, U. S. N., and Sarah (Bishop) Steedman.

They have a daughter,

129. **Marion Steedman Mason**, who was born at Pride's Crossing, Beverly, Mass., July 17, 1875; m., at Emmanuel Church, Boston, March 11, 1902, Richard Thornton Wilson, Jr., of New York, son of Richard Thornton and Clementine (Johnston) Wilson. He was born Sept. 11, 1866, obtained his early education at schools in New York, and graduated from Columbia University in 1887. He is a banker by profession, and has held the office of commissioner of municipal statistics in his native city. Residences, New York, Newport, R. I., and May River Bluff, S. C.

Amos Lawrence Mason is a descendant of General John Mason (b. in England about the year 1600; trained as a soldier in the Dutch Netherlands; emigrated to Dorchester, Mass., about 1630, thence to Connecticut, where he served with distinction in the war against the Pequot Indians; appointed major-general of the Connecticut forces and deputy-

[1] A Memoir of Fitch Edward Oliver, M. D., prepared by the Rev. Edmund F. Slafter, D. D., was privately printed in 1894. From this memoir chiefly, the information contained in the above sketch has been derived.

governor of the Colony; author of a history of the
Pequot war; d. at Norwich, Conn., in 1672). Dr.
Mason obtained his early education at the Public
Latin School and E. S. Dixwell's school in Boston.
He took the regular four years' course at Harvard
(A. B. 1863), and after graduation was for one year
a student of law at the Harvard Law School and in
the office of Mr. (afterwards Justice) Horace Gray.
He then engaged in literary pursuits until the spring
of 1865, when he sailed for Europe. In 1868 he entered the Harvard Medical School, where he remained four years, during the last of which he was
house-officer in the Massachusetts General Hospital,
and received the degree of M. D. in 1872. After a
year's study in Germany, he returned to Boston, and
since 1873 has practised his profession there, and at
Bar Harbor, Me.

Dr. Mason has served as one of the physicians of
the Boston City Hospital, Carney Hospital, Channing Home for Incurables, and Boston Dispensary;
has held the positions of clinical instructor in Aus-
cultation and associate professor of Clinical Medicine
in the Harvard Medical School, and has been president of the Suffolk District Medical Society and of
the Boston Society for Medical Improvement. He
has made several journeys to Europe for study and
travel, and one to the Nile and Syria in 1867–68.
Dr. Mason has written various articles for medical
publications, including the following: "Boston City
Hospital Reports: Two Hundred Cases of Pleura
Effusion, with Reference to the Operation of Tap-
ping the Chest," 1882. "Diseases of the Pleura,"

in Wilson and Eshner's " American Text-book of Applied Therapeutics," Philadelphia, 1896. " Bronchitis, Acute, Chronic, Plastic, Bronchiectasis," and " Asthma; Hay Fever," in Loomis and Thompson, " A System of Practical Medicine," New York, 1897. (1) " Subphrenic Abscess "; (2) " Gall-Bladder Infection in Typhoid Fever," Transactions of the Association of American Physicians, 1893 and 1897. " Diphtheria, Scarlet Fever, and Measles; " A Summary of Two Thousand Cases admitted to the City Hospital, 1880–1889." " Cases in which Typhoid Fever occurred twice in the same Patient," and various other articles on typhoid, typhus, and the acute fevers.

130. III. **Mary,** b. Nov. 22, 1844, at Salem; m., at Boston, Jan. 6, 1870, Howard Stockton, who was born at Philadelphia, Pa., Feb. 15, 1842. Residences at Boston and Wareham, Mass.

Their children:

131. 1. **Lawrence Mason,** b. at Springfield, Mass., Feb. 18, 1871.

Lawrence Mason Stockton prepared for college at St. Paul's School, Concord, N. H., and graduated at Harvard in 1891. He then studied law at the Harvard Law School, receiving the degree of LL. B. in 1894, and became a member of the firm of Lowell, Stimson & Stockton, afterwards Stimson & Stockton, 53 State Street, Boston. He holds various positions of responsibility, being a director of the New England Trust Company and clerk of the Essex Company. He was a member of the Boston Common Council in 1888 and 1889. Mr. Stockton has been court tennis champion of the United States.

132. 2. **Mary Remington,** b. at Brookline, May 10, 1872; m., Oct. 14, 1903, Wm. Amory, 2d.

133. 3. **Philip,** b. at Brookline, March 20, 1874.

Philip Stockton studied at Noble's school, Boston, after which he entered Harvard College, graduating in 1896. He then took a three years' course at the Massachusetts Institute of Technology, receiving the degree of S. B. in Civil Engineering, in 1899. After a year in the service of the Merrimac Manufacturing Company, Huntsville, Ala., he became treasurer of the Lowell Bleachery. He is now president of the City Trust Company, a new organization, incorporated in 1900, and having offices at 40 State Street, Boston.

134. 4. **Ethel,** b. at Beverly, Sept. 2, 1876.

135. 5. **Eleanor,** b. at Milton, Aug. 25, 1878.

136. 6. **Jane Mason,** b. at Boston, Nov. 27, 1880.

137. 7. **Howard,** b. at Boston, Dec. 18, 1883.

Howard Stockton, Jr., fitted for college at Groton School, Groton, Mass., and is a member of the Class of 1905 at Harvard.

Mrs. Mary (Mason) Stockton d. at Wareham, Mass., July 27, 1886.

Howard Stockton is a descendant, of the seventh generation, from Richard Stockton, who married Abigail —— in England, emigrated to America, and became a freeholder at Flushing, L. I., about the year 1656. He was appointed lieutenant of the horse company of Flushing in 1665, and lieutenant of the foot company of the same town in 1669. In 1690 he removed to Oneanickon, Burlington County, N. J.;

d. Sept., 1707. Richard, his eldest child, accompanied his father to New Jersey, and settled first at Piscataway in Middlesex County, but afterwards became a resident of Stony Brook, now Princeton, in Somerset County. He m., Nov. 8, 1691, Susanna Robinson. He d. in 1709. John Stockton, the fifth child of the above (1701–57), a resident of Princeton, was a judge of the Court of Common Pleas for the County of Somerset. He m., in 1729, Abigail Phillips. Their third child, Philip (1746–92), became a clergyman at Princeton, and m., April 13, 1769, Katharine Cumming. Lucius Witham, the second child of Philip (b. May 26, 1771), of Flemington, N. J., was clerk of the County of Hunterdon. He m. Eliza Augusta, daughter of Charles Coxe, Esq., of Sidney. Philip Augustus Stockton, the third child of the above, of Newport, R. I. (1802–76), was a lieutenant in the United States Navy and held for a time the office of consul-general to Saxony. He m. (first) Sarah Cantey, and had two sons. She d. and he m. (second), Dec. 3, 1840, at Philadelphia, Mary Ann Remington, daughter of J. B. and Hannah (Pym) Remington of Philadelphia.

Howard Stockton, their only child, was born at Philadelphia, Pa., Feb. 15, 1842. His early education was obtained at private schools in Newport, R. I., and at the Royal Saxon Polytechnic, Dresden, Saxony, where he graduated in 1862 (silver medallist). He was appointed captain and acting aide-de-camp, U. S. Volunteers, June 9, 1862; first lieutenant, Third Rhode Island Cavalry, March 17, 1864; second lieutenant, Ordnance Corps, U. S. A., May 23, 1864;

brevet first lieutenant and brevet captain, U. S. A.,
Sept. 14, 1866; first lieutenant, Ordnance Corps,
U. S. A., May 13, 1867. Mr. Stockton was admitted
to the Massachusetts bar, Sept. 20, 1871. Since then
he has held the following positions: Treasurer of the
Cocheco Manufacturing Company, from 1876 to
1887; treasurer of the Salmon Falls Manufacturing
Company, from 1880 to 1887; president of the American Bell Telephone Company, 1887–89; treasurer of
the Merrimac Manufacturing Company, 1889–1900;
treasurer of the Essex Company, 1882; actuary of
the Massachusetts Hospital Life Insurance Company,
1901; member of the Standing Committee, Diocese
of Massachusetts, 1890; delegate to the Diocesan
Convention, 1888 to 1892; vestryman in St. Paul's
Church, Boston, director in the Merchants' and Old
Boston National Banks, City Trust Company, and
Boston Manufacturers' Mutual Insurance Company;
vice-president of the American Mutual Liability Insurance Company; president of the Nashua Manufacturing Company, and of the Jackson Company;
trustee of the Boston Athenæum, and for many large
estates; member of the executive committee of the
corporation of the Massachusetts Institute of Technology.

138. IV. **Sarah**, b. Nov. 22, 1844, at Salem; m.,
at Boston, Oct. 15, 1868, Hasket Derby, M. D., who
was born at Boston, June 29, 1835. Residences,
Boston and Bar Harbor, Me.

Their children:

139. 1. **Charles Albrecht**, b. at Boston, Jan. 26,
1871; d. June 5, 1872.

140. 2. **Eloise**, b. at Brookline, July 3, 1873.

She has travelled much in Europe and elsewhere. In the autumn of 1902 she went to China with Mr. and Mrs. Thomas R. Wheelock, and spent a large part of the ensuing winter in Shanghai. She returned home in June, 1903.

141. 3. **George Strong**, b. at Boston, May 29, 1875; m., Aug. 5, 1901, at Falmouth Foreside, near Portland, Me., Mary Brewster Brown, daughter of Gen. John Marshall and Alida (Carroll) Brown.

George Strong Derby attended Mr. Noble's school in Boston, and entered Harvard, taking the regular course, and graduating in 1896. While in college he rowed on the University Crew. He received the degree of M. D. (Harvard) in 1900, and served for a year as surgical interne at the Massachusetts General Hospital. Dr. Derby was for a time a member of the Massachusetts Naval Battalion. Soon after his marriage he went abroad to complete his medical education, and passed the winter of 1901–02 in Vienna, Austria, studying pathology and ophthalmology. The following spring he went to Freiburg, in Breisgau, Germany, where he continued his work under Professor Axenfeld for seven months or more. At this writing he is studying at Utrecht under Professor Snellen, and expects to remain there several months, after which he intends visiting Paris and London, returning to Boston in the autumn of 1903 to practise his profession. Mrs. Derby accompanied her husband to Europe.

142. 4. **Stephen Hasket**, b. at Boston, Dec. 25, 1877.

Stephen Hasket Derby spent four years at St. Paul's School, Concord, N. H., and then went to Harvard, graduating in 1899. After leaving college he entered the Law School, taking a three years' course. He graduated *cum laude*, and was admitted to the Massachusetts bar in Oct., 1901. In July, 1902, he sailed from San Franciso for Honolulu, to engage in the practice of law. Since then he has been with the law firm of Kinney, McClanahan & Bigelow (formerly Kinney, Ballou & McClanahan). The inauguration of the Pacific cable, connecting the Hawaiian Islands with San Francisco, took place in Jan., 1903, and Mr. Derby has been appointed one of a committee of three to report on the subject of a suitable code. It is probable that he will make his home in Honolulu.

143. 5. **Robert Mason,** b. at Boston, Dec. 11, 1879.

Robert Mason Derby obtained his early education at Noble's school, Boston, and took a five years' course at the Massachusetts Institute of Technology, but left there at the close of the fourth year in 1901. He has a position in the freight department of the New York Central Railroad Company.

144. 6. **Augustine,** b. at Boston, Feb. 2, 1882.

Augustine Derby prepared for college at Noble's school, and is a member of the Harvard Class of 1903. He expects to enter the Law School in the autumn of that year.

145. 7. **Arthur Lawrence,** b. at Boston, March 3, 1884.

Arthur Lawrence Derby fitted for college at Noble's school, and was for a few months at the Massachusetts Institute of Technology. He entered Harvard in the autumn of 1901 as a member of the Class of 1905. He has been quite a traveller in his boyhood, having visited the West Indies and South America.

146. 8. **Francis**, b. at Boston, Jan. 15, 1886; d. Sept. 2, 1886.

THE DERBY FAMILY

Roger Derby, the emigrant, was born at Topsham, a seaport town of Devonshire, England, near Exeter, in the year 1643. His first wife was Lucretia Hillman, whom he married in England, Aug. 23, 1668. They came to America three years later, arriving in Boston, July 18, 1671, and soon after removed to Ipswich, Mass. "They were nonconformists, and affiliated to the Quakers, who at that time were terribly persecuted."[1] In 1681 they took up their abode in Salem. Mrs. Lucretia (Hillman) Derby died (probably at Salem), and Roger Derby m. (second), in 1681 (?), Elizabeth, widow of William Dynn, and daughter of Stephen and Elizabeth Hasket, — a native of England, — who d. at Salem about March, 1740. Roger Derby was by trade a chandler, and also dealt in dry goods. He d. at Salem, May 25, 1689.

Richard Derby, sixth of the eight children of Roger and his first wife, Lucretia, was b. at Ipswich, Mass., Oct. 8, 1679. He m., Feb. 25, 1702, Martha

[1] *The Driver Family*, compiled by Harriet Ruth (Waters) Cooke, p. 279.

Hasket, a sister of his stepmother. His occupation was that of a shipmaster. He d. Feb. 25, 1715.

Captain Richard Derby, a son of Richard, Sr., was b. at Salem, Sept. 12, 1712. At the age of twenty-four he became master of the sloop *Ranger*, sailing from Salem to Spanish ports, and in 1742 he had charge of the *Volant*, bound for Barbadoes. He m. Mary Hodges, Feb. 3, 1735. Captain Derby "re-tired from the sea" in 1757, and engaged in business as a merchant in Salem. He was a member of the General Court from 1769 to 1773. To him was in-trusted by the Provincial Congress an official account of the battle of Lexington, with other important pa-pers, which he dispatched by a swift vessel, com-manded by Captain John Derby, to London, where they arrived, May 29, 1775, eleven days in advance of the dispatches of General Gage.

"Captain Richard Derby owned at that time, a little fast-sailing schooner called the *Quero*, of sixty-two tons burden, a mere yacht. He offered her to the Provincial Congress. Captain Derby's two sons, Richard, Jr., and John, enlisted with him in the ven-ture. His younger son, Elias Hasket Derby, was in the counting-room, keeping books. Richard was to fit out, and John, who was thirty-four years old, to command, the *Quero*. In a very few days she was ready to weigh anchor. Gage's dispatch by the royal express packet *Sukey* had sailed April 24, but that gave no uneasiness, for the packet was slow and deep-laden. At length, on the 27th of April, sailing orders passed the Congress, and the *Quero* seems to have escaped during the night between the 28th and

29th. . . . No American's advent in London ever produced so real a sensation as did that of a Salem sailor, Captain John Derby, in May, 1775. He brought the news of Concord and Lexington in advance of the king's messenger, and made it known to the British public. Derby reached London on Sunday evening, May 28, 1775. On the next day the news was well abroad, and was received with consternation and the wildest comment."

Captain John Derby was not only the bearer of the first tidings of the beginning of the war to the mother country, but he was also the messenger, eight years later, in 1783, who brought home from Paris, in the ship *Astræa*, the first news of peace.

Captain Richard Derby d. at Salem, Nov. 9, 1783.

Elias Hasket Derby, Sr., son of the preceding, was b. Aug. 16, 1739. As a young man he had charge of his father's business accounts and correspondence, afterwards becoming extensively engaged in commerce on his own account. He was highly successful as a merchant, and founded the Salem East India trade. Mr. Derby assisted in the formation of the first colonial navy, in the early days of the Revolution, and many of the vessels of his large fleet, sailing under letters of marque, preyed upon British commerce on the high seas. He m. Elizabeth Crowninshield, April 23, 1761. He d. at Salem, Sept. 8, 1799.

His son, Elias Hasket Derby, Jr., was b. at Salem, Jan. 10, 1766. In early life he followed the sea, and made many voyages to foreign lands, among them one to India, where he spent three years. Return-

ing to Salem, he became a merchant, " succeeding to
the occupation of the home built by his father, and
after ten years of retirement was forced by reverses
in business, and the expenses incident to maintaining
a princely establishment, to resume trade." (See
Lamb's Biographical Dictionary.) The first broad-
cloth loom operated in Massachusetts was established by him in 1812. He m. Lucy Brown, June
10, 1797. Harvard College conferred upon him the
degree of A. M. in 1803. Mr. Derby removed his
residence to Londonderry, N. H., in Dec., 1815, and
there d. Sept. 16, 1826. " He was greatly respected
for his talents and extensive information, and beloved
for his generosity, benevolence, hospitality, and public spirit." (Londonderry epitaph.)

Elias Hasket Derby, third of the name, son of
Elias Hasket and Lucy (Brown) Derby, was b. in
Salem, Sept. 24, 1803. He attended the Boston
Public Latin School, and then entered Harvard Col-
lege, graduating with the Class of 1824. Afterwards
he studied law with Daniel Webster, who was a friend
of his father, and later engaged in practice as an
attorney in Boston. He m., Sept. 4, 1834, Eloise
Lloyd, daughter of George W. and Angelina (Lloyd)
Strong. Mr. Derby was admitted to the Court of
Common Pleas in Suffolk in Oct., 1827, and to the
Supreme Judicial Court in Oct., 1829. " He was a
broad, progressive man, and became a railroad lawyer. At one time he was the president of the Old
Colony Railroad Company." " While achieving legal
eminence, Mr. Derby has not forgotten the pleasant
walks of literature, which inspired and charmed his

college days. The 'Edinburgh Review' and 'Atlantic Monthly,' and indeed nearly all the leading magazines at home and abroad, have been enriched by articles from his pen. He is also the author of 'Two Months Abroad,' 'The Catholic,' 'The Overland Route to the Pacific,' and many reports on the British Provinces, the Fisheries, and kindred subjects, written while commissioner of the United States, all of which had wide circulation." ("Londonderry Celebration," p. 85.) Mr. Derby d. at Boston, March 31, 1880.

Dr. Hasket Derby, a son of Elias Hasket Derby, third, and Eloise Lloyd (Strong) Derby, was b. at Boston, June 29, 1835. He attended the Boston Latin School (1846–51) and Amherst College (A. B. 1855). He graduated from the Harvard Medical School in 1858, after which he spent more than three years in studying at the Universities of Vienna and Berlin, and in attending clinics and hospitals in London, Paris, and Utrecht. Upon his return to Boston he entered upon the practice of his profession, and has long been well known as one of our foremost occulists. He has held the positions of house-surgeon at the Mass. General Hospital, surgeon to the Mass. Charitable Eye and Ear Infirmary, and ophthalmic surgeon to Carney Hospital, and was at one time lecturer on Ophthalmology at the Harvard Medical School. During the civil war he was for a short time in the service of the Sanitary Commission at Fortress Monroe. Dr. Derby has made seventeen trips to Europe, usually during the summer months. He is the author of numerous articles in the "Boston Medical and Surgical Journal," and in periodicals devoted to ophthalmology. Among his publications are the following: " The Modern Operation for Cataract," Boston, 1871. " A Report on the Percentage of Near-sight found to exist in the Class of 1880, at Harvard College, with Some Account of Similar Investigations. An Account of the Phakometer of Snellen," Cambridge, 1877. " Holocain in Ophthalmic Surgery. Its Superiority over Cocaine; its Therapeutic Value," New York, 1899 (Reprinted from the " Archives of Opthalmology," vol. 28). Dr. Derby is a member of various medical organizations at home and abroad.

Charles Mason, the youngest son of the eminent statesman and jurist, Hon. Jeremiah Mason, and Mary (Means) Mason, was born at Portsmouth, N. H., July 25, 1812. He received instruction at the Portsmouth Academy, and prepared for college under the tuition of its preceptor, Rev. Andrew P. Peabody, D. D. Entering Harvard in 1829, he took a three years' course, graduating in 1832. He then began the study of theology at the Andover Seminary, and passed two years at the General Theological Seminary in New York. He was ordained deacon by Bishop Griswold in 1836, and became the rector of St. Peter's Church in Salem, May 1, 1837, retaining this position during ten years of successful ministry. In 1847 he assumed the charge of Grace Church, Boston, and remained its rector for fourteen years. During this period he was also engaged in philanthropic work among the poor. The Church Home for Orphan and Destitute Children, now at South Boston, originated in the parish of Grace Church, and Dr. Mason may properly be regarded as the founder of this institution. He received the degree of Doctor of Divinity from Harvard in 1858, and from Trinity College, Hartford, Conn., the same year. Dr. Mason was deeply afflicted by the death, at Salem, Dec. 2, 1844, of his wife Susanna, beloved daughter of Amos Lawrence. After an interval of nearly five years, he married Anna Huntington Lyman, tenth child of the Hon. Jonathan Huntington and Sophia (Hinckley) Lyman of Northampton, Mass. They had three children: Anna Sophia Lyman Mason, who married Professor John Chipman Gray; Rev. Charles Jeremiah Mason; and Harriet Sargent Mason. Dr. Mason died at Boston, March 23, 1862. Phillips Brooks thus wrote of him in the "Memorial History of Boston," vol. iii. p. 464: "The Reverend Charles Mason, rector of Grace Church, has left a record of the greatest purity of life and faithfulness in work." A Memoir of Dr. Mason was prepared by his friend and former instructor, Rev. A. P. Peabody, D. D., and printed in 1863.

FAMILY NO. 17

48. **Annie Bigelow,** m., Jan. 22, 1846, Benjamin Smith Rotch of New Bedford, Mass.

Their children:

147. I. **Edith,** b. at Boston, July 30, 1847; d. at Lenox, Mass., May 14, 1897.

148. II. **Arthur,** b. at Boston, May 13, 1850; m.,

at Bristol, R. I., Nov. 16, 1892, Lisette de Wolf Colt;
d. at Beverly, Mass., Aug. 15, 1894.

Arthur Rotch obtained his early education at
Epes S. Dixwell's school in Boston, and graduated
at Harvard College with the Class of 1871. He then
devoted himself to the study of architecture, taking
a two years' course at the Massachusetts Institute
of Technology and spending a year in the office of
Henry Van Brunt. In Feb., 1874, he went abroad,
and entered the Ecole des Beaux Arts in Paris.
During his stay at this institution he carried off
many honors, which were awarded him by examin-
ing juries for designs presented in competitions. In
the course of extensive travels in Europe he made a
specialty of the study of decorations.

Mr. Rotch returned to Boston in Aug,, 1880,
after an absence of more than six years, and formed
a partnership with George T. Tilden, under the name
of Rotch & Tilden, architects. This firm erected
numerous public buildings and churches. Among
these are the churches of the Messiah, Ascension, and
Holy Spirit, in Boston, the Art Museum and Art
School at Wellesley College, and public libraries at
Groton and Bridgewater, Mass., and at Eastport, Me.
They also designed and built numerous private residences in some of the principal cities and summer
resorts of the United States. The Suffolk County
Court House in Boston was erected under Mr. Rotch's
supervision. He was a member of the corporation of
the Massachusetts Institute of Technology and chairman of its Department of Architecture. He was also
a trustee of the Boston Museum of Fine Arts and of
the Massachusetts Eye and Ear Infirmary.

Mr. Rotch inherited from his father a taste for painting in water-colors, and was an artist of no mean ability. His death occurred at Beverly, Mass., Aug. 15, 1894. In his will he made handsome bequests to Harvard College for the formation of a Department of Architecture in the Lawrence Scientific School, to the Massachusetts Institute of Technology, to the Boston Museum of Fine Arts, and to the Massachusetts Charitable Eye and Ear Infirmary.

" IN MEMORY OF ARTHUR ROTCH. Resolutions adopted by the Corporation of the Massachusetts Institute of Technology.

" In the death of Mr. Arthur Rotch the Institute of Technology has lost one whose relations to it have been peculiarly intimate. Mr. Rotch attended the Institute as a student of architecture in the years 1872 and 1873; and, after his return from foreign study and travel to begin professional practice in Boston, he at once became a counsellor in regard to matters concerning the Institute, and especially the instruction in architecture. Elected a member of the Corporation in 1886, he became chairman of the Visiting Committee of that department. His interest in the work of the Institute and his warm personal regard for Professors Chandler and Létang drew him to visit the department with unusual frequency and to inspect its progress with the most careful scrutiny. His thorough mastery of his profession and his exquisite culture made his suggestions and recommendations always valuable. For years he remained the constant advisor of the instructors, on the one hand, while on the other he represented to the Corporation the needs of the department with a fulness of knowledge which always commanded assent to his views. On the occasion of the lamented death of Professor Létang, Mr. Rotch took an active interest in the appointment of a worthy successor; and when the growth of the department required the erection of a new and separate building, he not only gave to the work much time and attention, but contributed liberally of his means to the equipment of the building. The library of the Architectural Department will long remain a visible memorial of him."

Resolutions adopted by the Boston Society of Architects:

" The executive committee of the Boston Society of Architects desires to put on record its sense of the loss which the Society, in common with the whole profession of architects, has sustained in the death of its associate, Arthur Rotch.

" Mr. Rotch was not merely a successful architect; he was a man who, having great opportunities of usefulness, felt in an unusual degree the responsibility which they involved, and used them gladly and with enthusiasm for the elevation and purifying of the profession and for the enlightenment and education of the public, and his untimely death is to be deplored by all who have at heart the interests and dignity of architecture in the United States."

149. III. **Aimée**, b. at Paris, France, June 16, 1852; m., at Boston, Dec. 2, 1873, Winthrop Sargent of Boston.

Winthrop Sargent is of the seventh generation in descent from William Sargent of Exeter, England, who went from there to Bridgetown, Barbadoes, about the middle of the seventeenth century, afterwards returning to England. His wife's name was Mary Epes. His son William, called "second," also supposed to have been born in Exeter, was educated at Barbadoes, and settled, about the year 1678, at Gloucester, Mass., where he built a house at Eastern Point. He m., June 21, 1677, Mary, daughter of Peter Duncan, and they had fourteen children. He d. before June, 1707.

Colonel Epes Sargent, sixth child of William the "second" and Mary (Duncan) Sargent, was born July 12, 1690. He m. (first), April 1, 1720, Esther, daughter of Christian and Florence Macarty of Roxbury. She d. July 1, 1743. He m. (second), Aug. 10, 1744, widow Catharine Brown of Salem. Epes Sargent was a successful merchant, a magistrate, representative to the General Court of Massachusetts in 1744, and held the rank of colonel in the militia. He d. at Salem, Dec. 6, 1762.

Daniel Sargent, seventh child of Colonel Epes and Esther (Macarty) Sargent, was born March 18, 1731. He m., Feb. 3, 1763, Mary, daughter of John and Mary Turner. He d. Feb. 18, 1806.

Henry Sargent, fourth child of the preceding, was baptized Nov. 25, 1770; m., April 19, 1807, Hannah, daughter of Samuel Welles, a merchant of Boston.

Henry Winthrop Sargent, eldest child of the above-named, was born at Boston, Nov. 26, 1810. He was a graduate of Harvard, Class of 1830, and studied law for a time, afterwards engaging in business. Mr. Sargent had a fine country estate at Fishkill-on-the-Hudson, N. Y., and contributed many valuable articles on horticulture to current periodicals. He m., Jan. 10, 1839, Caroline Olmstead of New York. He d. at Fishkill, Nov. 10, 1882.

Winthrop Sargent, elder son of Colonel Henry Winthrop and Caroline (Olmstead) Sargent, was born at Fishkill, N. Y., April 3, 1840. He received his early instruction from private tutors, and entered Harvard in 1858 (A. B., Class of 1862, 1892; LL. B., 1864). He has spent many years in Europe. Mr. Sargent is trustee of several estates, and devotes much time to horticulture. Besides these interests, he has been president of the Highland Hospital and of the Howland Library at Matteawan, N. Y., and also a director of the First National Bank of Fishkill Landing. He m., at Boston, Dec. 2, 1873, Aimée, third child of Benjamin Smith and Annie Bigelow (Lawrence) Rotch.

150. IV. **Katharine**, b. March 9, 1856; d. March 12, 1856.

151. V. **Annie Lawrence**, b. at Boston, Feb. 14, 1857; m., at Boston, April 14, 1890, Horatio Appleton Lamb.

Their children:

152. 1. **Thomas**, b. at Boston, Jan. 19, 1892.

153. 2. **Aimée**, b. at Boston, May 23, 1893.

154. 3. **Benjamin Rotch**, b. at Boston, Jan. 7, 1895; d. at Boston, Feb. 22, 1895.

155. 4. **Rosamond**,   } b. at Boston, Dec.
156. 5. **Annie Lawrence**, } 17, 1898. Annie Lawrence d. at Milton, Dec. 6, 1899.

157. 6. **Edith Duncan**, b. at Milton, July 15, 1901.

Horatio Appleton Lamb is a son of Thomas and Hannah (Dawes) Lamb, and was born at Boston, Jan. 11, 1850. He fitted for college at W. Eliot Fettee's school, and at the Public Latin School, in Boston, and graduated at Harvard with the Class of 1871. He was for a time engaged in the dry goods commission business. Of late years he has held various positions of responsibility, having been treasurer of the New England Fibre Company and of the Riverside Water Company. He has also served as chairman of the Board of Trustees for Children of the City of Boston, as a park commissioner of the town of Milton, and as a trustee and director in various business organizations.

158. VI. **William**, b. Nov. 27, 1858; d. Oct. 3, 1859.

159. VII. **Abbott Lawrence**, b. at Boston, Jan. 6, 1861; m., at Savannah, Ga., Nov. 22, 1893, Margaret Randolph Anderson, daughter of Edward Clifford and Jane Margaret (Randolph) Anderson.

Their children, born at Boston, are:

159a. 1. **Elizabeth**, b. June 12, 1895; d. June 29, 1895.

159b. 2. **Margaret Randolph**, b. June 14, 1896.

159c. 3. **Arthur**, b. Feb. 1, 1899.

Abbott Lawrence Rotch pursued his early studies in Europe and at Chauncy Hall School in Boston, graduated at the Massachusetts Institute of Technology in 1884, as a mechanical engineer, and received the degree of A. M., *honoris causa*, from Harvard University in 1891. He founded in 1885, and has since maintained, the Blue Hill Meteorological Observatory, well known throughout the world for the cloud studies and researches in the upper air with kites that have been carried on there. He is a trustee of the Boston Society of Natural History, and of the Museum of Fine Arts, a member of the Corporation of the Massachusetts Institute of Technology, and librarian of the American Academy of Arts and Sciences. He is also a member of various American and foreign scientific societies and committees, and a Chevalier of the Legion of Honor. In the pursuit of his profession he has travelled extensively in the United States, South America, Europe, and Africa. From 1883 to 1892 he was a member of the First Corps of Cadets, M. V. M. Mr. Rotch was for ten years an associate editor of the " American Meteorological Journal," and is the author of numerous scientific publications. Among the more important of these are the following: " Blue Hill Observations," published in the Annals of Harvard College Observatory since 1887, and " Sounding the Ocean of Air," London, 1900. The latter work contains the lectures delivered before the Lowell Institute of Boston in 1898, Mr. Rotch having given in 1891 a course of lectures at this institution upon " Mountain Meteorology."

Benjamin Smith Rotch was of distinguished Quaker ancestry, being of the fifth generation from Joseph Rotch, who was born at Salisbury, Wiltshire, England, May 6, 1704, and emigrated to Nantucket, afterwards settling at New Bedford, Mass. He married Love Macy, daughter of Thomas and Deborah (Coffin) Macy. Joseph Rotch was the pioneer of the whale fishery business of Nantucket. He died at New Bedford, Nov. 24, 1784.

William Rotch, son of the preceding, was born on Nantucket Island in 1734, and continued there with success the industry inaugurated by his father, until it was practically ruined as a result of the Revolutionary war. England, then the chief market for sperm oil, had imposed upon that commodity an alien duty of £18 sterling per tun. In 1785, therefore, William Rotch transferred his business to Dunkirk, France, and his whaling-vessels, dispatched from that port, were the first to enter the Pacific Ocean. In 1794 he returned to Nantucket, and after a year's residence there made his home at New Bedford. He married Elizabeth, daughter of Benjamin and Lydia (Starbuck) Barney.

Benjamin Smith Rotch, second son of Joseph Rotch of New Bedford and Anne (Smith) Rotch, was born at Philadelphia, Pa., March 4, 1817, and in his childhood removed with his parents to New Bedford. He graduated at Harvard College in 1838, and began business as a merchant. In 1843 he was elected a member of the Massachusetts House of Representatives, and served as aide-de-camp on the staff of Governor George N. Briggs in 1845. He was one of the founders of the New Bedford Cordage Company, which was established in 1842. Mr. Rotch accompanied his father-in-law, Hon. Abbott Lawrence, when, in Sept., 1849, the latter went to England to assume the duties of United States Minister at the Court of St. James. He died at Milton, Aug. 19, 1882. The following is an extract from an obituary notice which appeared in the " Boston Daily Advertiser," Aug. 31, 1882 :

"During his visits to Europe, he had the opportunity to improve and cultivate that interest in the fine arts which rendered his influence in artistic matters most valuable in this community. Gifted with a refined taste and sensitive feeling for form and color, his careful study of foreign collections, supplemented by practical work, made him a competent and fastidious critic, as well as a painter, whose landscapes have shown to advantage in our local exhibitions. Though keenly alive to the impossibility of suddenly producing, in a strictly commercial community, works of art of the highest excellence, yet he was ever ready with a kind word and generous hand to help forward its cause. Many a struggling artist will remember gratefully the timely help which was so unostentatiously and freely given. His critical judgment was constantly appealed to in all artistic matters, and he was a prominent trustee of the Athenæum and of our Museum of Fine Arts, and chairman of its committee. He filled also most successfully the many other public and private offices which were confided to him. Of his excellence as the most devoted of husbands and fathers, it does not become me to speak. Though admired by all who knew him, yet so retiring and sensitive was his nature, that the privilege of his intimate friendship was extended to but few, but by those who were so fortunate as to have shared it he will long be remembered as a man preëminently worthy of love, confidence, and affectionate esteem."

FAMILY NO. 18

49. **James**, m., March 16, 1852, Elizabeth, daughter of William Hickling Prescott, the historian (H. U. 1814, LL. D. 1843) and Susan (Amory) Prescott. She d. May 24, 1864, at Boston.

Their children:

160. I. **James**, b. at Boston, March 23, 1853. Family No. 30. Groton.

161. II. **Gertrude**, b. Feb. 19, 1855; m. John Endicott Peabody. Family No. 31. Boston.

162. III. **Prescott**, b. at Boston, Jan. 17, 1861. Family No. 32. New York.

He m. (second), at West Roxbury, Dec. 4, 1865, Anna Lothrop Motley, daughter of Thomas and Maria (Bussey) Motley.

James Lawrence, eldest son of the Hon. Abbott and Katharine (Bigelow) Lawrence, was born at Boston, Dec. 6, 1821. He pursued his early studies at Chauncy Hall School, Boston, of which institution Gideon F. Thayer was the principal. Mr. Lawrence was admitted to Harvard, Sept. 5, 1836, and the date of his graduation was Aug. 26, 1840, as appears from the college records. He then studied law for two years at the Harvard Law School, after which he entered mercantile life, becoming a partner, with his father and Uncle Amos, in the house of A. & A. Lawrence & Co. He was afterwards the head of the firm for some years, and until obliged by illness to withdraw from active business. Mr. Lawrence served as an overseer of Harvard College from 1866 to 1875, and was a liberal benefactor of the Lawrence Scientific School, of which his father was the founder. He was one of the incorporators of the Boston Five Cent Savings Bank in 1854. His death occurred at Tunbridge Wells, England, Feb. 10, 1875.

An interesting reunion of some of the descendants of Major Samuel Lawrence was held Dec. 6, 1871, the occasion being the fiftieth birthday anniversary of James Lawrence, and also the wedding date, thirty-three years before, of Dr. and Mrs. William Richards Lawrence, at whose home in Longwood the meeting was held.

JAMES LAWRENCE

From the Boston Daily Advertiser, Feb. 12, 1875

" Opposed, alike from feeling and from principle, to everything approaching obituary eulogy, I can hardly let the grave close over a friend of a lifetime without the tribute of a word. Rare gifts, both of nature and of fortune, supplemented by the training of school, college, and law school, foreign travel and the opportunities of the best social culture at home and abroad, matured him as a man, while that nameless something of personal fascination, which some men have, drew about him a circle of such friends as a man keeps for his life. The pains which tore his frame, and left him physically in every part a wreck, never for a moment disturbed the poise of a brain wonderfully clear and exact to the end, and whatever the irritations of disease, they seemed rather to quicken than to obscure his outside sympathies. . . . At his bedside you found the latest news, and the latest book lay by him, or was minuted for order, while his conversation, singularly and felicitously rich, ranged broadly and freely everywhere, till you rose from your seat, feeling that he to whom you had come to minister, had ministered to you; while it shamed you to hear him say, 'You don't know how much good it has done me to see you.' . . . He got the keenest pleasure out of nature, conversation, books, and friendship; out of the glory of the dawn he so often saw; out of the birth of the last lamb at the Groton farm. With subtle zest did he enjoy all things; well did he use money and advantages. One does not look for blameless lives, but he will search long before he will find any in these respects more blameless than was his."

From the Boston Journal, Feb. 11, 1875

"Mr. Lawrence was in his early days an active business man, and for many years after the death of his father and uncle, Amos Lawrence, he was the head of the firm. His judgment upon men and business matters was keen, and during two years when he served in the Common Council, he gave promise of active participation in public affairs. He became trustee of his father's estate in 1855, and since then, with the exception of some special duties in connection with college associations, he has mingled but little beyond his immediate circle of friends."

THE PRESCOTT FAMILY

John Prescott, b. about 1604 at Shevington, Parish of Standish, Lancashire, m., Jan. 21, 1629, Mary

Platts of Wigan, in the same county. After his marriage he made his home at Sowerby, Parish of Halifax, in the West Riding of Yorkshire. "From conscientious motives," and to avoid persecution on account of his religion, he emigrated in 1638 to Barbadoes, and there passed two years. In 1640 he came to Massachusetts Bay, and settled at Watertown, where he owned considerable land. Of his subsequent history our chief sources of information are "The Prescott Memorial," by William Prescott, M. D., Boston, 1870, and the "History of Lancaster, Massachusetts," by Rev. Abijah P. Marvin. About the year 1643, Thomas King of Watertown, John Prescott, and others bought of Sholan, the chief of the Nashaway tribe of Indians, a large tract of land in the valley of the Nashua River. Here a settlement was made, which became incorporated in 1653 as the town of Lancaster, so called in honor of Mr. Prescott's native county in England. John Prescott was living there as early as the year 1646, and was one of the pioneer settlers. By occupation he was a blacksmith and miller. He d. in 1683.

Jonas Prescott, ninth and youngest child of John, was born at the Nashaway settlement, afterwards Lancaster, in June, 1648. He removed to Groton, where he became the owner of a mill in the south part of the town, which was afterwards annexed to Harvard. Jonas Prescott m., Dec. 14, 1672, Mary, only daughter of John Loker of Sudbury, and they had twelve children, of whom the tenth, Susanna, m., June 27, 1722, William Lawrence, a distinguished resident of Groton, and uncle of Major Samuel Lawrence. Mr.

Prescott was a blacksmith, and held the office of town clerk in 1692 and 1696. He served as a selectman several years, was representative to the General Court in 1699 and 1705, and a captain in the militia; d. Dec. 31, 1723. (See Butler's " History of Groton," pp. 286–289; and Dr. Green's " Groton Epitaphs," p. 249.)

Hon. Benjamin Prescott, twelfth and youngest child of Jonas, was born at Groton, Jan. 4. 1696. He m., June 11, 1718, Abigail, daughter of Hon. Thomas Oliver of Cambridge. In 1723 he was first chosen a representative to the General Court, and served as such during eight years. Lieutenant-colonel in the militia, 1732; justice of the Superior Court, 1735. He d. at Groton, Aug. 3, 1738.

Colonel William Prescott, fourth child of Benjamin, was born at Groton, Feb. 20, 1726, and in his youth settled in that part of the town now included in Pepperell. In 1755, as a lieutenant, he accompanied the provincial troops sent to remove the French Neutrals from Nova Scotia. In 1774 he was commissioned colonel of a regiment of minute-men from Pepperell and neighboring towns. Promptly upon news of the Lexington fight he marched with the men of his command to Cambridge. His subsequent military career, and especially his distinguished services as chief in command of the patriot troops at the battle of Bunker Hill, belong to the history of our country, and must ever be held in grateful remembrance. Colonel Prescott was publicly commended by General Washington for the excellent discipline maintained in his regiment during the retreat of the American forces after the battle of Long Island, which occurred, Aug. 27, 1776. In the autumn of the following year, he took part in the campaign which resulted in the surrender of General Burgoyne at Saratoga. Soon after this he retired from the army. Colonel Prescott served three years as representative from Pepperell, also as selectman and town clerk. He m., about the year 1756, Abigail Hale of Sutton. Notwithstanding the disparity in their years, an intimate friendship existed between Colonel Prescott and Major Samuel Lawrence, his former orderly in the early days of the Revolution. Colonel Prescott d. Oct. 13, 1795.

The Hon. William Prescott, only child of the above-named, was born at Pepperell, Aug. 19, 1762. He attended the district school and Dummer Academy, Byfield. Entering Harvard in 1779, he graduated with the Class of 1783, and afterwards taught school at Beverly for two years. Meanwhile he began the study of law, and was admitted to the bar in 1787. Two years after he removed to Salem, where he devoted himself to the practice of his profession for nineteen years. In 1808 he transferred his residence to Boston. Mr. Prescott served as representative to the General Court from both Salem and Boston. In 1815 he received from Harvard the degree of Doctor of Laws.[1] He m., Dec. 18, 1793, Catharine Green Hickling, daughter of Thomas Hickling, United States consul at the Island of St. Michael. He d. at Pepperell, Dec. 8, 1844. (See the " Prescott Memorial," pp. 75, 76.)

[1] This date is from the University Catalogue. In the *Prescott Memorial* it is given as 1824, and in Butler's *History of Pepperell*, 1814.

William Hickling Prescott, the eminent historian, a son of the Hon. William Prescott, was born at Salem, Mass., May 4, 1796, and graduated at Harvard College in 1814. During his Junior year he met with a sad accident, which deprived him of the sight of one eye, and rendered the other almost useless. Yet in spite of this great misfortune, with untiring energy and perseverance, and with the aid of capable readers and amanuenses, he pursued his literary studies and labors, and won for himself a wide reputation as an historical writer. His principal works are: "The History of Ferdinand and Isabella," published in 1837; "The Conquest of Mexico," 1843; "The Conquest of Peru," 1847; "The History of the Reign of Philip II. of Spain," 1855, which last was not completed.

Mr. Prescott m., May 4, 1820, Susan, fourth child of Thomas Coffin and Hannah (Linzee) Amory of Boston. His death occurred Jan. 28, 1859. (See the "Life of William Hickling Prescott," by George Ticknor, 1866.)

Elizabeth, the third child of the above-named, m., March 16, 1852, James Lawrence of Boston. (Family No. 18.)

FAMILY NO. 19

53. **Abbott**, m., at Boston, April 12, 1853, Harriette Story White Paige, daughter of James William and Harriette Story (White) Paige of Boston. Children:

163. I. **Abbott**, b. at Boston, Jan. 16, 1854.

Abbott Lawrence, Jr., received his preparatory instruction at Mr. Dixwell's school in Boston, and graduated at Harvard College in 1875. He then took a two years' course at the Law School, receiving the degree of Bachelor of Laws in 1877. Immediately thereafter he started on a tour around the world *via* San Franciso, Japan, China, Java, and India, arriving in Europe in April, 1878. He then boarded for six months in a French family at Paris, and for a like period in a German household at Dresden. Returning to Boston in Aug., 1879, he resumed the study of law and was admitted to the bar of the United States Circuit Court, Dec. 1, 1879. Mr. Lawrence served for a time on the staff of Brigadier-General Eben Sutton of the Second Brigade, M. V. M.; and was secretary of the Republican State Convention held at Worcester in 1881. He was taken ill in the autumn of that year, and died at Nassau, New Providence, Bahama Islands, March 15, 1882.

164. II. **Rosamond**, b. at Boston, May 17, 1856. Family No. 33. Hyde Park.

165. III. **William Paige**, b. at Lynn, Mass., Aug. 15, 1858.

William Paige Lawrence attended Mr. Noble's school in Boston, and was a student at the Harvard Law School for two years, from 1878 to 1880. He bought a farm in Groton in June, 1885, and took up his residence in that town. Mr. Lawrence was devoted to outdoor country life, was fond of horses and expert in their management. He was, moreover, an enthusiastic ornithologist, and well versed in the art of taxidermy. He made three visits to Europe. On June 4, 1891, he was appointed a justice of the peace, and held the office until his death, at Boston, Feb. 9, 1898.

166. IV. **John**, b. at Boston, April 27, 1861. Family No. 34. Groton.

167. V. **Robert Ashton**, b. at Boston, Nov. 4, 1865; m., at Hartford, Conn., Oct. 11, 1893, Caroline Ella, daughter of Rev. Eurotas Parmele and Anna (Cleveland) Hastings.

They had a son:

167a. **Abbott**, b. at Groton, Jan. 20, 1895, who d. two days after.

Robert Ashton Lawrence attended the private schools kept by Miss Hannah Adam and John Prentiss Hopkinson in Boston, and entered Harvard as a special student in 1885, remaining two years. In June, 1892, he removed to Groton, where he lived until the summer of 1895, when he went to Europe with his wife, and spent thirteen months in foreign travel and residence. In Dec., 1897, Mr. Lawrence removed to Chestnut Hill, where he lived until March, 1902. At this time he bought and occupied the fine estate of William Richardson Dupee, situated on Beacon Street in Newton, near the Chestnut Hill line. He has been for four years treasurer in the United States of the Naples Society for the Protection of Animals. He is also a director and life member of the Animal Rescue League, and president of the Boston Work-horse Parade Society. Mr. Lawrence served for six years as a member of the First Corps of Cadets, M. V. M. He has visited every European capital.

THE HASTINGS FAMILY

The name Hastings is of Danish origin, and appears on record at a very early period in English history, having been borne by many persons of title and distinction.

Mrs. Caroline Ella (Hastings) Lawrence is of the eighth generation from Thomas Hastings (b. in 1605), who sailed with his wife Susanna, from Ipswich, England, April 10, 1634, on the ship *Elizabeth*. He settled at Watertown, Mass., where he was for five years a selectman, town clerk three years, and a representative to the General Court in 1673. Mrs. Susanna Hastings d. Feb. 2, 1650, and he m. for his second wife, April 2, 1651, Margaret, daughter of William and Martha Cheney of Roxbury. Deacon Thomas Hastings d. in 1685.

Eurotas Parmele Hastings, a lineal descendant of Deacon Thomas, was b. April 17, 1821. He was a graduate of Hamilton College, N. Y., and of Union Theological Seminary. After being ordained, he went to Ceylon and was there engaged in teaching at Batticotta Seminary for five years. Returning to this country, he m., March 9, 1853, Anna, daughter of Rev. Richard F. Cleveland of Clinton, and sister of Hon. Grover Cleveland, afterwards President of the United States. Rev. Dr. Hastings was for forty-three years a missionary in Ceylon, and was the first president of Jaffna College, which was established in 1871; d. at Manepi, Ceylon, July 31, 1890. Of his seven children, the two youngest are Charles Edgar and his twin sister, Caroline Ella Hastings, who m., Oct. 11, 1893, Robert Ashton Lawrence.

168. VI. **Harriette Story**, b. at Boston, June 10, 1867. Family No. 35. Boston.

Abbott Lawrence received his early training at Chauncy Hall School, and was admitted to Harvard College, Sept. 1, 1845, graduating July 18, 1849; A. M., 1853. He took a course in the Law School, and received the degree of LL. B. in 1863, but did not engage in the practice of law. For many years he was actively interested in manufacturing affairs, and served as president and director of several business corporations, and also as actuary of the Massachusetts Hospital Life Insurance Company. He made several trips to Europe, and devoted some time to literary work, having edited the diary of his grandfather, Hon. Timothy Bigelow of Groton and Medford, Mass. Mr. Lawrence died at Nahant, July 6, 1893. His widow, Mrs. Harriette Story White (Paige) Lawrence, d. at Boston, Feb. 5, 1903.

THE PAIGE FAMILY

Nathaniel Paige came from England about 1685 with his wife and three children, and settled in Roxbury. He was appointed marshal of Suffolk County in 1686, and bought land in Billerica, where he appears to have resided for a brief time. In 1686 he became one of the eight Purchasers of Hardwick. He died, April 12, 1692, at Boston, probably while attending to his official duties. The name of this family is invariably spelled Paige, and has no known connection with any of the Pages in New England. The Rev. Dr. Lucius R. Paige, the historian of Cambridge and Hardwick, published in the History

of Hardwick a full account of the family, from which
abstracts are here made.

Nathaniel Paige and wife Joanna had at least five
children — Nathaniel, b. 1679; Elizabeth, b. 1681,
m. John Simkins; Sarah, m. Samuel Hill; James,
b. 1686, who died young; and Christopher, whose
birth is recorded in Billerica, Feb. 6, 1690–1. The
mother of the children died in 1724.

Christopher Paige, the youngest son, m. (first)
Joanna ———, who soon died, and he m. (second),
May 23, 1720, Elizabeth, daughter of Deacon George
Reed of Woburn. He resided in Billerica, in that
part which is now Bedford, but in 1735 became one
of the pioneer settlers of Hardwick, where his father
had secured proprietary rights a half century before. He d. March 10, 1774. The "Massachusetts
Gazette" has the following obituary: "At Hardwick,
Dea. Christopher Paige, aged 83 years and 21 days,
in a comfortable hope of a better life. He left a
widow, and has had 12 children, 9 now living and
3 dead; 81 grandchildren, 66 living and 15 dead."
Their son, William Paige, m., Jan. 12, 1744, Mercy,
daughter of James Aikens. He was a captain in the
French and Indian wars, chairman of the Committee
of Correspondence, representative, and delegate to
the convention at Cambridge for framing the state
constitution. He was likewise one of the committee
appointed by the General Court for the sale of confiscated estates in Worcester County. His brother,
Colonel Timothy Paige, served his fellow-townsmen
with ability in civil and military affairs. Christopher
Paige d. Feb. 14, 1790, and his wife d. Feb. 19,

1823, aged 102 years and 30 days. The following are their children: William, b. 1745; James, 1747; Rebecca, 1749, m. John Foster; Jesse, 1752; Mercy, 1754, m. Nathaniel Graves; Lucy, 1757, m. Daniel Ruggles; and Christopher, b. June 12, 1762.

Christopher Paige, Jr., graduated from Harvard College in 1784, and became a preacher of the standing order. He m. Rebecca Chamberlain, the widow of the Rev. Elijah Fletcher, pastor at Hopkinton, N. H. He preached for a brief season in Hopkinton and in Pittsfield, and in 1796 settled over the churches in Deering and Washington. In 1816 he was at Roxbury, N. H. His health failing, he removed to Salisbury, N. H., where Madam Paige d. July 9, 1821, and he d. Oct. 12, 1822. Rev. Christopher Paige was the father of three children: Elijah Fletcher, who was a graduate of Harvard College in 1810, and d. in Virginia in 1817; Christopher, who settled in Nashua, N. H.; and James William, who was b. in Pittsfield, N. H., July 2, 1792. There are accounts of Rev. Mr. Paige in the Histories of both Hopkinton and Salisbury.

James William Paige m. Harriette Story, daughter of Stephen White of Salem. She was b. Nov. 29, 1809, and d. Nov. 25, 1863. Their daughter, Harriette Story White Paige, m., April 12, 1853, Abbott Lawrence.

Mr. Stephen White maintained intimate relations for many years with Daniel Webster. Mr. White in his will, which was made in Dec., 1839, devises to Mr. Webster "all my muskets, fowling pieces and other apparatus thereto pertaining, as a slight manifestation of the deep sense I entertain of his high and exalted talents, but more especially of what is to me far more estimable, that kindness and goodness of heart which endears him to all those who best know his qualities." And further, Mr. White devises, " as a slight testimonial of the regard and respect which I entertain for the virtues and high character of Mrs. Daniel Webster, my Executors will return to her the signet ring, which was her own gift, and which will not be withdrawn from my finger until the voice which dictates this will shall be silent." Under date of Aug. 22, 1841, Mr. Webster writes to Mrs. Paige: " The death of your father affected me much. It seemed sudden, notwithstanding his long continuance of feeble health. He is a loss to me; I hardly expect to find others more agreeable for their extent of information, softness of manners and pleasant conversation. We have passed much happy time together." (Webster's " Life and Letters," vol. ii. p. 108.)

Mr. Paige, when a young man, became a merchant in Boston. He was closely associated with men who had been successful, and with a like spirit became one of them. His intimacy with the Hon. Daniel Webster was almost lifelong, and he and the son of Mr. Webster married sisters, daughters of Mr. Stephen White of Salem and afterwards of Boston. Mr. White was a near friend of Mr. Webster, so that with loyalty they stood by each other in all their affairs. No biography of Mr. Webster can be written without allusion to Mr. White and Mr. Paige. Mr. and Mrs. Paige waited upon Daniel Webster in his dying hours at Marshfield. The Paige home at 122 Summer Street was Webster's headquarters in Boston; and it was from this home that the funeral of Colonel Daniel Fletcher Webster took place in Sept., 1862. The last years of Mr. Paige were spent in infirmity and retirement. He d. May 19, 1868. A Boston newspaper at the time of his death said: " Mr. James W. Paige, formerly senior partner of an extensive commission house in this city, died Tuesday, after a long illness, at the age of 75 years. He was for many years the honored head of one of the largest wholesale commission houses. Hon. Daniel Webster married for his first wife the half-sister of Mr. Paige, and his connection with the distinguished statesman was of long continuance and of the most intimate character. He was active in the management of several corporations, but with the exception of being a member of the Constitutional Convention of this State in 1853, held no official position. Mr. Paige retired from business a year or two since in feeble health." Another newspaper said of the funeral: " There was a large congregation present [at King's Chapel], embracing many of the leading merchants and business men of Boston, anxious to pay a last tribute of respect to one of their number. The dry goods commission merchants and jobbers closed their places of business at the hour of the funeral, as a mark of respect, and attended the funeral in considerable numbers. The services, of an impressive character, were conducted by the Rev'nds H. W. Foote and Chandler Robbins of the Second Church." Another newspaper said: " The mercantile community lose a prominent man in the death of Mr. Paige."

THE WHITE FAMILY

Henry White, a son of John White, was born in that part of Salem which is now Danvers. Henry White m., Oct. 8, 1776, Phebe Brown. He was a merchant and died about 1824; the widow survived until June 17, 1840, aged 83 years. They had two or three daughters, and sons Joseph; Stephen, b. July 10, 1787; and Francis. The son Joseph was always called "junior," in distinction from his uncle, Captain Joseph White. He m., in 1808, Betsy, daughter of Dr. Elisha Story, and had three daughters, (1) Elizabeth Story White, who m. Samuel C. Gray of Boston; (2) Mary Barrow White, who m. George W. Pratt; and (3) Charlotte Sophia. Captain Joseph White, Jr., d. in 1819. The son Francis died unmarried. The son Stephen White m., Aug. 19, 1808, Harriette Story, a sister of Joseph's wife.

Captain Joseph White, Sr., was a wealthy merchant-mariner of Salem, who was brutally murdered in his bed in April, 1830. After vigilant efforts, the perpetrators were brought to justice, one of them committing suicide. In the celebrated trial which followed, the Commonwealth was represented by the Hon. Daniel Webster, in the prosecution of the murderers and in the defence of the White family, who had been systematically maligned. The noble and eloquent service rendered by Daniel Webster not only extended his already wide repute, but deepened the friendship existing between him and Stephen White. Immediately after the trial Mr. White employed Mr. Samuel Lorenzo Knapp, editor of the " Boston Gazette," to prepare and publish a biography of Daniel Webster. The rapidly extending fame of Mr. Webster as an interpreter of the Constitution, in the Senate of the United States, soon called for a new and enlarged edition of the book.

Stephen White inherited large interests from his uncle, Captain Joseph White, and managed them with great skill. He was public-spirited, and entered into the affairs of his native town, and of the Commonwealth. He was elected several times to both branches of the legislature, and was often called upon to render service in behalf of the people, and to take positions calling for integrity and confidence. He removed to Boston about 1830.

In a poem by Mr. William W. Story, which was read on the occasion of the 250th anniversary of the landing of Governor Endicott at Salem, Sept. 18, 1878, Mr. Story says : —

> " There too are Phillips, Silsbee, Saltonstall :
> Putnam and Crowninshield and King and White,
> Good men and true to battle for the right,
> At bar, bench, and the Nation's Council Hall."

Health began to fail Mr. White about 1835. He died in New York city, Aug. 10, 1841. His death called forth a filial letter from Daniel Webster to his daughter, Mrs. Paige. Mr. White had three daughters: (1) Harriette Story, b. Nov. 29, 1809, who m. James W. Paige; (2) Caroline Story, who m. Colonel Daniel Fletcher Webster, son of Daniel Webster; and (3) Ellen, who m. John B. Joy.

Elisha Story and his sister Sarah, who m., at Boston, Mr. Thomas Dawse, in the year 1702, are the
first of this family of whom we have an authentic
record. Elisha Story m., in 1706, Lydia Emmons,
who died a few years later without surviving issue.
He m. (second) Sarah (Stocker), widow of Charles
Renouf. She had two children by her first husband,
and four children by Mr. Story. He d. in 1725, aged
42 years, and the widow in 1742, aged 58 years.
Their only surviving son, William, b. April 25, 1720,
m., at Boston in 1741, Elizabeth Marion, by whom
there were two children: Elisha, b. Dec. 3, 1743,
and Elizabeth. William Story m. (second) Joanna
Appleton of Ipswich, and had other children, among
them the Rev. Isaac Story, who m. Rebecca, daughter of Rev. Simon Bradstreet, and succeeded his
father-in-law in the pastorate of the church in Marblehead. Mr. William Story m., in 1776, Madam
Abigail Marshall. He was deputy register of the
Court of Admiralty at Boston, but resigned in Aug.,
1765. He then removed to Marblehead. His sympathies were doubtless with the royal party, but he
continued to reside in Marblehead until his death,
Nov. 24, 1799, aged 80 years.

Dr. Elisha Story was born Dec. 3, 1743, and m. (first)
Ruth, daughter of Major John Ruddock of Boston;
she d. March 21, 1778, aged 32 years. He m. (sec-
ond), Nov. 29, 1778, Mehitable, daughter of Captain
John Pedrick by his wife Mehitable Stacy. Dr.
Story d. Aug. 27, 1805, aged 62 years, and the widow

Mehitable survived until Aug. 9, 1847. By his first wife there was a son William, who m., in 1797, Elizabeth Patten, and they were the parents of Augustus Story, b. in 1812, and who graduated at Harvard College in 1828. Dr. Story and his wife Mehitable had: (1) Joseph, b. Sept. 18, 1779, who was a justice of the United States Supreme Court, whose legal learning and decisions are of extended repute; (2) Mehitable, who m., in 1804, William Fettyplace; (3) Betsy, who m., in 1808, Captain Joseph White, Jr.; (4) Horace, who d. in 1823 while journeying to New Orleans; and (5) Harriett, who m., Aug. 19, 1808, Stephen White, a brother of Joseph White, Jr., who m. her above-named sister Betsy. The White and Story families, thus intimately connected in home life, were also intimate in social and political affairs. Madam Mehitable (Pedrick) Story was a woman of excellent qualities. She used to relate a most romantic account of her youth and the efforts of an officer of the British army to obtain her hand in marriage. His advances were rejected, and at the age of nineteen she became the wife of the patriot, Dr. Elisha Story. This romance is published in " Essex Institute Collections," vol. 17, p. 192.

FAMILY NO. 20

54. **Katharine Bigelow,** m., at Boston, June 1, 1854, Augustus Lowell. She d. April 1, 1895.
Their children are :
169. I. **Percival,** b. at Boston, March 13, 1855.
Percival Lowell pursued his early studies at pri-

vate schools in Boston and in France, after which he took the regular academical course at Harvard, receiving the degree of A. B. in 1876. He then spent a year in foreign travel, and on his return was for a time engaged in the management of trust funds in Boston, serving also as treasurer *pro tem.* of the Massachusetts Cotton Mills, and as treasurer of the Lowell Bleachery. Early in the year 1883 he went to Japan, and spent some months at Tokio, and in the interior of the country, studying the language and customs of the people. He then accepted the position of foreign secretary and counsellor of the Korean Special Mission to the United States, which was the first embassy sent by Korea to a western power. The embassy arrived in San Francisco, Sept. 2, 1883, and proceeded to New York, where it was received by President Arthur. After a visit of six weeks in the United States, the embassy returned to Korea, accompanied by Mr. Lowell, who passed the ensuing winter as a guest of the king at the capital city, Soül. He again visited Japan, and came home by way of Singapore and the Red Sea in the summer of 1884. Mr. Lowell has since visited Japan several times. In 1894 he established the Lowell Observatory on Flagstaff Hill, in Arizona. He is a Fellow of the American Academy of Arts and Sciences, member of the Royal Astronomical Society, and of the Asiatic Society of Japan. He is the author of the following works: " Chosön, the Land of the Morning Calm. A Sketch of Korea," Boston, Ticknor & Co., 1886. " The Soul of the Far East," Houghton, Mifflin & Co., 1888. " Noto, an Unexplored Corner of Japan," Houghton, Mifflin & Co., 1891. "Mars," Houghton, Mifflin & Co., 1895. "Occult Japan, or the Way of the Gods," Houghton, Mifflin & Co., 1895. "New Observations of the Planet Mercury," Cambridge, 1898.

170. II. **Abbott Lawrence**, b. at Boston, Dec. 13, 1856; m., at Boston, June 19, 1879, Anna Parker Lowell, daughter of George Gardner and Mary Ellen (Parker) Lowell.

Abbott Lawrence Lowell obtained his preparatory training at schools in Paris, France, and Boston. After graduation at Harvard in 1877, and from the Law School three years later, he continued his professional studies in the office of Russell & Putnam, Boston. Since 1880 he has practised law with Francis C. Lowell, and in 1891 he formed a law partnership with the latter and F. J. Stimson. Mr. Lowell was for some years a member of the Boston School Committee, and has since been active in the interests of the Boston Public School Association. He succeeded his father as trustee of the Lowell Institute, and is now professor of the Science of Government in Harvard University, and a member of the corporation of the Massachusetts Institute of Technology. He is also a member of the American Academy of Arts and Sciences. In 1884 he published (jointly with Francis C. Lowell) a work on the "Transfer of Stock in Corporations." He is also the author of the following named books: "Essays on Government," Houghton, Mifflin & Co., Boston, 1889. "Governments and Parties in Continental Europe" (2 vols.), Houghton, Mifflin & Co., 1896.

"Oscillations in Politics," Philadelphia, 1898. [American Academy of Political and Social Science.] "Colonial Civil Service," Macmillan & Co., New York, 1900.

171. III. **Katharine,** b. at Boston, Nov. 27, 1858; m. (first), Dec. 5, 1882, at Brookline, Alfred Roosevelt, son of James Alfred and Elizabeth (Emlen) Roosevelt of New York, and cousin-german to President Theodore Roosevelt. He d. in 1891.

They had:

172. 1. **Elfrida,** b. Dec. 22, 1883.

173. 2. **James Alfred,** b. Feb. 23, 1885.

174. 3. **Katharine Lowell,** b. Aug. 18, 1887.

Mrs. Katharine (Lowell) Roosevelt m. (second), at Chestnut Hill, Nov. 24, 1902, Thomas James Bowlker (M. A., Cambridge; ordained priest, 1894), formerly assistant master at Haileybury College, Hertfordshire, England (The Hon. and Rev. Canon Edward Lyttelton, M. A., master).

175. IV. **Elizabeth,** b. at Boston, Feb. 2, 1862; m., at Brookline, June 9, 1888, William Lowell Putnam.

Their children born at Boston:

176. 1. **George,** b. June 4, 1889.

177. 2. **Katharine Lawrence,** b. Dec. 15, 1890.

178. 3. **Roger Lowell,** b. Dec. 19, 1893.

179. 4. **Harriet Lowell,** b. Aug. 30, 1897; d. March 7, 1900.

179a. 5. **Augustus Lowell,** b. at Brookline, June 25, 1899.

William Lowell Putnam, the eldest child of George and Harriet (Lowell) Putnam of Boston, and grandson of Rev. George Putnam, D. D., and Elizabeth (Ware) Putman of Roxbury, was born at Roxbury, Nov. 22, 1861. He obtained his early education at private schools in Cambridge and at the Cambridge High School, and graduated at Harvard in 1882. Immediately after leaving college he went abroad and spent fifteen months in travel in Great Britain and on the Continent. Returning to this country in Sept., 1883, he entered the Harvard Law School, where he took the regular course. During the summer of 1884 he studied in the office of Ropes, Gray & Loring. After leaving the Law School he practised law in Boston for some years with Messrs. Russell & Putnam, having an office at 50 State Street, and later with his father and brother, under the firm name of Putnam & Putnam, in the Ames Building. Mr. Putnam is a director and trustee of various organizations. He served for three years in the First Corps of Cadets, M. V. M. He wrote an article on "Fraudulent Imitation by Deceptive Use of One's Own Name," for the "Harvard Law Review," Oct., 1898.

180. V. **Roger**, b. at Boston, Feb. 2, 1862; d. Aug. 31, 1863.

181. VI. **May**, b. May 1, 1870; d. same day.

182. VII. **Amy**, b. at Brookline, Feb. 9, 1874. Resides in the Lowell homestead in that town.

THE LOWELL FAMILY[1]

The Lowells in the United States are of Norman descent, and their remote ancestors are believed to

---

[1] The arms of Lowell are : Sable, a dexter hand, couped at the wrist, grasping three pointless darts, one in pale, and two in saltire argent.

have accompanied William, Duke of Normandy, to England in 1066. The name was originally Lowle, and continued in this form for several centuries. Authentic family records are wanting for the period between the Conquest and the early part of the thirteenth century, but the lineage has been traced from William Lowle, who was born at Yardley, Worcestershire, probably before 1250. In this region and in the County of Somerset, members of the Lowle family resided for nine generations. Percival Lowle or Lowell, son of Richard, and a native of Somersetshire, was born in 1571. His mother was a daughter of Edmund Percival, of distinguished ancestry, and Elizabeth Panthuit of Weston-in-Gordano. Percival Lowell was a merchant of Bristol. In 1639, when sixty-four years of age, he emigrated to this country, with his wife Rebecca, his sons John and Richard, and his daughter Joan, on the ship *Jonathan*. They arrived at Newbury, Mass., in the month of June, and became residents of that town, where Percival Lowell died, Jan. 8, 1665, at the age of 93.

John Lowell, eldest child of Percival and Rebecca, was born in England in 1595. When 24 years of age, he apprenticed himself to Richard Baugh, a Bristol glover, and in 1619 he was "admitted a citizen of Bristol." His first wife was Mary ——, whom he m. in England. She d. in 1639, and during the same year he accompanied his parents to America, and m. for his second wife, Elizabeth Goodale. John Lowell "was a man of good education for those days, and prominent in the community." He d. at Newbury, Mass., July 10, 1647.

John Lowell, second of the name, of the third generation, son of the above-named John and his first wife, Mary, was born in England in 1629, and was therefore ten years old when he came to the new world. He m. (first), Jan. 3, 1653, Hannah, daughter of George and Edith Proctor. She d. and he was afterwards twice married. John Lowell followed the trade of a cooper. He removed early from Newbury to Boston, and afterwards lived at Scituate and Rehoboth, returning later to Boston, where he d. Jan. 7, 1694.

Ebenezer, the fifteenth child of John and Hannah (Proctor) Lowell, was b. at Boston in 1675. He m., Jan. 30, 1694, Elizabeth, daughter of Michael and Hannah Shailer of Hingham. Ebenezer Lowell was a cordwainer, and was reputed to be "a man of much energy of character." He d. at Boston, Sept. 10, 1711.

The Rev. John Lowell, fifth child of the last-named, was born at Boston, March 14, 1704. Graduate of Harvard in 1721; ordained pastor of the Third Church of Newbury, Mass., Jan. 19, 1726, and retained the position for forty-two years. According to the Boston records, John Lowell and Sarah Champney (daughter of Noah and Sarah (Tunnel) Champney) were m., Dec. 23, 1725, by Mr. William Waldron, the first pastor of the "New Brick Church" on Hanover Street. She d. June 28, 1756, and he m. for his second wife, in 1758, Elizabeth (Cutts) Whipple, widow of Rev. Joseph Whipple of Hampton Falls, N. H. Mr. Lowell was a scholarly man, of liberal theological views. He d. at Newburyport, Mass., May 15, 1767.

Judge John Lowell, only son of the preceding, was b. at Newburyport, Mass., June 17, 1743. Grad. Harvard, 1760. Upon leaving college he was said to have taken a vow of celibacy. Within a few years thereafter he was otherwise minded, for he m. (first), Jan. 3, 1767, at Salem, Sarah, daughter of Stephen and Elizabeth (Cabot) Higginson. She d. May 5, 1772, and he m. (second), May 31, 1774, Susanna, daughter of Francis and Mary (Fitch) Cabot of Salem. She d. March 30, 1777, and he m. for his third wife, at Dunstable, Mass., June 27, 1778, Rebecca, daughter of Judge James and Katharine (Graves) Russell of Charlestown, Mass., and widow of James Tyng of Dunstable. Mr. Lowell at first practised law at Newburyport, but removed to Boston in 1777. He was a member of the Continental Congress in 1782–83, and was appointed by President Washington, in 1789, judge of the United States District Court for Massachusetts. In 1801 he was appointed by President Adams justice of the U. S. Circuit Court for Maine, Massachusetts, New Hampshire, and Rhode Island. Judge John Lowell "enjoyed a great and deserved reputation, equally in respect of his professional ability, and of his high character." (" Memorial History of Boston," iv. p. 586.) He received the degree of LL. D. from Harvard in 1792. He d. at Roxbury, Mass., May 6, 1802.

John Lowell, third of the name, second child of Judge John and Sarah (Higginson) Lowell, was b. at Newburyport, Oct. 6, 1769, and graduated at Harvard in 1786, before he had reached the age of seventeen. He then studied law, was admitted to the Suffolk bar in 1789, and practised his profession with marked success until 1803, when he retired owing to impaired health. After three years' travel and sojourn in Europe, he returned home and engaged in literary work. Mr. Lowell " acquired fame as a political writer, wielding a trenchant pen." He was a Fellow of Harvard College, 1810–32 ; LL. D. 1814. He m., June 8, 1793, Rebecca, daughter of John and Katherine (Greene) Amory. He was one of the founders of several noted institutions : the Massachusetts General Hospital, Boston Athenæum, and Massachusetts Hospital Life Insurance Company. He d. at Boston, March 12, 1840.

John Amory Lowell, second child of John and Rebecca (Amory) Lowell, was born at Boston, Nov. 11, 1798, and graduated at Harvard College in 1815, at the age of sixteen. He then entered the store of Kirk Boott & Sons, importers of English goods, remaining with them about four years. In Jan., 1822, he formed a partnership with John W. Boott (under the style of Boott & Lowell), which was dissolved in July, 1824. Mr. Lowell served as an official of the Suffolk Bank for fifty-nine years. Treasurer of the Boston Manufacturing Company, at Waltham, from 1827 to 1844. He built the Boott Cotton Mills (of which he was the treasurer, and afterwards president), and also the Massachusetts Cotton Mills, of which he was also treasurer and a director. President of the Pacific Mills, 1871–77. Fellow of Harvard College, 1837–77; LL. D. 1851. Mr. Lowell was the first trustee of the Lowell Institute, which was founded by his cousin, John Lowell, Jr., 1799–1836, and inaugurated in 1839. He m. (first), at Boston, Feb. 14, 1822, Susan Cabot, second child of Francis Cabot and Hannah (Jackson) Lowell. She d. at Cambridge, Aug. 15, 1827, and he m. (second), at Salem, April 2, 1829, Elizabeth Cabot, daughter of Judge Samuel and Sarah (Gooll) Putnam. The Hon. John Amory Lowell d. Oct. 31, 1881.

Augustus Lowell, a son of John Amory and Elizabeth (Putnam) Lowell (daughter of the Hon. Samuel Putnam of Salem), was born at Boston, Jan. 15, 1830. He lived in his boyhood at the ancestral country home in Roxbury, and drove with his father every morning to Boston, where he attended the Public Latin School. Entering Harvard in 1846, he took the regular course, graduating with the Class of 1850. He then went to Europe with his father, and remained abroad until the autumn of the following year, the latter part of the time being devoted to travel in Germany and Switzerland, with his classmate, Mr. Lincoln Baylies. Upon his return home he took a position in the counting-room of Bullard & Lee, East India merchants, Boston, where he remained for two years. He was then sent to Lowell (named after his great-uncle, Francis C. Lowell) to obtain a practical knowledge of the running of cotton manufactories, and here he passed a year, after which he entered the office of J. M. Beebe, Morgan & Co., in Boston. June 1, 1854, he was married at Boston to Katharine Bigelow Lawrence, youngest child of the Hon. Abbott Lawrence. After this he was almost constantly officially connected with the mills at Lowell and Lawrence, and was also engaged in the East Indian trade in partnership with Mr. Franklin H. Story. In 1864 Mr. Lowell went abroad with his wife and family, and was absent from home two years and a half, the summers being spent in travel for the benefit of Mrs. Lowell's health, which had become impaired. Returning to Boston in the autumn of 1866, he gradually assumed various business cares, devoting himself chiefly to manufacturing interests and the management of trusts. Many were the positions of responsibility held by him at different times. He served as treasurer of the Boott Cotton Mills for eleven years ; as a member of the executive committee of the Board of Directors of the Massachusetts Hospital Life Insurance Company ; president of the Provident Institution for Savings, and of the Boston Gas Light Company ; treasurer and president of the Merrimac Manufacturing Company ; president of the following named manufacturing companies : the Massachusetts Mills in Georgia, Massachusetts Cotton Mills, Pacific Mills, Boott Cotton Mills, Lowell Bleachery, Lowell Machine Shop, Glendon Iron Company. Mr. Lowell was also a director of the following : Everett Mills, Middlesex Company, Lawrence Mills, Lowell Manufacturing Company, Suffolk National Bank, Cranberry Iron Company, Plymouth Cordage Company, and a trustee of the Union Trust Company of New York.

Besides these varied and important business interests, he found time to devote to matters affecting the public welfare. Thus he served for many years as a trustee of the Massachusetts Eye and Ear Infirmary and of the Boston Museum of Fine Arts, and for one term as a member of the Boston School Committee.

He succeeded his father in 1881 as the trustee of the Lowell Institute, which greatly prospered under his able administration; and for more than a quarter of a century he was prominent in the management of the Massachusetts Institute of Technology, first as a member of its Corporation, and from 1883 as one of its executive committee. After his return from Europe in 1866, Mr. Lowell made his summer home in Brookline, where he took great pleasure in gardening, devoting also much attention to the greenhouses on his fine estate. His death occurred there, June 22, 1901.

In a Memoir of Augustus Lowell, prepared by his son, Percival Lowell, and reprinted from the "Proceedings of the American Academy of Arts and Sciences," vol. xxxvii., some leading traits of Mr. Lowell's character are thus described: " Three qualities he possessed to an unusual degree; will, ability, and integrity. . . . He was noted for his determination. To his lot, in consequence, fell many necessary and thankless tasks. He likewise escaped many empty honors. For where he went, he worked. No one ever thought of preferring him to a post merely *honoris causa*. For people knew that in getting him they got not a figurehead, but a man who was certain to make himself felt; not because he tried to do so, but because it was in him to do it. He entered concerns not by the postern-gate of popularity, but by the portal of inevitableness. He was chosen because he was necessary. And he stayed for the same reason." " He was apt to be right, that is, to be wise. His judgment of things within his own field was excellent. It was essentially sound. His was that uncommon sense-possession, the possession of common sense. Instinctively his mind worked correctly. It was the exact opposite of the mind of the crank, which may often hit off a brilliant conception, but which is too unsafe to be trusted. With him no one idea ever usurped the right of way to the exclusion of others. Each had its due effect; which fundamental balance makes the only safe foundation for superstructure."

FAMILY NO. 21

67. **Mary Nisbet**, m., at Staten Island, N. Y., June 2, 1863, Malcolm Graeme Haughton.

Their children:

183. I. **Lawrence**, b. at Clifton, Staten Island, March 9, 1864. He attended Bishops College School, and the Institute of Technology in Boston. Cotton buyer. He was for four years a member of the First Corps of Cadets, M. V. M., and served during the Spanish war in the Twelfth Regiment of the National Guard of the State of New York.

184. II. **Malcolm Graeme, Jr.**, b. at Clifton, S. I., April 5, 1866. Attended Bishops College School, and studied with a private tutor. Was for one year a member of the Class of 1886, H. U. Since 1884 he has been engaged in business as a cotton buyer, in Columbus, Miss., Rockdale, Milam County, Texas, and as a member of the firm of Haughton & Co. in Boston. He was for seven years from 1893 agent in Texas for Messrs. Ralli Bros. of New York.

185. III. **Alan Randolph**, b. at Clifton, S. I., Feb. 1, 1869; d. at Chestnut Hill, Mass., Nov. 23, 1883.

186. IV. **Alison Turnbull Lawrence**, b. at Clifton, S. I., July 12, 1871. She has devoted several years, at home and abroad, to the cultivation of her voice in singing, with great success.

187. V. **Percy Duncan**, b. at Grymes Hill, S. I., July 11, 1876; educated at Groton School. Graduate of H. U., Class of 1899. Has been prominent in college athletics. Member of First Corps of Cadets, M. V. M. He is with Messrs. E. H. Rollins & Co., bankers, Boston.

Malcolm Graeme Haughton, Sr., son of Benjamin and Rachel Haughton, was born in Banford, near Lawrencetown, in the north of Ireland, Nov. 2, 1831. He received early instruction from private tutors and at schools in Dublin. Coming to this country, he engaged in business as a merchant in New Orleans and New York, and later in Boston as a cotton buyer. Residence at Brookline.

EIGHTH GENERATION

FAMILY NO. 22

111. **Arthur**, m., at Stockbridge, Mass., June 12, 1877, Alison Turnbull Lawrence, second daughter of Samuel and Alison Turnbull Lawrence of Stockbridge. She d. May 22, 1884.

Their children:

188. I. **William Richards**, b. at Stockbridge, July 3, 1878. He received his early education at Groton School, Groton, Mass. Graduated at Harvard in 1901. While in college he was an editor of the "Crimson." Master in Groton School. In 1902 he went to Germany to study languages and the science of teaching.

189. II. **Susan Dana**, b. at Stockbridge, Aug. 20, 1879; d. Sept. 16, 1888.

Arthur Lawrence received his early training at Lawrence Academy, Groton; M. Keller's private school in Paris, France; Boston Public Latin School, Epes S. Dixwell's school, and at Norwich (Vt.) University. After graduation at Harvard, in 1863, he was for a short time in the counting-room of E. R. Mudge, Sawyer & Co., where he remained until Feb., 1864, when he entered the service of the United States Christian Commission, and continued therein as delegate and agent until the close of the war. He was a volunteer aide of General O. O. Howard, commanding the right wing of General W. T. Sherman's army, during the famous march from Atlanta to the sea. On Dec. 13, 1864, Generals Sherman and Howard, with their staffs, watched from Cheves' rice-mill, on the opposite bank of the Ogeeche River, the assault on Fort McAllister, which was captured after sunset by Brigadier-General William B. Hazen's Division. The two generals, with their orderlies, and Colonel Strong of Howard's staff, Major George Ward Nichols, and Mr. Lawrence, embarked in a small boat having three oars, the three last named being the oarsmen. The trip was thus described by Mr. Lawrence: " General Sherman sat in the stern, steering with a paddle, to counteract the inequality of the two sides. It was moonlight, and he was in the highest spirits. We shouted and sang; then his lame arm gave out (he had been wounded at the first battle of Bull Run), and I took his place in the stern. We took our chances as to torpedoes, and pulled down to the fort. General Hazen met us on the sands, and we went to his quarters and had supper. Then Major Anderson, the late commander of the fort, was brought in. He and his men had fought with great gallantry. His colored servant was waiting upon us at table, and Sherman said to him, ' Now, Robert, remember, you 're a free man; don't be afraid to speak out.' And he was not. And as Major Anderson was brought in, the two men, no longer master and slave, as they had been two hours before, stood face to face. It was most dramatic."

In Oct., 1865, Mr. Lawrence entered the Theological Seminary at Gambier, O., where he remained two years. He then went abroad, and spent the winter of 1867–68 in travelling in Egypt and in the Holy Land with his cousin, Dr. A. Lawrence Mason. Reaching home in Oct., 1868, he resumed his studies at the Episcopal Theological School in Cambridge, and was ordained deacon at Longwood, March 2, 1869. Soon after, he sailed for Colon, Isthmus of Panama, with his brother Robert, *en route* to California, and for several months was in charge of St. Paul's Church, Virginia City, Nev. From Dec., 1870, to April, 1872, he was assistant minister of Calvary Church, New York. He became rector of St. Paul's Church, Stockbridge, Mass., July 7, 1872, and still holds the position. In 1893 he received the degree of Doctor of Divinity from Williams College. At the present time he is archdeacon of Springfield, a member of the Board of Trustees of Donations of the Diocese of Massachusetts, of the Standing Committee of the Diocese of Western Massachusetts, and vice-president of the Berkshire Industrial Farm. He has served as a delegate to the General Conventions of the Episcopal Church in 1888, 1892, 1895, and 1901.

Dr. Lawrence has made numerous Atlantic voyages, and has travelled extensively in the United States and Europe, Africa, Egypt, and the East. He has also visited Cuba, Jamaica, and the Bermudas. He is the author of an illustrated article in the " Century Magazine " for 1895, entitled " Bryant and the Berkshire Hills," and of an article on the " Origin of the Names of Berkshire Towns," in the " Collections of the Berkshire Historical and Scientific Society," vol. ii., 1895.

FAMILY NO. 23

112. **Robert Means**, m., at Brookline, June 30, 1870, Katharine Lawrence Cleaveland, b. at Brooklyn, N. Y., March 6, 1845; daughter of Nehemiah Cleaveland, LL. D., and Catherine Atherton (Means) Cleaveland, who was a daughter of Colonel David McGregor and Catherine (Atherton) Means of Amherst, N. H. (b. May 22, 1817; d. at Brooklyn, L. I., Aug. 27, 1846).

Their children:

190. I. **Madeleine,** b. at Boston, Aug. 15, 1871.

191. II. **Isabel Cleaveland,** b. at Boston, Jan. 14, 1873.

192. III. **Helen Atherton,** b. at Paris, France, May 12, 1876; d. at Boston, July 31, 1879.

193. IV. **Robert Means,** b. at Boston, July 19, 1877; d. at Boston, April 2, 1878.

Nehemiah Cleaveland was a descendant of Moses Cleveland or Cleaveland, the common ancestor of all those of New England origin who bear the name. Moses Cleveland was a native of Ipswich, the shire town of Suffolk County, England, and came to this country when a youth, about the year 1635, making his home in Woburn, Mass., where he became a freeholder in 1643.

Rev. John Cleaveland, great-grandson of Moses, grandson of Josiah, and son of Josiah and Abigail (Paine) Cleaveland, was born at Canterbury, Conn., April 22, 1722. He m. (first), at Ipswich, Mass., July 15, 1747, Mary, youngest child of Parker and Mary (Choate) Dodge. She d. April 21, 1768, and he m. (second), Sept. 28, 1769, at Salem, Mrs. Mary (Neale) Foster, widow of Captain John Foster. Rev. John Cleaveland was a graduate of Yale (Class of 1745) and studied theology. In 1747 he became pastor of the Sixth Parish in Chebacco (now called Essex, but at that time a part of the town of Ipswich), and his ministry there lasted fifty-two years. He was commissioned by Governor Thomas Pownall, March 13, 1758, chaplain of a regiment of foot, commanded by Colonel Jonathan Bagley, and served during the French and Indian war, and in the early part of the Revolution. It was a traditional saying of him that "he preached all the young men among his people into the army, and then went himself, taking his four sons with him." Rev. John Cleaveland d. April 22, 1799.

Dr. Nehemiah Cleaveland was the fourth son of Rev. John and Mary (Dodge) Cleaveland, and was born at Ipswich, Mass., Aug. 26, 1760. When sixteen years old he attended his father during the siege of Boston, afterwards enlisting and being in active service at West Point, Ticonderoga, and other places. At the age of twenty-one he began the study of medicine with his brother at Byfield, and afterwards with Dr. Manning of Ipswich. In 1783 he entered upon practice in Topsfield and the adjacent towns. Dr. Cleaveland served five years in the State Senate. In 1814 he was appointed a session justice of the Court of Common Pleas. From 1820 to 1822 he was associate justice of the Court of Sessions for Essex County, and from 1823 to 1828 he was chief justice. In the latter year he retired from all public business. Dr. Cleaveland m. (first), Oct. 6, 1787, Lucy, daughter of Dr. John and Lucy (Bowles) Manning. She d. June 6, 1791, and he m. (second), July 1, 1792, Experience, daughter of Dr. Elisha and Mrs. Tamersine (Coit) Lord, née Kimball, who d. Jan. 21, 1845, at Manchester-by-the-Sea. Dr. Cleaveland d. at Topsfield, Feb. 26, 1837.

Nehemiah Cleaveland, third child of the last-named, was born at Topsfield, Aug. 16, 1796. He fitted for college at Dummer Academy, Byfield, Mass., and graduated at Bowdoin in 1813. He then taught school at Portland, Me., and at Dedham, Mass.; and from 1817 to 1820 was classical tutor at Bowdoin College. For the ensuing nineteen years he was principal of Dummer Academy, and afterwards occupied the positions of headmaster of the Lowell, Mass., High School and professor of Ancient Languages in Phillips Exeter Academy. At a later period he conducted a school for young ladies at Brooklyn, L. I. Mr. Cleaveland's death occurred at Westport, Conn., April 17, 1877, in his eighty-first year. He was a fine classical scholar, a graceful writer and orator, and a successful teacher. " In his tastes and habits, a gentleman of the old school ; an ever faithful and sympathizing friend ; hospitable, courteous, and generous ; reticent of his religious thoughts and feelings, but a man of deep piety." Mr. Cleaveland's first wife was Abby Pickard Manning, daughter of Dr. Joseph and Elizabeth (Pickard) Manning of Charleston, S. C. She was b. at Ipswich, Mass., April 15, 1794; d. July 2, 1836. He m. (second), Nov. 25, 1842, Catherine Atherton Means, daughter of Colonel David McGregor and Catherine (Atherton) Means of Amherst, N. H. She d. at Byfield, Mass., Aug. 27, 1846.

THE MEANS FAMILY

The Meanses are probably of Huguenot descent. The name was anciently written Mayne, Maine, or Magne, and appears in Domesday Book, and in various local records in Great Britain. The name is believed to be derived from the ancient French Province of Le

Maine, and in the form of *magne* it has the same meaning as the Latin *magnus;* as, for example, in the name Charlemagne. On a stone in Glasgow Cathedral is inscribed the name of John Main, who died in 1684. The ancestors of the Meanses of Amherst, N. H., are believed to have taken refuge in Ireland, to avoid religious persecution, probably towards the close of the seventeenth century.

Colonel Robert Means (son of Thomas Means), b. at Stewartstown, County of Tyrone, Ireland, Aug. 28, 1742, came to America as a young man in 1766, and engaged in the business of weaving at Merrimac, and afterwards settled at Amherst, N. H. After a few years he abandoned the pursuit of weaving and entered upon a successful mercantile career. He became widely known throughout that region, and established a reputation for honesty and fair dealing. Colonel Means served as a representative from Amherst in the General Court of New Hampshire during several sessions, also for two years as a state senator, and as treasurer of Hillsborough County for a long period. He m., Nov. 24, 1774, Mary, daughter of Rev. David McGregor of Londonderry, N. H. Colonel Means d. at Amherst, Jan. 24, 1823. He had nine children, of whom the second, Mary, b. Oct. 20, 1777, m., Nov. 6, 1799, Hon. Jeremiah Mason, whose youngest child, the Rev. Charles Mason, m., at Boston, June 11, 1838, Susanna, daughter of Amos Lawrence. (Family No. 16.)

Elizabeth, the next younger daughter (b. Sept. 8, 1779), m., Sept. 28, 1800, Rev. Jesse Appleton (Dartmouth, 1792 ; pastor at Hampton, N. H.; president of

Bowdoin College). Their daughter Jane m. Hon. Franklin Pierce, afterwards President of the United States.

David McGregor Means, the fourth child of Colonel Robert Means (b. Sept. 28, 1781), m., Jan. 12, 1808, Catherine, daughter of Hon. Joshua Atherton. They had nine children, of whom the fifth, Catherine, b. May 22, 1817, m., Nov. 25, 1842, Nehemiah Cleaveland, LL. D. She d. at Byfield, Mass., Aug. 27, 1846. Their only child, Katharine Lawrence Cleaveland, m., June 30, 1870, Robert Means Lawrence. (Family No. 23.) David McGregor Means d. at Amherst, March 5, 1835.

Nancy, the fifth child of Colonel Robert Means (b. Oct. 28, 1783), m. (first), Feb. 4, 1816, Judge Caleb Ellis. He d. and she m. (second), April 16, 1821, Amos Lawrence of Boston. (Family No. 4.)[1]

THE McGREGOR FAMILY

The lineage of the McGregors is purely Scottish. According to one authority, the ancestors of some of the founders of Londonderry, N. H., emigrated from Argyleshire about the year 1612, and settled in the extreme north of Ireland. But the greater number are believed to have left Scotland in the latter part of the seventeenth century, on account of the relentless persecution of Claverhouse. Some of the elder ones among the emigrants to New Hampshire had taken

---

[1] There are many families of the name of Maynes or Maines in County Tyrone and other portions of northern Ireland at the present time.

an active part in the defence of Londonderry, Ireland, during the famous siege of that Protestant stronghold in 1689, when its inhabitants successfully resisted the forces of James II.

The Rev. James McGregor was born in Ireland about the year 1677. He was a Presbyterian minister of old Londonderry, who came to America in 1718, accompanied by his family and the members of his congregation. Before embarking, Mr. McGregor preached a sermon to his flock, and enumerated the reasons which induced him to leave Ireland. They were: (1) "to avoid oppression and cruel bondage; (2) to shun persecution and designed ruin; (3) to withdraw from the communion of idolaters; and (4) to have an opportunity to worship God according to the dictates of conscience and the rules of his inspired Word." (Willey's "Book of Nutfield," p. 49.) Mr. McGregor, with his large company, arrived in Boston, Aug. 4, 1718, and after some vicissitudes settled at Nutfield, N. H., as the district which now includes the town of Londonderry was then called. Here was formed, in May, 1719, "the First Church in Derry," of which Mr. McGregor was the pastor. He m., in old Londonderry, Aug. 29, 1706, Maryanne Cargyl, and they had ten children. Besides his official duties, Mr. McGregor devoted considerable time to school-teaching. He d. March 5, 1729.

Rev. David McGregor, third child of James, was b. in Ireland, Nov. 6, 1710. He was ordained in 1737, and became the first minister of the West Parish of Londonderry, in 1739, holding the position for nearly forty years. His wife's maiden name was

Mary Boyd. She d. Sept. 28, 1793, aged 70 years. His death occurred, May 30, 1777. Their ninth and youngest child, Mary McGregor, m., Nov. 24, 1774, Colonel Robert Means of Amherst, N. H.

A gun, formerly the property of Rev. James McGregor, and which was used during the siege of Londonderry, Ireland, in 1689, was in the possession of A. F. Hall, Esq., of Manchester, N. H., in 1870. This weapon is doubly interesting as a relic, having been carried into the pulpit every Sunday by Mr. McGregor, " loaded and primed, to be ready in case of sudden attack by the Indian enemy." (" Londonderry Celebration," p. 114.)   " The surname of MacGregor, once a numerous name, hath of a long tract of time been accounted one of the ancient Scottish surnames, being a known, ancient, proper Scottish name." (" An Inquiry into the Genealogy and Present State of Ancient Scottish Surnames, by William Buchanan of Auchmar.   Edinborough, MDCCLXXV.")

Robert Means Lawrence received early instruction at the Boston Latin School (one year) and at the schools of Marlborough Churchill at Sing Sing, N. Y. (one year), and Epes S. Dixwell, in Boston (six years).   In 1865 he spent five months in a French household at Melun, Seine-et-Marne, France, and in the autumn of that year he studied under a tutor at Cambridge, Mass., and entered the Harvard Class of 1869 at the beginning of the Sophomore year, remaining until the close of the first Senior term.   He received the degree of A. B. some years later.   After leaving college he travelled in the Southern States,

California, and Japan. Returning to Boston, he entered the Harvard Medical School in the fall of 1869, taking a four years' course, and graduating in 1873. The following year he went abroad with his wife and children, and spent twenty-eight months, mostly in Vienna and Paris, in attendance at lectures and clinics. On his return he took an office on Essex Street, Boston. From 1876 to 1886 he was one of the physicians of the Boston Dispensary; assistant surgeon and surgeon of the First Regiment of Infantry, M. V. M., 1877–82, and member of the Board of Medical Examiners, M. V. M.; trustee of the Wells Memorial Workingmen's Club, and of the Workingmen's Coöperative Bank; treasurer of the Episcopal Church Association (1880–93). In 1882 he bought a farm in Lexington, Mass., and there made his home for eight years, serving as chairman of the Town Board of Health, selectman (1884–86), member of the School Committee (1888–90), vice-president of the Lexington Savings Bank, medical examiner of Independence Lodge, Ancient Order of United Workmen (1882–88), and senior warden of the Church of Our Redeemer, Lexington. After nearly two years in Europe with his family, and three winters in Washington, he again settled in Boston, and of late years has devoted much time to the study of family history and folk-lore. Fellow of the Massachusetts Medical Society and member of the Boston Society for Medical Improvement; member of the American Folk-Lore Society and National Geographic Society; life member of the New England Historic Genealogical Society. Author: "The Therapeutic Value of the Iodide of Ethyl" (reprinted from the "New York Medical Record," June 19, 1880). "Phonic Paralysis, with rapid respiration" ("Boston Medical and Surgical Journal," July 20, 1882). "Historical Sketches of Some Members of the Lawrence Family," 215 pages, Boston, Rand-Avery Co., 1888. "The Magic of the Horse-shoe," 344 pages, Houghton, Mifflin & Co., 1898.

FAMILY NO. 24

113. **Marianne Appleton,** m., at Brookline, May 12, 1864, Robert Amory, M. D., and had one daughter:

194. **Alice,** b. at Waban Farm, Newton, May 8, 1865. She m., at Longwood, Oct. 12, 1892, Augustus Thorndike, M. D., and had these, all born at Boston:

195. 1. **Mary,** b. Oct. 19, 1893.
196. 2. **Alice Cornelia,** b. March 6, 1895.
197. 3. **Augustus,** b. March 13, 1896.
198. 4. **Charles,** b. March 13, 1898.
199. 5. **Robert Amory,** b. Dec. 19, 1900.

Augustus Thorndike, son of Charles and Mary Edmundson (Edgar) Thorndike, was born at Paris, France, April 27, 1863. His preparatory training was received in Brookline, and at Mr. Noble's school in Boston. After graduation at Harvard with the Class of 1884 he spent three months in European travel, and on his return to this country he entered the Harvard Medical School, and received the degree of M. D. in 1888. He then began the practice of his profession in Boston, devoting himself to the specialty of orthopedic surgery, and was interested in the establishment of the Industrial School for Crippled and Deformed Children, which was founded in 1893 and incorporated the following year. Dr. Thorndike was for several years one of the visiting physicians to St. Luke's Home for Convalescents in Roxbury, and was a district physician and surgeon to the Boston Dispensary from 1890 to 1896. He is at present a visiting surgeon to the House of the Good Samaritan, assistant surgeon to the West End Infants' Hospital, and junior assistant surgeon to the Children's Hospital in Boston. He is a member of the Massachusetts Medical Society, American Medical Association, American Orthopedic Association, Boston Society for Medical Improvement, and Boston Society of Medical Sciences. Among his contributions to medical literature is the following: " Three Cases of Spastic Hemiplegia treated by Open Tenotomy or Myotomy in the Forearm and Hand," Boston, 1892.

THE AMORY FAMILY

The lineage of the Amorys of Boston has been traced from Hugh Amory, who was living at Wrington, a market-town of Somersetshire, England, in the year 1605. His youngest son, Thomas (baptized June 5, 1608), served a seven years' apprenticeship at Bristol, with Robert Elliott, whose eldest daughter, Ann, he married Nov. 7, 1631. Thomas Amory became a prominent merchant of Bristol. In 1660, he was appointed " Chief Commissioner of the Navy in Ireland" and removed with his family to Galy,

Listowel, in the County Kerry. He d. about June, 1667.

Jonathan, the youngest of ten children of Thomas and Ann (Elliott) Amory, was b. March 14, 1654, at Bristol, and was for a time engaged in business at Dublin, where he married the widow Rebecca Houston in 1677 (license dated May 31). About the year 1683, they emigrated with their young children to Barbadoes, West Indies, where Rebecca d. and he m. (second), Martha ———. Within a few years after, Jonathan removed to South Carolina, and became a resident of Charleston, where he was known to be living in Nov., 1691. Here he held important official positions, being speaker of the Assembly, advocate-general, and treasurer of the Province. He d. of yellow fever in 1699.

Thomas Amory, second child of Jonathan and Rebecca, was b. at Dublin in May, 1682. When a very young child he accompanied his parents to Barbadoes, and later to Charleston. In 1694, when twelve years of age, he was sent to the care of relatives in England, and attended Westminster School, London. After this he entered the employ of a French merchant named Nicholas Oursel, who sent him, in 1706, as supercargo, to the Azores, where he became a merchant, and was appointed Dutch and English consul, having his residence at Angra, the capital of the islands. In the summer of 1719 he sailed for Boston, and thence proceeded to South Carolina, where he passed the ensuing winter, returning to Boston in the spring of 1720. Mr. Amory m., May 9, 1721, Rebecca, daughter of Francis

Holmes, and engaged in business as a merchant. He d. June 20, 1728.

Thomas, eldest child of Thomas and Rebecca (Holmes) Amory, was born at Boston, April 23, 1722. He entered the Public Latin School in 1735, and graduated at Harvard in 1741. Afterwards he studied theology, although he was not ordained to the ministry, but became a merchant. Thomas Amory m., in 1764, his cousin Elizabeth, tenth child of William and Ann (Holmes) Coffin. He d. in Aug., 1784.

Jonathan, the third of nine children of Thomas and Elizabeth, was b. July 7, 1770. H. U. 1787. He entered the counting-house of his uncles Jonathan and John Amory, afterwards engaging in business with James Cutler, and still later forming a partnership with his elder brother, Thomas Coffin Amory. He m. (first), in 1793, Ann Wier, who left no issue. She d. in 1795, and he m. (second), in 1801, Mehetable, daughter of Governor James Sullivan and widow of James Cutler, above-mentioned. He d. at Boston in 1847.

James Sullivan, third child of Jonathan Amory and his second wife, was born at Boston, May 14, 1809. He attended the private school of Captain Partridge near Boston, and was for two years a member of the Harvard Class of 1829, receiving the degree of A. B. out of course. Mr. Amory was m., at Trinity Church, Boston, Nov. 28, 1837, to Mary Copley, daughter of Gardiner and Elizabeth (Clark) Greene. He was treasurer of the Nashua and Jackson manufacturing companies (cotton goods) and of

the Lancaster Mills, and held the office of president
of the Provident Institution for Savings. He was
also a director of various business organizations.
When a young man he made two voyages to Calcutta as supercargo, and later he visited Europe frequently. Mr. Amory was at one time colonel of the
Independent Corps of Cadets, M. V. M. He d. at
Boston, June 8, 1884.

Robert Amory, the third son of James Sullivan
and Mary Copley (Greene) Amory, and a descendant
of Hon. James Sullivan, the fifth governor of Massachusetts (1744–1808), was b. at Boston, May 3,
1842. He attended E. S. Dixwell's school at Boston, graduated at Harvard in 1863, and at the Medical School in 1866. After spending a year abroad
in the study of his profession, during which time he
visited the Paris hospitals and served as externe at
the Dublin Lying-in Hospital, he took up his residence at Longwood, and there began the practice of
medicine, which he continued for about twenty years.
In April, 1868, he was appointed lecturer at the
Harvard Medical School, and instituted with the
authority of Prof. Edward H. Clarke, M. D., a class
for the study of the physiological action of drugs upon
animals; and in 1873 he was appointed professor
of Physiology at the Medical School of Bowdoin
College. Dr. Amory has been a trial commissioner
and councillor of the Massachusetts Medical Society,
president of the Norfolk County Medical Society,
and medical examiner of Norfolk County. He is a
member of the Massachusetts Medical Society, American Academy of Arts and Sciences, American Medi-

cal Association, Boston Society of Medical Sciences, Boston Society of Natural History, and a corresponding member of the New York Therapeutic Society. He was president of the convention for revising the U. S. Pharmacopœia, 1860–70. Dr. Amory was commissioned assistant surgeon of the First Battery of Light Artillery, M. V. M., July 28, 1875, resigning April 28, 1876. Commissioned surgeon of the First Battalion of Cavalry, Aug. 14, 1876, and on Aug. 15, 1878, medical director, with the rank of lieutenant-colonel, on the staff of Brigadier-General Eben Sutton, commanding the Second Brigade, M. V. M. He was a physician to the Boston Dispensary in 1869–70, and was for nine years a member and secretary of the School Committee, and a trustee of the Public Library of Brookline. Dr. Amory retired from the practice of medicine in Oct., 1887, and for ten years thereafter was president of the Brookline Gas-light Company.

Mrs. Marianne Appleton (Lawrence) Amory died May 15, 1882, and he m., Sept. 4, 1884, at Boston, Katharine Leighton Crehore, daughter of George Clarendon and Lucy (Daniel) Crehore. They have these children: (1) Robert, Jr., b. at Boston, Oct. 23, 1885; (2) Mary Copley, b. at Bar Harbor, Me., July 3, 1888; (3) Katharine Leighton, b. at Boston, Oct. 21, 1891; (4) Margery Sullivan, b. at Boston, Oct. 21, 1897.

Dr. Amory was for several years a member of the staff of the "Boston Medical and Surgical Journal," as reporter on therapeutics. In 1886, together with Dr. Edward H. Clarke, he prepared a treatise on

the Physiological and Therapeutical Action of the
Bromides. He also wrote a book on the Action of
Nitrous Oxide Gas as an anæsthetic (Boston, 1870),
and translated and edited the Lectures on Physiology of Professor Küss of the Strasburg School of
Medicine. He revised and edited the volume on
Poisons, in Wharton and Stillé's Medical Jurispru-
dence (third edition), published by Kay & Brother,
Philadelphia. With Professor Edward S. Wood of
the Harvard Medical School he revised and edited
the fourth edition of the same work, which was published in 1884, and he is now engaged in revising
the fifth edition, which is to appear in 1904. Dr.
Amory was one of the organizers of the Massachusetts Medico-legal Society, and was elected its first
recording secretary in 1878, and its second president
in 1880 and 1881. He is at present an honorary
member of the Society.

FAMILY NO. 25

114. **Sarah**, m., at Brookline, Oct. 4, 1866, Peter
Chardon Brooks. Residences at Boston and West
Medford, Mass.

Their children:

200. I. **Eleanor**, b. at West Medford, Sept. 18,
1867; m., at West Medford, Oct. 17, 1891, Richard
Middlecott Saltonstall, and has these, born at Chestnut Hill:

201. 1. **Leverett**, b. Sept. 1, 1892.
202. 2. **Eleanor**, b. Oct. 19, 1894.
203. 3. **Muriel Gurdon**, b. March 26, 1896.

204. 4. **Richard**, b. July 23, 1897.

Richard Middlecott Saltonstall, second son of Leverett Saltonstall and Rose, daughter of John Clarke and Harriet (Rose) Lee, was b. Oct. 28, 1859. He received early instruction at Chestnut Hill, and at Noble's school in Boston, and is a Harvard graduate of the Class of 1880. In the fall of that year he entered the Harvard Law School, and was admitted to the Suffolk bar, Jan., 1884. In 1887 he was appointed general solicitor of the New York and New England Railroad Company, holding this position until Feb., 1890, since when he has been engaged in the general practice of the law. At a meeting of the Alumni Association of Harvard College, in June, 1888, Mr. Saltonstall was chosen a member of the committee to nominate overseers. In 1889 he built a house at Chestnut Hill, which has since been his residence. On the first day of Nov., 1898, he formed a partnership with William A. Gaston, his classmate, and Frederic A. Snow, with an office at 15 Congress Street, Boston. Except for the usual summer vacations and a short trip to Europe in 1896, Mr. Saltonstall has been steadily engaged in his regular work. He is also trustee of various estates.

Richard Middlecott Saltonstall is a descendant, in the ninth generation, of Sir Richard Saltonstall (b. 1521), who was knighted by Queen Elizabeth in 1598. He was a member of the Merchant Adventurers and Furriers' Hall, sheriff of London, 1588, lord mayor, 1597–98, and member of Parliament for the City of London. He was lord of the Manor of Moorhall in Yardley and Barkway, Northamptonshire. Sir Richard Saltonstall m. Susanna, daughter of Thomas Poyntz of North Okenden. They had five sons and ten daughters.

Leverett Saltonstall, father of Richard M. Saltonstall, was a graduate of Harvard College in 1844, and of the Law School in 1847. He was admitted to the Suffolk bar in 1850, and continued to practise law until 1862, when he retired, devoting himself to agricultural pursuits and the management of trusts. In Dec., 1885, he was appointed collector of customs for the port of Boston by President Cleveland, and retained the office for more than four years. He was an overseer of Harvard College from 1876 to 1888, and was reëlected in 1890.

205. II. **Lawrence**, b. at Boston, Nov. 9, 1868.

Lawrence Brooks attended Mr. Noble's school in Boston and took the regular academic course at Harvard, graduating in 1891. In the early winter of 1896 he became a resident of Groton, and two years afterwards he bought an estate in that town, where he has been interested in farming. He has devoted attention especially to the development and improvement of worn-out land, and to the planting of timber-trees in places unfit for tillage. Mr. Brooks has travelled over a large part of Europe at different times, and visited the West Indies in 1892. More recently he spent several months at Yokohama, Japan, and returned to this country towards the close of 1902.

THE BROOKS FAMILY

Peter Chardon Brooks, son of Gorham and Ellen (Shepherd) Brooks, was born at Watertown, now

Belmont, Mass., May 8, 1831. He is of the eighth generation from Captain Thomas Brooks, the emigrant ancestor, who settled in Watertown, Mass., about 1631, and was admitted a freeman, Dec. 7, 1636. Two years later he removed to Concord, where he became a large landowner. He was appointed constable, and held the rank of captain in the militia. He also served seven years as representative from Concord to the General Court. Captain Thomas Brooks m. Grace ——, who d. May 12, 1664. His death occurred at Concord, May 21, 1667.

Caleb Brooks, the third child of the preceding, was born at Watertown in 1632. He m. (first), April 10, 1660, Susanna, daughter of Thomas Atkinson, and had five children. She d. in 1669, and he m. (second) Hannah Atkinson, younger sister of his first wife. Caleb Brooks removed in 1680 from Concord to Medford, Mass., where he d. July 29, 1696.

Captain Samuel Brooks, the younger of two sons of Caleb by his second marriage, was born at Concord, Sept. 1, 1672. He m. Sarah, daughter of Dr. Thomas and Mary (Gardner) Boylston of Muddy River, now Brookline. Captain Samuel Brooks d. July 3, 1735.

Samuel Brooks, elder child of the preceding, was born in Medford, Sept. 3, 1700. He m. Mary Bontwell; owned several slaves; died July 5, 1768.

Rev. Edward Brooks, the fourth child of Samuel, was born at Medford, Nov. 4, 1733. Graduated, Harvard College, 1757. Ordained in North Yarmouth, Me., July 4, 1764, and remained there five years, removing to Medford, Mass., in 1769. He was a participant in the engagements with the British troops on their return from Lexington, April 19, 1775, and was chaplain of the frigate *Hancock* in 1777. He m., Sept. 23, 1764, Abigail, daughter of Rev. John and Joanna (Cotton) Brown of Haverhill. He d. at Medford, May 6, 1781.

Peter Chardon Brooks, the second child of Rev. Edward, was born at North Yarmouth, Me., Jan. 6, 1767. His boyhood was spent on the ancestral farm in Medford. At the age of twenty-one he established himself as an insurance broker in Boston, and remained in business until the year 1804 or thereabouts, when he retired. Mr. Brooks was a member of the Common Council of Boston in 1822, the year of the organization of the first city government. He also served in the Massachusetts Senate several years. He was named after Pierre Chardon, a friend and classmate of his father, the son of a prominent Boston merchant, and of French Huguenot ancestry. Peter Chardon Brooks m., Nov. 26, 1792, Anna, daughter of Hon. Nathaniel Gorham of Charlestown. He d. at Boston, Jan. 1, 1849.

Gorham Brooks, the second of thirteen children of the preceding, was b. at Medford, Feb. 10, 1795. He entered Phillips Academy, Andover, in 1805, and graduated at Harvard College in 1814. After studying law for a while, he devoted himself to mercantile affairs. In 1833 he entered the firm of W. C. Mayhew & Co., and later that of Brooks & Harrison, at Baltimore, Md. Returning to Medford in 1840, he became interested in agriculture. Mr. Brooks m., at Watertown, April 20, 1829, Ellen, daughter of

Rezin Davis Shepherd of Shepherdstown, Va. He d. Sept. 10, 1855.

Peter Chardon Brooks, the subject of this sketch, a son of Gorham and Ellen (Shepherd) Brooks, was b. at Watertown, May 8, 1831. He prepared for college under Samuel Eliot, was admitted to Harvard, Aug. 22, 1848, graduating in 1852, and has devoted himself largely to agricultural pursuits, forestry, and art. He is also a trustee of valuable estates. Mr. Brooks has travelled extensively. His Boston residence for many years was on Arlington Street, at the northerly corner of Marlborough Street, but he has recently occupied a new house on Bay State Road. His summer home is at West Medford.

FAMILY NO. 26

115. **Amory Appleton,** m., June 1, 1871, Emily Fairfax Silsbee, daughter of John Boardman and Martha Mansfield (Shepard) Silsbee, and had these:

206. I. **Amos Amory,** b. at Boston, Dec. 1, 1874.

Amos Amory Lawrence pursued his preliminary studies at St. Paul's School, Concord, N. H. He then took the regular four years' course at Harvard, graduating in 1896, after which he was for one year a student at the Massachusetts Institute of Technology. He has made several trips to Europe, and at the present time (1902) is studying Architecture at the Ecole des Beaux Arts in Paris.

207. II. **John Silsbee,** b. at Nahant, Sept. 6, 1878.

John Silsbee Lawrence attended the private

schools of Messrs. Noble and Greenough in Boston,
and is a Harvard graduate of the Class of 1901.
While in college he was the trainer of the successful
Freshman football elevens in 1900 and 1901. Mr.
Lawrence has visited Europe twice. He is a member of the First Corps of Cadets, M. V. M., and is to
be a merchant. At present he is in the counting-
room of Messrs. Lawrence & Co. in Boston, being
engaged, with his father, in the business of distribut-
ing New England cotton mill products.

208. III. **Edith,** b. at Boston, Nov. 10, 1879; m.,
at Longwood, Feb. 19, 1903, Harold Jefferson Coolidge of Boston, son of Joseph Randolph and Julia
(Gardner) Coolidge. He was born at Nice, France,
Jan. 22, 1870, and is a lineal descendant of Thomas
Jefferson, third President of the United States. Mr.
Coolidge attended Chauncy Hall School and the
private school of John P. Hopkinson in Boston; he
studied also in Germany, and graduated from Harvard with the Class of 1892. He is a lawyer by profession, having an office at 22 Congress Street, Boston.
In 1893–94 he made a trip around the world, and
besides this he has visited Europe several times.
Mr. Coolidge was admitted to the bar in 1896, and
at this writing (1903) he is a member of the law firm
of Loring & Coolidge. They have (208a) Harold
Jefferson Coolidge Junior, b. Jan. 15, 1904.

Mrs. Emily Fairfax (Silsbee) Lawrence d. at Bos-
ton, April 4, 1895. Amory Appleton Lawrence m.
(second), at Groton, Mass., June 12, 1900, Gertrude
Major, daughter of Francis Blake and Sallie Blake
(Austin) Rice of Boston. Residences at Boston,
Groton, and Beverly, Mass.

Amory Appleton Lawrence pursued his early studies at schools in Brookline and Boston, graduating at Harvard in 1870. He decided upon a mercantile career, thus following the honorable examples of his grandfather and father, and in Sept., 1870, he entered the house of Lawrence & Co., dry goods commission merchants, becoming a member of the firm the next year. He was chosen a director of the Massachusetts National Bank in Jan., 1873, resigning after ten years' service. In 1887 he became a director of the National Union Bank. He has been president of the Salmon Falls Manufacturing Company, and of the Ipswich and Gilmanton Mills, a director of the Pacific Mills, of the Dwight and Cocheco manufacturing companies, and treasurer of the Groton Water Company. Mr. Lawrence was elected president of the Boston Merchants' Association in Feb., 1901, and has been for many years treasurer of the Boston Episcopal Charitable Society, and chairman of the class committee of the Harvard Class of 1870. In March, 1902, he was one of three Boston merchants selected as a committee to settle an important strike which was paralyzing the city's trade. Under the leadership of Governor Crane, the strike was settled in a night. Mr. Lawrence has made several trips to Europe and has twice visited California.

April 1, 1883, Messrs. Lawrence & Co. assumed the selling agency of the Pacific Mills. Henry Saltonstall Howe became a member of the firm in 1887, and Henry Coffin Everett in 1893. The latter is a nephew of Henry Brainard Mather, who was for many years a partner. Edward 'Sturgis Grew and Cyrus J. Anderson, who became partners in the firm in 1884 and 1887 respectively, have since retired.

THE SILSBEE FAMILY

The Silsbees of Salem, Mass., trace their lineage from Henry Sillsbey or Silsbee, who was born in England before 1618, came to this country and settled first at Salem in the year 1639, afterwards removing to Ipswich, and becoming an inhabitant of Lynn in 1651. He was a shoemaker by trade. His first wife, Dorothy, d. Sept. 27, 1676, and he m. (second), Nov. 18, 1680, Grace, widow of Jonas Eaton of Reading, Mass.

Nathaniel Silsbee, third child of Henry, the emigrant, and Dorothy, was b. about the year 1651. He was a carpenter. He m. (first), Nov. 5, 1671, Deborah, daughter of John and Margaret Tompkins. She d. before 1697, and he m. (second), Elizabeth, daughter of Jonathan and Jane (Cromwell) Pickering. He d. about 1717.

Nathaniel, third child of the preceding, was born at Salem, Oct. 23, 1677. He m. (first), May 27, 1703, Hannah Pickering, who was probably a sister of his father's second wife. She d. and he m. (second) Martha ———. He d. Jan. 2, 1769.

William, baptized Aug. 14, 1715, was the only child of Nathaniel by his second marriage. He m., Oct. 17, 1735, Joanna, daughter of Zachary and Ruth (Ingalles) Fowle. William Silsbee followed the trade of a carpenter. He d. about July, 1783.

Captain Nathaniel Silsbee, third child of William

and Joanna, was b. Nov. 9, 1748. He m., Nov. 1, 1770, Sarah, daughter of John and Rebecca (Beadle) Becket. Captain Silsbee was master-mariner and owner of several vessels engaged in the business of trading with the West Indies.

Zachariah Fowle Silsbee, seventh child of Captain Nathaniel and Sarah, was b. Aug. 9, 1783. He m., Nov. 27, 1810, Sarah Boardman. In early life he "followed the sea," and was for many years engaged in foreign trade, as a member of the firm of Stone, Silsbee & Pickman of Salem. He was also president of the Salem Savings Bank. He d. July 3, 1873.

John Boardman Silsbee, son of the preceding, was b. April 10, 1813. He graduated at Harvard in 1832 and became a merchant. He m., May 10, 1849, Martha Mansfield Shepard, seventh child of Michael and Harriet Fairfax (Clark) Shepard. He d. April 1, 1867.

Emily Fairfax Silsbee (b. at Salem, June 7, 1850), eldest of four children of the above-named, m., at Boston, June 1, 1871, Amory Appleton Lawrence. She d. at Boston, April 4, 1895. (Family No. 26.)

THE RICE FAMILY, AND OTHER FAMILIES ALLIED THERETO

Edmund Rice, the emigrant from England, settled in Sudbury in 1639, and soon removed to Marlborough. His wife Tamazine d. June 13, 1654, and he d. May 3, 1663. They were the parents of eleven children, of whom Edward, the second child, m. Agnes Bent, and in turn they had eleven children, and the seventh child was Jacob, b. in 1660, who d. Oct. 30, 1746, aged 86 years. Jacob Rice had wife Mary,

who d. Oct. 6, 1752, aged 80 years. They resided at
Marlborough, where their gravestones are to be seen.
Jacob and Mary Rice had nine children, of whom
Obadiah was the third child, b. Nov. 13, 1698. Obadiah Rice m., Sept. 22, 1722, Esther Merrick. They
settled in Brookfield and were the parents of eleven
children. The mother d. April 10, 1761. Their second child was Tilly, b. Nov. 8, 1724, who m., Nov. 21,
1748, Mary, the daughter of Thomas and Sarah (Baxter) Buckminster. She d. June 21, 1795, aged 67
years, and he d. Nov. 6, 1803, aged 79 years. They
had seven children, the fifth of whom was Thomas, b.
May 30, 1767. Thomas Rice m. Sally Makepeace,
July 12, 1792. They resided in Brookfield and Warren, and had three daughters, Sally, Caroline, and
Mary, and one son, George Tilly Rice, b. Feb. 19,
1796. George Tilly Rice m., in 1829, Elizabeth C.,
daughter of the Hon. Francis Blake. The family resided in Worcester. There were born to them three
sons: George Tilly, b. 1831, Francis Blake, b. April
12, 1835, and Arthur W., who died in infancy.

Francis Blake Rice m., Jan. 9, 1861, Georgiana
DeV., daughter of Captain George Lincoln. She d.
Dec. 28, 1861, aged 21 years. He m. (second), June
20, 1869, Sallie Austin. They had four children, of
whom the second, Gertrude Major, b. Sept. 10, 1871,
m. Amory Appleton Lawrence.

William Blake settled in Dorchester; his wife
was Agnes, who d. July 22, 1678. He d. Oct. 25,
1663, aged 69 years. He was a member of the
Ancient and Honorable Artillery Company. They
had at least five children: William, b. in 1620, who

m. Hannah ——; James, b. 1623, m. Elizabeth
Clapp; John, b. 1626; Mary, who m. Jacob Leager;
and Edward, who m. Patience, daughter of John Pope.
Edward and Patience Blake had nine children, the
first five of whom were born in Boston. The son
Solomon was the seventh child, b. about 1675, m.,
in 1704, Abigail Arnold, and had thirteen children.
Joseph was the fourth child, b. Aug. 10, 1709. The
family resided in Boston. Joseph Blake m., in Boston, May 18, 1738, Mary Welland. They had five
children. He d. Sept. 17, 1745. Their eldest son,
Joseph, was b. Feb. 5, 1739, and m. Deborah, daughter of Samuel Smith of Sandwich. They resided in
Hingham and had twelve children. He was a lieutenant in the French and Indian war. He later had
two other wives. He d. in Billerica, July 21, 1818,
aged 79 years. Their ninth child was the Hon.
Francis Blake, who was b. Oct. 14, 1774. He was a
graduate of Harvard College, 1789, and settled in
Rutland, but in 1802 removed to Worcester. He
was a lawyer, prominent in political circles, and an
editor of the " National Ægis " (in support of Thomas
Jefferson) from its establishment in 1801. He m.,
1794, Elizabeth, daughter of Gardiner Chandler, and
had eight children. She d. Sept. 22, 1839. He d.
at Worcester, Feb. 23, 1817, in the fulness and prime
of life. Their daughter, Elizabeth C., b. Sept. 21,
1819 m., April 16, 1829, George Tilley Rice.

Deborah Smith, the mother of the Hon. Francis
Blake, was the daughter of Samuel Smith of Sandwich, by his wife Bethia Chipman. She was the
granddaughter of John Chipman, who married the

daughter of John Howland of the Mayflower Company.

Thomas Buckminster was a descendant of John of Peterborough, Northamptonshire, England. He settled in Boston, and thence removed to Brookline. His wife was named Joan. Their son Joseph m. Elizabeth, daughter of Hugh Clarke. They had children: Joseph, b. July 31, 1666, and Elizabeth. He d. Nov. 20, 1668. Joseph settled in Framingham. He was colonel of a regiment in the expedition against Port Royal, and prominent in all the affairs of Framingham and the politics of the Province. His first wife was Martha, daughter of John Sharp, whom he married in 1686. They had eight children, of whom the second son was Thomas, b. in 1699. Thomas Buckminster removed, when a young man, to Brookfield. He was a captain in the provincial militia, and saw slight service in the French and Indian war. He m., in 1722, Sarah, daughter of the Rev. Joseph Baxter of Medfield. They had ten children, of whom Mary, the fourth child, b. Nov. 5, 1728, became the wife of Tilly Rice.

There is a full account of the Buckminster family in the histories of Framingham. See also the volume entitled "The Descendants of William Blake of Dorchester," and the History of Hingham, for information regarding this branch of the Blake family. For particulars concerning the Rices, see the family genealogy, and the histories of Marlborough and North Brookfield.

William Chandler settled at Roxbury in 1637, with his wife Annis, and to them were born five children.

He d. Jan. 16, 1641. Apostle John Eliot, in his church records, styles him a " Godly Brother." The widow m. (second) John Dane, and m. (third) John Parmenter. The fourth child was John, b. about 1635, who m. Elizabeth, daughter of William Doug-las, and who died in 1705. He was among the pro-moters and settlers of Woodstock, Conn. The third of their eight children was John, b. in 1665, who con-tinued his residence at the homestead and became eminent as a judge. His wife was Mary, the daugh-ter of Joshua Raymond and wife Elizabeth, the daughter of Nehemiah Smith. They had ten chil-dren, of whom John, the eldest, was b. Oct. 18, 1693. Judge Chandler d. Aug. 10, 1743, aged 79 years. John, the son, m., Oct. 23, 1716, Hannah, eldest daughter of John Gardiner of Gardiner's Island. She d. in 1739, and he m. (second) Sarah, widow of Hon. Nathaniel Paine and daughter of Timothy Clarke of Boston. He d. at Worcester, Aug. 10, 1762, aged 69 years. He was eminent in political and military circles. An extended account of his useful career is to be found in the History of the Chandler Family, p. 115 and onward. There were nine children by the first wife; the son John, third child, was b. Feb. 26, 1721. He m. (first) Dorothy, daughter of Colonel Nathaniel Paine of Bristol, R. I. (to whom were born four children), and d. in 1745. He m. (second), 1746, Mary, daughter of Colonel Charles Church and grand-daughter of Colonel Benjamin Church, the famous Indian fighter. She was the mother of thirteen chil-dren. The Hon. John Chandler was a leading citi-zen and eminent man in Worcester before the war for independence, and during the war he went to England. He was one of the six men of Worcester included in the Act of Banishment. He died in London, Sept. 26, 1800. His sixth child by the second wife, Gardiner, was b. Jan. 27, 1749, and m., in 1772, Elizabeth, daughter of Brigadier-General Timothy Ruggles of Hardwick. He was a Loyalist in the war of the Revolution, and his estate was confiscated by the State. He removed from Worcester to Brattleborough, Vt., and thence to Hinsdale, N. H., where he died. There were three children, the second of whom was Elizabeth, who m., Dec. 14, 1794, the Hon. Francis Blake.

Romeo Austin was born in Orwell, Vt., in 1805, the son of Josiah and Mary B. Austin. He came to Boston and married Sarah C., daughter of Joshua Blake. Mrs. Austin died at Boston on May 20, 1864, aged 53 years; and Mr. Austin died March 1, 1888, aged 83 years. The ancestors of Romeo Austin were from Suffield, Conn., and his father was born there, and removed before 1795 to Orwell, where he engaged in business with his brother, Apollo Austin, a widely known merchant and a man who often served his fellow-townsmen in official affairs. Josiah Austin died in 1824, in Orwell. To Romeo Austin and his wife Sarah were born two children: Gertrude Blake, born about 1838, who died unmarried in July, 1902, and Sallie Blake, who married Francis Blake Rice, whose daughter, Gertrude Major Rice, married Amory Appleton Lawrence.

FAMILY NO. 27

116. **William**, m., May 19, 1874, at Boston, Julia, daughter of Frederic and Sarah Maria (Parker) Cunningham. Residences at Boston, Cambridge, and Bar Harbor, Me.

Their children:

209. I. **Marian**, b. at Boston, May 16, 1875.

210. II. **Julia**, b. at Lawrence, Mass., Feb. 4, 1877.

211. III. **Sarah**, b. at Boston, March 22, 1879.

212. IV. **Rosamond**, b. at Lawrence, Dec. 2, 1882 ; d. Feb. 18, 1883.

213. V. **Ruth**, b. at Cambridge, Jan. 27, 1886.

214. VI. **William Appleton**, b. at Cambridge, May 21, 1889.

215. VII. **Elinor**, b. at Boston, Jan. 31, 1894.

216. VIII. **Frederic Cunningham**, b. at Cambridge, May 22, 1899.

William Lawrence was born at Boston, May 30, 1850, and was baptized in St. Paul's Church, Boston. In 1851 his father removed to Cottage Farm, now Longwood, Brookline. He first attended a small private school, then the Pierce Grammar School in Brookline, and later the private school of Epes S. Dixwell, Boston. He was confirmed in St. Paul's Church, Brookline, during the rectorship of Rev. Dr. Francis Wharton. In 1866–67 he had a tutor, Professor Flagg of Harvard College, and was for a few months in Europe, entering Harvard in Sept., 1867. He took the regular academic course, graduating in

1871, after which he spent a year in study at home and in Cambridge. During that year he decided to enter the ministry of the Protestant Episcopal Church. The years 1872–74 he passed at Andover Theological Seminary, and 1874–75 at the Philadelphia Divinity School and the Episcopal Theological School at Cambridge, Mass., receiving from the latter the degree of B. D. in 1875. He was ordained deacon in St. John's Memorial Chapel, Cambridge, by Bishop Paddock, June 20, 1875. After a severe illness from typhoid fever, he entered upon his duties, April 1, 1876, as assistant to the Rev. Dr. George Packard, rector of Grace Church, Lawrence. In that church he was ordained priest, June 11, 1876. Upon the death of Dr. Packard, William Lawrence succeeded him as rector in March, 1877. Jan. 1, 1884, he became professor of Homiletics and Pastoral Care in the Episcopal Theological School, Cambridge. He was also the colleague of Dean Gray in charge of St. John's Memorial Chapel, and had for his spiritual charge the Harvard students worshipping there. In 1888 he was made vice-dean, and upon the death of Dean Gray in 1890, succeeded him in office. He was appointed preacher to Harvard University in 1888, and received the honorary degrees of S. T. D. from Hobart College in 1890, of S. T. D. from Harvard University in 1893, and LL. D. from Lawrence University, Appleton, Wis., in 1898. He was elected Bishop of the Protestant Episcopal Church in Massachusetts, to succeed Bishop Phillips Brooks, May 4, 1893, and was consecrated in Trinity Church, Boston, Oct. 5. In 1894 he was elected an overseer of Harvard College, and was reëlected in 1900.

Bishop Lawrence was for several years a trustee of Smith College, and is now president of the boards of trustees of Wellesley College, of Groton School, and of St. Mark's School at Southborough, Mass. He is a member of the Massachusetts Historical Society, of the American Antiquarian Society, and of other historical organizations. He is the author of the "Life of Amos A. Lawrence" (Houghton, Mifflin & Co., 1888). In 1896 he published (Houghton, Mifflin & Co.) a volume entitled "Visions and Service," containing sermons preached in Cambridge. He is also the author of various pamphlets and sermons which have been printed at different times. His Memoir of Roger Wolcott appeared in the autumn of 1902. Bishop Lawrence has made several trips to Europe.

FAMILY NO. 28

118. **Hetty Sullivan**, m., in Brookline, Mass., Dec. 11, 1877, Frederic Cunningham, and has these:

217. I. **Hetty Sullivan,**[1] ⎱ b. at Nahant, Mass.,
218. II. **Harriet Cutler,** ⎰ June 27, 1885.

219. III. **Constance**, b. at Nahant, Sept. 8, 1886.

220. IV. **Frederic**, b. at Cottage Farm, Brookline, Dec. 28, 1888.

221. V. **Susanna**, b. at Cottage Farm, March 19, 1890.

222. VI. **Lawrence**, b. at Cottage Farm, Dec. 29, 1892.

[1] Died Aug. 29, 1903.

THE CUNNINGHAM FAMILY

Frederic Cunningham is of the seventh generation in the line of descent from Andrew Cunningham, who came from Scotland to these shores about the year 1680, and settled in Boston. He was by trade a glazier. At a meeting of the Scots' Charitable Society of Boston, Feb. 4, 1695, he was chosen " keeper of the money box."

Andrew Cunningham was appointed constable at a Boston town meeting, May 14, 1705, but was excused from serving on account of his having a lame arm. He m., probably in the latter part of 1685, Sarah, eldest daughter of William Gibson, a Scotchman, and they had nine children. He d. after 1730.

William Cunningham, fifth child of the preceding, was born at Boston, Nov. 17, 1694. In early life he followed his father's trade. At a town meeting held in Boston, May 5, 1725, he was chosen a constable, and took the oath of office. William Cunningham was one of the founders of Hollis· Street Church, which was established in 1732. He m., Nov. 27, 1716, Elizabeth, daughter of William Wheeler, and had ten children. He d. Nov. 11, 1744, at Boston.

James Cunningham, second son of the above, was born at Boston, April 24, 1721. He too served as a constable of his native town, having been chosen to that office and sworn in, March 9, 1746. He was captain of the South Engine Company for five years from 1756, and served also as one of the fire wards, who were selected by reason of their fitness as " prudent persons of known fidelity." James Cunningham was commander of the Ancient and Honorable Artillery Company in 1768, major of the Boston Regiment of the State Militia from 1767 to 1772, and was in military service during the Revolutionary war. He m. (first), at Boston, June 4, 1742, Elizabeth (daughter of Peter and Ann) Boylston, whose sister Susannah was the wife of Deacon John Adams and mother of John Adams, second President of the United States. Mrs. Elizabeth (Boylston) Cunningham d. June 23, 1769, and James Cunningham m. for his second wife, at Boston, Martha, widow of John Chaloner and daughter of Deacon Benjamin Church. He d. at Dedham, June 6, 1795.

Andrew, eighth and youngest child of James and Elizabeth, was born at Boston, Feb. 16, 1760. He served in 1777 as a private in Colonel Brook's regiment. In 1799 he was appointed secretary of the Massachusetts Mutual Life Insurance Company, and held the office until his death. He was also secretary of the Board of Fire Wards of Boston, and commander of the Ancient and Honorable Artillery Company in 1793, adjutant of the Boston Regiment, 1787–89, and quartermaster of the First Division, Massachusetts Volunteer Militia, 1789–93. Andrew Cunningham m. (first), at Dedham, Oct. 2, 1783, Mary, daughter of Joseph Lewis of that town. She d. May 9, 1809, and he m. for his second wife, at Raynham, Mass., July 11, 1811, Abigail, daughter of Colonel Zephaniah Leonard of that town and widow of David West of Boston. Andrew Cunningham d. at Roxbury, Aug. 29, 1829.

Charles, the fourth in age of ten children of Andrew

and Mary, was born at Boston, April 6, 1791. He was a merchant and ship-owner, and engaged in business with his elder brother Andrew, under the firm name of A. & C. Cunningham. He m., at Fayal, Azores, Jan. 17, 1822, Roxalina, daughter of John Bass Dabney, who was for many years United States consul at Fayal. They had four children. Charles Cunningham d. at Boston, Dec. 7, 1871.

Frederic, second son of the last-named, was born at Boston, June 11, 1826. He was a Harvard graduate (Class of 1845), and member of the firm of Dabney & Cunningham, merchants, who were engaged in trade with the Levant. He m., March 4, 1850, Sarah Maria, daughter of William and Julia Maria (Stevens) Parker, and granddaughter of Right Rev. Samuel Parker. Their second child, Julia, m., at Boston, May 19, 1874, William Lawrence, now seventh Bishop of the Episcopal Church in the Diocese of Massachusetts. (Family No. 27.) Frederic Cunningham, Sr., d. at Boston, March 27, 1864.

Frederic Cunningham, third child of Frederic and Sarah Maria (Parker) Cunningham, was born at Cohasset, Mass., Aug. 23, 1854. He took the full course of six years at the Boston Public Latin School, and four years at Harvard College, graduating in 1874. He then spent nearly a year in Europe, of which five months were passed in Berlin, studying German. Returning home in the autumn of 1875, he entered the Harvard Law School, where he remained two years, receiving the degree of LL. B., June 27, 1877. He was admitted to the Suffolk bar, Nov. 9, 1878, and has since been engaged in the practice of law, and especially of marine law, having offices with Lewis S. Dabney (Harvard, 1861).   Mr. and Mrs. Cunningham went abroad in 1901, and established their residence in Paris, in order that their children might enjoy the superior educational advantages there afforded.   In the fall of 1902 they returned to this country, and Mr. Cunningham resumed the practice of law.   He is one of the founders, and a member of the Board of Directors, of the Boston Legal Aid Society, which was organized and incorporated in the year 1900.

FAMILY NO. 29

119. **Harriett Dexter,** m., at Longwood, Dec. 28, 1881, Augustus Hemenway of Boston.   Residences, Boston and Milton.

Their children :

223. I. **Augustus,** b. at Boston, Oct. 6, 1882. He attended private schools in Boston, and Groton School.   A member of the Harvard Class of 1905.

224. II. **Hope,** b. at Canton, Mass., Oct. 16, 1887.

225. III. **Charlotte,** b. at Canton, Oct. 14, 1888.

226. IV. **Hetty Lawrence,** b. at Boston, Dec. 3, 1890.

227. V. **Lawrence,** b. at Boston, Dec. 28, 1891.

228. VI. **Mary,** b. at Boston, Oct. 3, 1893.

THE HEMENWAY FAMILY

Ralph Hemenway was a resident of Roxbury in 1633, and was devoted to all the interests of Apostle Eliot's church and of this historic town.   He m., in

1644, Elizabeth Hewes, who d. in 1686, aged 82 years.

They had, among others, Samuel, who removed to New Haven; John, who m. Mary Trescott, and settled in Roxbury; and Joshua, who was baptized April 9, 1643, and who d. at Roxbury in 1716. Joshua m. (first), in 1668, Joanna Evans. He m. (second) Mary, who died in 1703, and his third wife was Elizabeth Weeks, who survived until 1737. Their son Joshua was born Sept. 15, 1668. His first wife, Margaret, d. in 1694, and his second wife was Rebecca ——, by whom were most of his children. Joshua Hemenway, Jr., removed from Roxbury to Framingham in 1693. He was for many years a prominent man in the affairs of the church and town. His interest in religion led him to sympathize with the "Great Awakening," and he was one of the founders of the Second Church of Framingham. Among his children was Phineas Hemenway, who was b. April 26, 1706, and graduated at Harvard College in 1730. He settled in the Christian ministry over the church in Townsend, Mass., where the sacred relation was maintained until his death. He m., May 8, 1739, Sarah, daughter of Samuel Stevens of Marlborough, who, after his death, became, in 1761, the wife of David Taylor of Concord. The following is the inscription upon the burial tablet in Townsend: "Erected by the Town. To the Memory of Rev. Mr. Phineas Hemenway, the First Pastor of the Church Here, Who Departed this Life May 20 1760, Aged 55. In the 27th Year of his Ministry. He was sound in the faith, zealous in the Cause of God, meek and patient under trials, Diligent in improving his talents, faithful to his Lord, and to the souls of his people. From Death's arrows, no age or station is free." Rev. Phineas Hemenway made his will the day before he died, in which he mentions his wife Sarah, and children Ebenezer, Sarah, Phineas, Elizabeth, Samuel, and Joseph. Concerning them we can briefly say that Ebenezer m., in 1758, Elizabeth Moors, and settled in Ashburnham; Sarah m. Nathaniel Sawtell of Chelmsford; Phineas m. Elizabeth Taylor of Groton. He was a minute-man from Groton and responded to the alarm from Concord and Lexington, and thereafter rendered military service. Concerning Elizabeth we have not learned. Samuel m. Sally Fitch; and Joseph settled in Groton, and was a soldier in the war for independence.

Lieutenant Samuel Hemenway, the son of Rev. Phineas Hemenway, m., at Groton, April 26, 1774, Sally, the daughter of Zachariah Fitch of Pepperell. She was b. Jan. 2, 1755, and d. at Groton, April 15, 1826; and he d. March 15, 1818, aged 70 years. They purchased, soon after marriage, the Fitch homestead, near " Fitch's Bridge " on the Nashua River, where they continued to reside until their decease. Lieutenant Samuel Hemenway made his will July 18, 1817, and the same was proved March 30, 1818; in which document he mentions his wife, and children Samuel, Joseph, Jeremiah, Mary, Bela, and Artemus, who was executor with his mother; and daughters Sarah, wife of Joseph Warner, and Lucy, who m. Asa Lawrence, Jr. In his will he is styled " Gentleman."

The widow of Lieutenant Hemenway survived until 1826, and in her will, made a few weeks before her death, she mentions the five children of her deceased son Samuel. Their daughter Mary d. Oct. 9, 1863, aged 75 years; and their son Jeremiah d. Nov. 16, 1834, aged 52 years. Samuel Hemenway was a minute-man and answered the alarm from Lexington and Concord, afterwards serving as sergeant in a campaign against the British forces in the region of Fort Ticonderoga in the autumn of 1777, and shortly after was commissioned lieutenant.

Dr. Samuel Hemenway, son of Lieutenant Samuel Hemenway, was b. at Groton, and while in Salem a medical student in the home and office of Dr. Edward A. Holyoke, he became acquainted with and married, Nov. 13, 1803, Sally, daughter of Captain Jeduthun Upton. He continued his residence in Salem a few years, when he removed to Boston. He d. Jan. 8, 1823, aged 45 years; the widow d. Nov. 16, 1865, aged 78 years. The burial place of the family is at Groton. Their children were: (1) Edward Augustus Holyoke, b. at Salem, April 25, 1805 (in early manhood he assumed the single name Augustus); (2) George Washington, b. June 26, 1807, and d. Sept. 5, 1830, having settled in business in Concord; (3) Samuel Charles, b. May 18, 1809; (4) William H., b. May 25, 1811, and settled in Machias, Me.; (5) Charles P., b. June 14, 1818, and became a merchant in Boston. Dr. Samuel A. Green, in his "Groton Historical Series," vol. iii. p. 47, says: "Dr. Samuel Hemenway was a son of Samuel and Sarah (Fitch) Hemenway, and was born at Groton on Nov.

16, 1777. He attended school at Groton Academy in the year 1797, and afterwards studied medicine under the tuition of Dr. Edward Holyoke of Salem. He began the practice of his profession in that town, and was married on Nov. 13, 1803, to Sally, daughter of Captain Jeduthun and Mary Upton of Salem. He joined the Massachusetts Medical Society in 1808. About the year 1817 he removed to Boston, where he died on Jan. 8, 1823. See 'Groton Epitaphs' (p. 154) for the inscription on his tombstone. He was the father of Augustus Hemenway of Boston."

Augustus Hemenway, eldest son of Dr. Samuel Hemenway, was b. at Salem, Mass., April 25, 1805. His baptismal name was Edward Augustus Holyoke Hemenway, in honor of the eminent physician with whom his father studied, but in young manhood he assumed the single name. He entered the employ of Mr. Benjamin Bangs, a wealthy ship-owner and merchant of Boston, and for a series of years was his agent and partner in South American trade. He finally became owner of extensive silver mines in Valpariso, which yielded large returns. Mr. Hemenway m., June 26, 1840, at New York, Mary, daughter of Thomas Tileston, one of the wealthiest merchant-mariners of New York city. Their children were Charlotte Augusta, who d. in 1865 ; Alice, who d. in infancy; Amy, the wife of Louis Cabot ; Edith, the wife of W. E. C. Eustis; and Augustus, who was b. Oct. 10, 1853. Mr. Hemenway died June 16, 1876, while on a trip to Cuba, and Mrs. Hemenway survived until March 6, 1894.

The gift of giving has ever been finely manifest in

the Hemenway home.   Mrs. Hemenway during her entire life enjoyed rendering favors where they not only would be appreciated, but where they would accrue to the benefit of the world.   She fully believed in training and education as the great conservators of good living and character.   Educational and philanthropic institutions were ever cherished by her. The Tileston Normal School of Wilmington, N. C., so named in memory of her honored father, was an object of her care.   In 1876 she liberally assisted the Old South Association in preserving the historic Old South Meeting-house, and this was followed by the establishment of a course of lectures upon American history, which is maintained, and eminent scholars are summoned to portray to the growing youth the heroism of former generations. The late Mr. John Fiske was one of the earliest lecturers upon this foundation.   In 1881 she instituted four annual prizes for pupils of the high schools of Boston for the best essays upon chosen subjects of American history.   She was also interested in promoting better training among young women, and established cooking and sewing schools and kitchen gardens, and also the Normal schools of Boston and Framingham, where special attention was given the practical industries of womanhood.   She was a patroness also of the American Archæological Institute, the "Journal of American Ethnology and Archæology," and the Boston Teachers' Mutual Benefit Association.   These are but a few of her helpful charities.   On her death, tributes were paid her wherever the higher life of humanity is regarded.   The

Boston public schools cherish her memory in many ways.

Augustus Hemenway, a son of Augustus and Mary (Tileston) Hemenway, was b. at Boston, Oct. 10, 1853. He attended the private schools of Messrs. Fette and Dixwell in Boston, after which he took the regular course at Harvard, graduating in 1875. He was elected an overseer of Harvard College in 1888, and served as representative to the General Court from Milton and Canton in 1890 and 1891. He was appointed a member of the Metropolitan Park Commission by Governor Greenhalge in 1895. The Hemenway Gymnasium was presented by him to Harvard University in 1878, and he built an addition thereto in 1895. He also gave to the town of Canton a new library building. Mr. Hemenway usually passes the winter in Boston, and the summer months at his Readville residence. He is a trustee of valuable estates, having an office at 10 Tremont Street, Boston. Mr. and Mrs. Hemenway and family travelled in Europe in 1884 and 1902.

THE TILESTON FAMILY

Thomas Tileston, the New England immigrant, was in Dorchester in 1634. Among his children was Timothy, who in turn had a son Timothy, who was the father of Ezekiel Tileston, born in 1731. He m., in 1753, Sarah, daughter of Edward Belcher. Ezekiel Tileston and wife Sarah were the parents of Lemuel, b. in 1763, who m. as his second wife, Mary, daughter of William Minns. She d. at Cambridge in 1826, and he d. at Haverhill in 1836. He was a dealer in India goods. Their son Thomas was b. at Boston, Aug. 13, 1793. In Haverhill, Mass., Thomas Tileston learned the printer's trade, and had editorial experience upon the " Merrimac Intelligencer." In 1822 he formed a partnership with Mr. Paul Spofford, and they became agents of a Boston and New York line of packets. In 1826 Mr. Tileston began developing the South American and Cuban trade, which he continued. He was also interested in a line of packets between New York and Liverpool. In 1840 he was elected president of the Phœnix Bank of New York, and chairman of the Clearing House Association; and he was also a leading spirit in the American Insurance Company. The " New York Tribune," on the occasion of his death, Feb. 29, 1864, said: " He was emphatically a thorough business man, ' born to lead and command.' When sloops were used, he built schooners; when brigs were the fashion of the times, he launched ships; when ships became the chief craft at our ports, he ordered steamships. He was an active, busy, enterprising man, whose industry and energy have been crowned with a princely fortune, and he leaves it with the odor of an enviable reputation."

Thomas Tileston m., in Haverhill, April 11, 1820, Mary, daughter of Dudley Porter. They had nine children, the eldest of whom was Mary, b. Dec. 20, 1821, who m., June 26, 1840, Augustus Hemenway; and Ellen Louise, who in 1866 m. Charles Porter Hemenway, a brother of Augustus Hemenway. Their home in New York city was on the corner of Fifth Avenue and East Fourteenth Street. Mr. Tileston and Mr. Spofford were partners in business for forty-six years. Mr. Spofford resided in the next house to Mr. Tileston. The Genealogy of the Spofford Family (p. 144) contains an account of the firm, and their lifelong intimacy.

THE UPTON FAMILY

John Upton and wife Eleanor were the progenitors, through their fourteen children, of the Upton family of New England. They were of that part of Salem which is now Peabody certainly as early as 1658. His son John was b. in 1655, and the probabilities are that the father had been some years in New England. John Upton d. July 11, 1699, in Reading, to which place he had removed. He was a thrifty and prosperous husbandman. Their son, William Upton, was b. June 10, 1663, and m., in 1701, Mary Maber, and had ten children, the youngest of whom was Caleb. Caleb Upton was b. Feb. 4, 1722. The name of his wife was not known to the compiler of the Upton Memorial, but they had at least seven children. He was a settler of Amherst, N. H., and probably d. at Fitchburg, Mass. Jeduthun was the eldest son of Caleb Upton and was b. in Reading in 1746, and m., 1783, Mary Brown, widow of —— Austin. He resided in Salem a large part of his life, but removed to Steuben, Me., where his wife d. in 1815, and he d. in June, 1823. He was a prosperous merchant, and was styled "captain." The wife had three children by her first husband, Mr. Austin, and six children by Mr. Upton. Their daughter Sally, b. at Salem, Feb. 19, 1787, became,

Nov. 13, 1803, the wife of Dr. Samuel Hemenway, then a medical student in Salem, where he resided for a number of years. There is an account of this family on pages 102 and 107 of the Upton Memorial.

THE PORTER FAMILY

John Porter, the immigrant, was in Roxbury, and became a freeman in Nov., 1633. From 1635 to 1644 he resided in Hingham, and thence removed to that part of Salem which is now Danvers. His children were John, who died unmarried, Samuel, Joseph, Benjamin, Israel, Mary, Jonathan, and Sarah. The son Samuel m. Hannah, daughter of William and Elizabeth Dodge, and had a son John, b. in 1658. Samuel Porter made his will, Feb. 10, 1658, "being bound to the Barbadoes," and the same was proved before court, June 28, 1660. The widow m., in 1661, Thomas Woodbury, and became the mother of nine children. John Porter inherited his father's homestead in the present town of Wenham. He m. Lydia, daughter of Henry and Lydia Herrick. She d. in 1737, aged 77 years, and John Porter d. in 1753, aged 95 years. They had eleven children, whose united ages at the time of their deaths was 955 years, an average of 87 years.

Samuel Porter, the eldest, b. in 1681, resided at the homestead and m., in 1707, Sarah, daughter of John and Sarah (Perkins) Bradstreet, who was the mother of his children. The Wenham town records say: " September 13, 1770, died Sergeant Samuel Porter, who was born Feb. 17, 1681 ; *ætatis* 89 years and seven months lacking four days. What man is he yt liveth, and shall not see death." Their eldest son, Samuel Porter, b. 1711, settled in Wenham, where he d. in 1786. His wife Anna d. in 1805, aged 90 years. They had twelve children, the fifth of whom was Dudley, b. in 1744, who d. in Andover in 1816. His wife Sally d. in 1792, aged 43 years. He was a merchant in Haverhill for a number of years. They had seven children, the first of whom was Dudley, b. in 1770, who m., in 1793, Polly Austin, and had Dudley, who d. in young manhood; Eleazer A., a merchant in New York city, and from 1837 in Haverhill; and the daughter Mary, who m. Thomas Tileston of New York city. Most of these items concerning the Porter family are from the Genealogy by Hon. Joseph W. Porter, Bangor, edition of 1878, where the families are treated at length.

THE BRADSTREET FAMILY

Governor Simon Bradstreet was b. at Hobling, England, in 1603. He came to New England with Winthrop in 1630, together with wife Ann, daughter of Governor Thomas Dudley. Governor Bradstreet was for many years an assistant to the governor, deputy governor five years, and governor from 1679 to 1686 and from 1689 to 1692. He resided for the greater part of his life at Andover. His wife Ann, who d. in 1672, was an early writer of poetry in New England. She was a woman of superior worth and ability, and a fit companion of Simon Bradstreet, who was a tower of strength among the people of Massachusetts Bay Colony. He d. in Salem, 1697, aged 94 years. Their son, John Bradstreet, m., in 1679, Sarah,

daughter of Rev. William Perkins of Topsfield, and
had sons and daughters, among whom was Sarah who
in 1707 became the wife of Samuel Porter of Wenham.
There is much literature upon Governor Thomas Dudley and Simon Bradstreet in various histories and historical studies of the founding of New England.

THE FITCH FAMILY

Deacon Zachary Fitch was at Lynn in 1633, and
about 1640 settled in that part of Reading which is
now Wakefield. He was a deacon of the First Church
from 1645 until his death, June 9, 1662. His wife was
Mary ——. They had eight children: Thomas, Jeremiah, Benjamin, Sarah, Joseph, John, Samuel, and
Zachariah. The son Samuel was b. in 1645, and m.,
in 1673, Sarah, daughter of Job Lane, and their son
Samuel, b. March 4, 1674, m., in 1695, Elizabeth,
daughter of Joseph and Sarah (Wyman) Walker of
Billerica. She was b. in 1678 and d. in 1716, and was
the mother of eight children, the last of whom, Zachariah, was b. Feb. 13, 1713. Zachariah Fitch m., Oct.
1, 1733, Elizabeth, daughter of William Grimes of
Lexington. Mr. Fitch resided in Bedford. He d.
Dec. 8, 1800, and the wife d. March 12, 1790. They
had fourteen children, the ninth of whom was Sarah,
or Sally, as she was styled. She was b. Jan. 2, 1755,
and on April 26, 1774, m. Lieutenant Samuel Hemenway of Groton. There is a history of the Fitch family in the " New England Historical and Genealogical Register," volumes lv. and lvi., by the Hon. Ezra
S. Stevens, and also in the History of Bedford, p. 10,
genealogical section, by Mr. Abram English Brown.

160. James, m., at Boston, Jan. 16, 1875, Caroline Estelle, daughter of Enoch Redington and Caroline Augusta (Patten) Mudge of Boston. Residence at the Lawrence homestead in Groton, Mass.

Their children:

229. I. Elizabeth Prescott, b. at Swampscott, Mass., July 29, 1876.

230. II. James, b. at Boston, Feb. 7, 1878.

James Lawrence, Jr., attended Groton School, and was admitted to Harvard in Sept., 1897, graduating in June, 1901. He was president of his class, and prominent in college athletics, being a member of the University Crew and of the football eleven. Upon leaving college he entered the office of George Mixter, banker and note broker, at 28 State Street, Boston.

231. III. Richard, b. at Groton, Sept. 19, 1879.

Richard Lawrence received his preparatory training at Groton School, and took the regular collegiate course at Harvard, graduating in 1902. His present residence is at the homestead in Groton.

James Lawrence spent his boyhood in Boston, and received instruction at the schools of W. Eliot Fettee and Epes S. Dixwell. After graduation at Harvard in 1874, he devoted several months to European travel, and on his return entered the Harvard Law School, where he attended lectures during two terms in 1875–76. He then took up his residence in Groton, where he has since been engaged in farming and stock-raising on an extensive scale. Mr. Lawrence has been vice-president of the American Shropshire Sheep Association, a trustee of the Middlesex Agricultural Society, of Lawrence Academy since 1876, and of Groton School since its foundation. He is also a life member of the Massachusetts Horticultural Society, of the Guernsey and Ayrshire societies, and of the English Shropshire Association, besides which he has served as a director of several manufacturing companies, of the Bowker Fertilizer Company, and of the Worcester and Nashua Railroad. He has been a member of the committees appointed to visit the Lawrence Scientific School and Bussey Institution, and is a life member of the Harvard Law School Association. Mr. Lawrence is also a member of the Republican Club of Massachusetts, and has several times been a delegate to the Republican State Convention. He was a member of the Massachusetts House of Representatives in 1897, from the twenty-fourth Middlesex district, and served on the Committee of Ways and Means. Mr. Lawrence has been in every State and Territory, and in every capital city of the Union, and has travelled throughout Mexico, and in British Columbia, to the northernmost point accessible by railroad.

THE MUDGE FAMILY

The family of Mudge is of considerable antiquity in England, as the name, which was originally written Mugge, may be found on record as early as the beginning of the fifteenth century. Thomas Mudge, born in England about 1624, is believed to have been a native of Devonshire. Embarking from Plymouth, he crossed the seas, and became a resident of Malden, Mass., in 1654, or earlier. His wife's name was Mary, and they had a family of eight children.

John Mudge, fourth child of Thomas and Mary, was b. at Malden in 1654. He was a farmer and tanner, and a soldier in King Philip's war. He m., in 1684, Ruth, daughter of Robert and Hannah Burditt of Malden, and d. Oct. 29, 1733.

Deacon John Mudge, second son of the above, was b. at Malden, Nov. 21, 1686. He was a farmer. His wife's name was Lydia. He d. Nov. 26, 1762.

John, third of the name, eldest child of Deacon John and Lydia Mudge, was b. at Malden, Dec. 30, 1713. He also was engaged in farming, at first in Malden, afterwards in Lynnfield. He m., May 4, 1738, Mary, daughter of Samuel and Anna Waite of Malden. He d. at Lynnfield, Nov. 26, 1762.

Enoch, seventh child of John and Mary (Waite) Mudge, was b. at Lynnfield, Aug. 1, 1754. He m., Jan. 6, 1773, Lydia, daughter of John and Abigail Ingalls. He was a soldier of the Revolution, by trade a shoe manufacturer, and a highly respected citizen of Lynn. He d. there Jan. 30, 1832.

Rev. Enoch Mudge, second son of Enoch and Lydia, was b. at Lynn, June 28, 1776. He m., Nov. 29, 1797, the widow Jerusha Hinckley of Orrington, Me., who was a daughter of John and Ruth Holbrook of Wellfleet, Mass. Mr. Mudge was the first native Methodist preacher of New England. He d. at Lynn, April 2, 1850. A biographical account of this excellent man may be found in the Appendix to the

" Memorials of the Mudge Family in America," by Alfred Mudge, Boston, 1868.

Enoch Redington, son of Rev. Enoch and Jerusha Holbrook (Hinckley) Mudge, was b. at Orrington, Me., March 22, 1812.   He was for a time a merchant at Portland, and lived in New York from 1836 to 1840. In the latter year he went to New Orleans, where he opened the St. Charles Hotel, of which he was the manager for five years.   Then he returned to New York, and devoted himself to mercantile pursuits. About the year 1850 he came to Boston, where he was in business for many years, at first as a partner in the firm of Fay, Mudge & Atwood, and later as senior member of the firm of E. R. Mudge, Sawyer & Co., dry goods commission merchants.   Mr. Mudge was a very prominent layman of the Episcopal Church. He m., May 9, 1832, Caroline Augusta, daughter of John and Olive Patten of Portland, Me.   Their sixth child, Caroline Estelle, b. at Lynn, Mass., July 9, 1850, m., at Boston, Jan. 16, 1875, James Lawrence of Boston, and resides at Groton.   (Family No. 30.)   Enoch Redington Mudge d. at Swampscott, Mass., Oct. 1, 1881.

FAMILY NO. 31

161. **Gertrude**, m. at Boston, June 15, 1878, John Endicott Peabody.

Their children :

232. I. **Marion Lee**, b. at London, England, July 6, 1879.

233. II. **Harold**, b. at Boston, Dec. 7, 1880.

Mrs. Gertrude (Lawrence) Peabody d. May 2, 1883.

Mr. Peabody m. (second), at Beverly, Mass., Aug. 25, 1887, Martha Prince Whitney, daughter of William Michael and Anne Augusta (Nourse) Whitney. They have:

233a. III. **Samuel Endicott**, b. at Lausanne, Switzerland, Aug. 27, 1895.

THE PEABODY FAMILY

John Endicott Peabody, Francis Peabody, Jr. (Family No. 33), and Mrs. Martha Endicott (Peabody) Lawrence (Family No. 34) are descendants in the eighth generation from Lieutenant Francis Peabody of St. Albans, Hertfordshire (b. in 1614), who came to New England in the ship *Planter* in 1635, lived for a time at Ipswich, Mass., and was one of the first settlers, in 1639, of Hampton, N. H., where he remained for about eighteen years. He was made a freeman in 1642, and served several terms as one of the " selected men " of Hampton. In 1657 he removed to Topsfield, Mass., where he had previously bought a farm. According to the town records, " Ffrances Pabodye " was first chosen a selectman of Topsfield in 1659, and was often reëlected. He also served as town clerk many years, and was appointed lieutenant of the local military company, May 27, 1668. In 1664 the town gave him permission to set up a grist-mill, and eight years later he built a saw-mill. The old Peabody house, " by the mill, where Lieutenant Peabody lived in 1660," was torn down in 1846. His wife was Mary, daughter of Reginald Foster of Boxford, and their children numbered fourteen. Lieutenant Francis Peabody d. at Topsfield, Feb. 23, 1697-8, and his wife's death occurred there, April 9, 1705.

Isaac Peabody (1648-1726), fourth child of the preceding, was a resident of Topsfield, and his name appears frequently in the early town records. It is also found in a list of residents who took the oath of allegiance and fidelity to their sovereign, Charles II., in 1677. At a " Lawfull Towne meeting ye 3 March, 1684, Isacke pebody and Isacke Estey were chosen fence Veveeres," and he was a selectman in 1693. His wife's Christian name was Sarah.

Cornet Francis Peabody, eldest of twelve children of Isaac, was b. Dec. 1, 1694, and became a wealthy resident of Middleton, Mass. Although having the title of cornet, he ranked as " Captain of the troop of Horse of the County." On Jan. 27, 1715, he m. Dorothy Perkins. He d. April 23, 1769.

Deacon Francis Peabody, eldest of eleven children of Cornet Francis Peabody, was b. at Middleton, Sept. 21, 1715, and became a prominent citizen of the town. He m. Margaret Knight, March 26, 1739; d. Dec. 7, 1797. They had twelve children, of whom the ninth was

Joseph Peabody, b. at Middleton, Dec. 9, 1757. In his youth he found occupation in farming in his native town and at Boxford. His name appears on a muster-roll of Captain William Perley's company in Colonel James Faye's regiment of minute-men, and he marched with his company to Lexington, April 19, 1775. He also enlisted for eight months in the following year, and again in 1777. After this he entered the service of the American "private armed marine," and made several cruises. In 1782, when he was second officer of the *Ranger*, Mr. Peabody was severely wounded during an engagement with the enemy. After the war he made many business trips to different parts of the world, and in the early part of the nineteenth century he became a large ship-owner, having at one time no less than eighty-three vessels. Mr. Peabody m. (first), Aug. 28, 1791, Catherine, daughter of Rev. Elias Smith of Middleton. She d. after about two years, and he m. (second), Oct. 24, 1795, Elizabeth Smith, sister of his first wife. He d. Jan. 5, 1844.

Colonel Francis Peabody, fourth child of Joseph, was b. at Salem, Dec. 7, 1801. His early education was obtained at Dummer Academy, Byfield, and at the private school of Jacob Newman Knapp in Brighton. When eighteen years of age he made a voyage to Russia for his health. In 1825 he received a commission as colonel of the First Regiment, Massachusetts militia, and later was engaged for some years in the business of refining sperm oil on an extensive scale. He was elected president of the Essex Institute in 1865. Colonel Peabody m., July 7, 1823, Martha, daughter of Samuel Endicott, and a lineal descendant of Governor John Endicott. Colonel Peabody d. Oct. 31, 1867.

Samuel Endicott Peabody, second child of the above-mentioned, was b. at Salem, April 19, 1825. He attended the private schools of Messrs. Henry K. Oliver and Samuel Carlton in Salem, and entered

Harvard with the Class of 1846, but left college at the close of the Sophomore year and made an extensive tour in Europe and the East. He has been a partner in the business firms of Curtis & Peabody, Boston, and J. S. Morgan & Co., London, and has also been president and chairman of the Board of Directors of the American Loan and Trust Co., Boston. Mr. Peabody at one time held the rank of captain, afterwards of major, in the Salem Light Infantry. He m., Nov. 23, 1848, at Salem, Marianne Cabot Lee, daughter of John Clarke Lee and Harriet Paine (Rose) Lee, and has a fine residence, " Kernwood," in Salem, near the Peabody line. Their eldest son, John Endicott Peabody, was b. at Salem, Jan. 6, 1853. He received instructions at Mr. William W. Richards' private school in that town, and entered Trinity College, Cambridge, England, in Oct., 1871, taking the degree of B. A. after a three years' course. He was then for sixteen months in a commission house at Antwerp, Belgium, and for two years with Messrs. Drexel, Morgan & Co., bankers, in New York. Mr. Peabody is an artist by profession, and has travelled extensively in Europe. He has been twice married. (See Family No. 31.)

FAMILY NO. 32

162. **Prescott**, m., at New York, June 23, 1886, Katharine Bulkley, daughter of Edward Henry and Katharine Bulkley.

They have a daughter:

234. **Katharine,** born at Paris, France, April 12, 1887.

Prescott Lawrence was born at Boston, Jan. 17, 1861. He was for a time a member of the Harvard Class of 1882. After leaving college he travelled in Europe, chiefly in England, returning to Boston in the fall of 1881. He made another trip abroad in the following spring. For some years he had a farm in Groton, Mass., which was also his residence. In 1890 he sold this farm to Amory Appleton Lawrence, and removed to New York city and later to Newport, R. I., where he has since lived. Mr. Lawrence has been for many years prominent at the New York and Boston Horse Shows, as one of the judges of various classes of horses, carriages, and appointments, and driving competition. He is a member of several of the principal clubs in the metropolis.

FAMILY NO. 33

164. **Rosamond,** m., at Boston, Jan. 13, 1881, Francis Peabody, Jr. Residence in Milton.

They have these children:

235. I. **Rosamond,** b. at Boston, Oct. 7, 1881.
236. II. **Martha,** b. at Boston, Jan. 14, 1886.
237. III. **Sylvia,** b. at Boston, April 1, 1893.

Francis Peabody, Jr., son of Samuel Endicott and Marianne Cabot (Lee) Peabody, was born at Salem, Mass., Sept. 1, 1854. He accompanied his father to England in 1871, and was for two years a student at Cheltenham College, Gloucestershire. He then spent two years at Trinity College, Cambridge, receiving the degree of B. L. in 1876. After a year in the office of a prominent barrister of Lincoln's Inn and the Middle Temple, he returned to this country and entered the law office of Morse, Stone & Greenough in Boston.   In Nov., 1879, he was admitted to the Suffolk bar, after a year's attendance at the Harvard Law School, and has since been engaged in the practice of law.   Mr. Peabody held the office of judge advocate general on the staff of Governor William E. Russell, and was at one time the Democratic candidate for mayor of Boston.   He is trustee of several estates.

FAMILY NO. 34

166. **John,** m., at Salem, Mass., June 16, 1887, Martha Endicott Peabody, daughter of Samuel Endicott and Marianne Cabot (Lee) Peabody.   Residence at Groton.

They have these:

238. I. **Hester,** b. at Cambridge, April 4, 1888.

239. II. **Mary,** b. at Boston, Oct. 7, 1890.

240. III. **Geraldine,** b. at Groton, June 1, 1893.

241. IV. **Harriette Paige,** b. at Groton, Dec. 24, 1898.

John Lawrence attended school in his native city, and graduated at Harvard College in 1885.   Early in July of that year he left Boston on a trip around the world.   Journeying westward, he visited the Yellowstone Park and Yosemite Valley, and then sailed from San Francisco for Yokohama.   The following account of his travels is given in his own words:

" I spent six weeks in Japan, a good deal of the

time up country, making the ascent of Fujiyama. Then I went to Shanghai, and from there sailed to Tientsin. At the latter place I hired two ponies and a Chinese boy, who spoke a little pigeon-English, and with these rode to Pekin, making the journey of eighty-five miles in twenty-nine hours. At Pekin I stayed with Sir Robert Hart, and so had an opportunity of meeting many of the foreign residents there. After a few days at the capital I started north for Kalgan, about one hundred and forty miles distant, passing through the Great Wall on my way. Kalgan, as you may remember, is the most northern city of China before you get to the great plain of Mongolia, over which the tea-carriers pass to Kiachta. I made a day's journey into the plain, spending the night with some wandering Mongols in their felt huts; then I returned to Pekin by a road more to the eastward, passing through many large walled towns whose names I have forgotten. The country all through this region is very hilly, and the road terrible, frequently nothing better than an old dried watercourse. From Pekin I went back to Tientsin, thence to Shanghai and Hong Kong, spending a few days at Canton. From Hong Kong I went to Singapore, then to Batavia. In Java I stayed a fortnight, a good deal of the time in the centre of the island among the coffee plantations, and then back to Singapore and on to Colombo. After a few days at Ceylon, I sailed to Madras and from there went to the hill towns in the Neelgherry Mountains; then back again to Madras and on to Calcutta, thence to Darjeeling. From Darjeeling I made an expedition to the Nepaul frontier in order to get a better view of Mount Everest. Afterwards I went to Agra and Delhi and as far north as Peshawur, where I had an opportunity to ride up the Khyber Pass.

"I then went to Bombay, sailing from thence to Bassorah, and stopping on the way at Muscat and other ports in the Persian Gulf. After a week in a river steamer I arrived at Bagdad. From there I visited the ruins of Babylon; then hiring a Bedouin and two camels I started across the desert for Damascus. This was a long and tiresome journey, occupying twelve days. We travelled all day and part of each night, as the watering places were few, and the distance had to be covered between them." We carried our drinking water in pig-skins, which were infested with every kind of insect, and the water was not improved by the burning sun and the joggling alongside the camel.

"I was told before leaving Bagdad that I should certainly be robbed on the way, so I was prepared by having practically nothing with me, except a new pair of boots, which the Bedouins promptly seized.

"I spent about ten days in Damascus, and then hiring a dragoman, a muleteer, and three horses I went north through Baalbec, Aleppo, Marash, Cæsarea, Zeitoun, and Angora. This journey occupied from the 10th of May until the 18th of June, when I arrived at Constantinople. Asia Minor at that time seemed to be comparatively safe, if you were only well armed, as we were. From Constantinople I went to Greece, spending a fortnight at Athens, then sailing to Trieste *via* Corfu. From there I went straight to London and home, where I arrived about the middle of August, 1886, having been nearly fourteen months on the trip."

In the autumn following his return, Mr. Lawrence entered the office of Francis Peabody, Jr., as a student of law, and in Oct., 1887, he began attending lectures at the Harvard Law School, but on account of his health did not finish the course. In 1890 he became a resident of Groton, where he has been prominent in town affairs, holding the office of chairman of the Board of Selectmen. He was commissioned lieutenant in the Naval Brigade, M. V. M., in Sept., 1892, resigning in July, 1894. During the war with Spain Mr. Lawrence held a commission as ensign in the United States Navy, serving also as executive officer of the *Inca*.

FAMILY NO. 35

168. **Harriette Story,** m., at Boston, March 8, 1893, Reginald Foster of Boston.

Their children:

242. I. **Ruth,** b. Jan. 3, 1894.

243. II. **Dorothy Dwight,** b. Sept. 30, 1895; d. March 23, 1898.

244. III. **Lawrence,** b. Aug. 9, 1898.

245. IV. **Reginald,** b. Nov. 10, 1899.

246. V. **Maxwell Evarts,** b. Aug. 27, 1901.

THE FOSTER FAMILY

Reginald Foster is of the ninth generation from his emigrant ancestor of the same name, who came from Little Badow, Essex, England. He was a member of the Foster family of Bamborough and Etherstone Castle, Northumberland, and came to America in 1638, settling at Ipswich, Mass.

Abraham Foster, third child of Reginald " the first," was born at Exeter, Devonshire, England, in 1622. He accompanied his father to the new world and became a yeoman of Ipswich.

Ephraim Foster, son of the last named, was born at Ipswich, Oct. 9, 1657. He m., in 1677, Hannah, daughter of Robert Eames, and settled in that part of Andover which is now North Andover, where he became a prominent citizen. He d. Sept. 21, 1746.

Ephraim Foster, son of Ephraim and Hannah (Eames) Foster, was b. at Andover, March 12, 1688. He m., Jan. 17, 1716, Abigail, daughter of Joseph Poor of Newbury, Mass. He d. April 8, 1738.

Hon. Jedediah Foster, son of the preceding, was b. at Andover, Oct. 10, 1726. He m., May 18, 1749, Dorothy, daughter of Brigadier General Joseph Dwight. Grad. Harvard College, 1744. He was a justice of the Superior Court of Judicature of Massachusetts, and during the Revolution held the rank of colonel. He also served sixteen years in the state legislature. He d. Oct. 17, 1779.

Hon. Dwight Foster, son of Jedediah and Dorothy (Dwight) Foster, was b. at Brookfield, Mass., Dec. 7, 1757. He m., May 7, 1783, Rebecca, eldest daughter of Colonel Francis Faulkner of Acton. Mr. Foster graduated at Brown University, Providence, R. I., in 1774, and practised law, first at Providence, afterwards at Brookfield. He served as a representative and senator from Massachusetts in Congress, and was chief justice of the Court of Common Pleas for the County of Worcester. In June, 1792, he was appointed sheriff of the county. He d. April 23, 1823.

Hon. Alfred Dwight Foster, fourth child of Hon. Dwight and Rebecca (Faulkner) Foster, was b. at Brookfield, July 26, 1800. He attended Leicester Academy, graduated at Harvard in 1819, and was admitted to the bar in 1822. Two years later he removed from Brookfield to Worcester, and retired from practice in 1827. Mr. Foster was judge of probate, a representative to the General Court of Massachusetts from 1831 to 1833, and was for many years treasurer of the State Lunatic Asylum. He m., Feb. 14, 1828, Lydia Stiles. He d. Aug. 3, 1852.

Hon. Dwight Foster, eldest child of the above, was b. Dec. 13, 1828. He fitted for college at the public schools of Worcester, and graduated at Yale in 1848. He then studied law, was admitted to the bar in 1849, and practised his profession in Worcester. During the civil war, he was attorney-general of Massachusetts, and from Aug. 31, 1866, to Jan. 12, 1869, he was an associate justice of the Supreme Court, and thereafter practised law until his death. He m., Aug. 20, 1850, Henrietta Perkins Baldwin, daughter of Governor Roger Sherman Baldwin. He d. April 18, 1884.

Reginald Foster of Boston, sixth child of the preceding, was b. at Worcester, Mass., Jan. 2, 1863, and received his early training at the Boston Latin School and Mr. Noble's private school, after which he took the regular collegiate course at Yale, graduating in 1884. He received the degree of LL. B. from Boston University in 1886, was admitted to the Suffolk bar in the following year, and has since been engaged in the practice of law at 87 Milk Street, Boston. Mr. Foster m., in Boston, March 8, 1893, Harriette Story, youngest child of Abbott and Harriette White (Paige) Lawrence.

APPENDIX

APPENDIX

GRANT OF CREST TO THE ANCIENT ARMS
OF LAWRENCE

From the Herald's Visitation of Huntingdonshire in the year
1562

To ALL and Singular as well Kinges, Herauldes and officers of Armes, as Nobles, Gentilmen and others which these presents shall see or here. William Hervye Esquire, otherwise called Clarencieulx, principall Heraulde, and kinge of Armes of the Southe East and West parties of England from the Ryver of Trent Southward: Sendeth due commendaĉons and greating. Forasmoche, as auncientlie from the begynnyng the valyaunte and vertuous actes excellent parsons have been commended to the worlde with sondry monuments and remembrances of their good desertts, Emonges the which of the chefist and moste usuall hath ben the bearinge of signes and tokens yn Shilds called Armes, the which ar none other thinges than evydences and demonstraĉons of prowes and valoure dyverslie distributed according to the quallities and deserttes of the parsons, that suche signes and tokens of the diligent, faythfull and couragious, myght apere before the negligent cowarde and ignorante, and be an efficient cawse to move, styre and kyndle the hartes off men to the ymytaĉon of vertue

and noblenes, even so hath the same ben and yett ys
continuallye observed to thintent that such as have
don comendable servyce to their Prince or Contrey
eyther yn warr or peace, may both receyve due honor
yn their lyves, and also deryve the same succesyvelie
to their postertie after them   And beinge required
of William Lawrence of Seint Ives yn the Countie
of Huntington Esqyre to make searche in the Register, and Records of myne office for the Armes to
him belonginge, and I found the same. And so con-
sideringe the antiquytie thereof, coulde not without
his great Injurye assigne unto hym any other Armes,
then those which belonged to the howse and famelie
whereof he is descended. And in perpetuall memorye off the same, I have confirmed, assigned, geven
and graunted unto hym the saide armes with the ap-
purtenannces hereafter followinge. That is to saye
Argent, a crosse ragge gulz, on a cheife azure a lyon
passant regardant golde. And for as moche as I
found no Creast unto the same as comonlie to all
auncient armes their belonged none, I have geven
unto hym by way of encrease for his Creaste and
Cognyssaunce on a wreathe, gold and azure, a Rowe-
buckes head, raised sables bezante horned gold a
Crowne abowte the neck argent, mantellid gules
dubled argent, as more playnlie apeareth depicted yn
this margent. Which armes and creaste I the saide
Clarencieulx king of Armes yn manner and forme
above saide, by power and auctoritie to myne office
annexed and granted by Letters pattents under the
greate Seale of England, have ratifyed, confirmed,
geven and graunted, and by theise presents doe rati-

fie, confirme, gyve and graunte unto the saide William Lawrence of Seint Ives yn the Countie of
Huntington, Esquyre, and to his posteritie with their
due difference to use, beare and shewe forevermore
hereafter the saide armes and Creaste yn Shilde Cote
Armoure or otherwise, and therein to be revested at
his and their libertie and pleasure, without ympedi-
ment or ynterruption of any person or persons. In
witness whereof I the saide Clarencieulx king of
Armes have signed theise presents with my hande and
putt therunto the seal of myne office and the seal of
myne Armes yeven at London the XXXth daye of
October In the Yeare of oure Lorde God a thousand
fyve hondred sixtie and two and in the fourth yeare
of the reigne of oure most dread Sovereigne Ladye
Elizabeth, by the grace of God Quene of England,
France and Ireland, deffender of the faithe.

W. HERVY als Clarencieuls
King of Armes.

Transcribed from and compared
  with the original. 18th Aug. 1688.
      HEN: ST. GEORGE Clarenceuls.

William Lawrence of St. Ives, in Huntingdonshire, was a descendant of Richard Lawrence, who
was the younger son of Thomas of Rumburgh, Suffolk (d. 1471). The latter's elder son, John (of the
eleventh generation from the first Sir Robert Lawrence of Ashton Hall, Lancashire), was the progenitor
of Major Samuel Lawrence of Groton, Mass.

EXTRACTS FROM THE WILL OF THOMAS LAWRENCE OF RUMBURGH

Of the tenth generation from the first Sir Robert of Ashton Hall. The original is in Latin

In the name of God Amen, I Thomas Lawrence, of Rumburgh, of sound mind, this seventh day of July, in the year of our Lord 1471 (1461) make my testament and last will.

I give to the order of Friars Preachers of Dunwich, thirteen shillings and four pence.

Also I give to the high altar of the Church of All Saints of South Elmham twenty shillings.

Also to the reparation of the same church twenty shillings.

Also I give to my servant, Agnes Elye, thirteen shillings and four pence.

Also I give to every grandchild, the children of my son John Lawrence, six shillings and eight pence.

Also I give to John Wolett, my servant forty pence.

Also to the repair of the Bachelor's Light Rumburgh Street, six shillings and eight pence.

Also I give and devise all my lands and tenements, arable, meadow and pasture, lying in the towns and fields of Rumburgh, Spexhall, and parish of St. Michael in South Elmham, after my decease, to John my son, his heirs and assigns for ever. Also to the same John, all my lands and tenements in the parish of All Saints in South Elmham. Also I will and require my feoffees to enfeoff John, my son, after my decease in all my lands and tenements, on the request of the said John.

The residue of my estate I give to John Lawrence, and Richard Lawrence, my sons.

Proved at Cratfield, in Suffolk.

Nov. 6, 1461 (1471)   Deposited at Ipswich.

EXTRACTS FROM THE WILL OF JOHN LAWRENCE OF RUMBURGH

Of the eleventh generation from the first Sir Robert of Ashton Hall

In dei noīe amen, the x day of July the Yer of our Lord Mccccciiij. I John Lawrens of Rumburgh, w^t an hooll mend make my will in this manner.

First I commend my soule to Allmyghty god, to our lady seynt Mary and to all the saints in heaven, my body to be buryed in the parishe churche of Seynt Mihill tharchanngell of Rumburgh forsaid.

Itm of my goods I geff to the high auter for tithes forgotyn iij^s iiij^d.

Itm I bqth to the Repacōn of the saide Churche where most nede ys XX^s.

Itm I bequeth to the grey Frers in Dunwiche iij^s iiij^d.

Itm to the black frers of the same towne iij^s iiij^d.

Itm I bequeth to the white Freres in Norwich iij^s iiij^d.

Itm I bequeth to the Frers in Orford, iij^s iiij^d

Itm I bequeth to the Repacon of the Causey in Rumburgh strete vj^s viij^d

Itm I gef and bequeth to Margery Lawrens my wyf, her heires and assignes, my tenent called Besill, w^t all the lands y^s to in any wise belongyng, as well free as bond.

Itm I gef and bequeth to Margery Lawrens my wyff her heires and assignes, my tenent called Brayes, w.ᵗ all the lands yˢ to in any wise belongyng, as well free as bond.

Itm I bequeth and gif to Margery my wyf, hir heres and assignes, my tenent called Cranes, w.ᵗ all the lands yˢ to in any wise belongyng, as well free as bond.

Itm I wull that my tenent called Gooles be sold by myn executrice and the mony comyng yˢ of I wull that Robard Lawrens my sone have yt.

Itm I gef and bequeth xxvj.ˢ viij.ᵈ to be disposed to poure folk where most nede ys. That ys to say, in Rumburgh, Wysset, Spectyshall, and holton, by even porīons.

Itm I wull and charge Feffes which stand and be infeffed to myn use, that the delyeˢ estate of all my tenents and lands accordyng to this my last will when they be desired or requyred yˢ to be myn executrice.

The Residue of all my goods and catalls, not bequethed nor given, I put into the good disposicion of myn sooll executrice, whom I ordeyn, and make the said Margery my wyff, she to dispose them to the plesure of god and for the helthe of my soule, my frends soules, and our benefactours soules.

Made the day and yer abovesaid.

Proved at Norwich August 3, 1504, and deposited there in the Bishop's Registry.

EXTRACTS FROM THE WILL OF JOHN LAWRENCE OF RUMBURGH

Great-grandfather of John of Wisset, and of Watertown and Groton, Massachusetts

In dei nomie Amen; the xxvij^{ti} daie of Aprill in the year of our Lord god 1590 and in the xxxij^{tie} of the Raigne of our Sovereigne Ladie Elizabeth. By the grace of God of England France and Ireland quene, Defender of the faith etc. I John Lawrence of Romberough, in the Countie of Suff. Yeoman, and in the dioces of Norwich, Beinge whole of Mynd and of perfecte Memorye & Remembrance,

Item I doe gyve & bequethe to John Lawrence my son all that my Tenement wherein I now doe inhabit, and dwell, together with all my Lands, Medowes, Pastures & feadings, with their appetennes whatsoev^r to them belonging wheresoev^r they lye, in Romberough and Wisset, or nigh either of them: To have and to hold the said Tent, lands, Pasturs and feadings, wth their appurtennes whatsoev^r, to the said John and to the heires of his bodie Lawfullie begotten for ever, with and upon condic̄on that he the said John his heires and executors or ass^s shall doe all such act and acts, thinge and things and pforme such legac̄es, gifts and bequests as I shall assigne and appoint the said John my son in and by this my Last Will and Testament and to paye my debts and discharge Richard my sone of such obligac̄on or obligac̄ons as he standeth bownden wth me in them for the payment of anie some, or somes whatsoev^{r.}

Item I doe give and bequeth to Richard Lawrence

my sone, the some of three skore pounds, of Lawfull englishe money To be paide unto the said Richard, his heires execut'rs or ass^s in mann^r and forme following, viz. wth in two years next after my decease, Fifteen pounds, and at such daie xij moneth then next ensuinge other fiften pounds. And at suche daie fyve Years after the said second payment other fifteen pounds, and at such daie twelve moneth after the thirdd payment other XV^{ti} in full satisfaction for the said three skore pounds.

Item I do gyve unto Richard my sone the some of twenty shillings, to be paied by John my sone, his executos, ass^s at the feast of St. Michaell tharch— next after my decease, and such daie xij moneths other xx^s as his annuitie till he Receyve his first legacie of xv^{ti} wch is dewe to be paide within two years after my decease.

Item I give and bequeth to Susane Lawrence my daughter the some of Twentie fyve pounds of lawfull englishe money To be paid unto the said Susane her heires, executo's or assignes by the said John my sone, his heires executo's ass^s in mann^r and forme following viz within fower yeares next after my decease xij^{li} x^s and at suche daie twelve moniths then next ensuinge, other xij x^s in full payment of the said xxv^{ti}

Item I doe gyve & bequeth to Elizabeth my Daughter nowe wief of Symon Sheldrak the some of Fifteen pounds of Lawfull englishe money To be paied unto the said Elizabeth her heires, executo's or ass^s, by the said John, his heires, executo's or ass^s within seven years next after my decease, tene pounds and suche tyme fower years after fyve pounds, in full payment of the said xv^{li}

Item I doe give and bequeth to Margerie my daught.^r now wief of Robert Blithe, thi some of xv^{li} of Lawfull englishe money, to be paied unto the said Margerie, her heires, executors or ass^{s.} by the said John my sone, his heires, executors or ass^{s.} within eight Years next insuinge my said decease tenne pounds, and at such tyme fower years after fyve pounds, in full payment of the said xv^{li.}

Item I doe give and bequeth unto Willm̄ Blithe, sone of the said Robt Blith, my sone in lawe, and unto the two children of Symon Sheldrak, my son in law, wch he haith by my daughter Elizabeth, to eche of them twentie shillings of Lawfull money of England. To be paied by the said John my sone, his heires, Executo's or ass^{s.} when that they come to their severall ag^s of xxj^{ti} years.

Item I do geve and bequeth also to the Children of John Bullimnt of the said towne of Romberough to eche of them tene Shillings of Lawfull Englishe Money To be paied unto them by the said John my sone, his heires, executo's or assigns, when that they shall accomplishe and come to their severall ag^s of xxj^{ti} years.

Item I gyve and bequeth unto the said John my sone, the Posted bedd with all the furniture therunto belonging, as it standeth in the Chamber belowe, and the Table and Cobard with two joined forms in the Hall.

Item I gyve and bequeth to Richard my sone, one posted bedd with all the furniture therunto belonging as it standeth in the chamber over the Hall.

Item I gyve and bequeth unto Susane my dawgh-

ter, my Gese with all the Goslings that I now have
and all the laxen yarne that she latlie did spyne for
her to convert to her owne use, and also one bedd
with the furniture thereto belonging, as it standeth
in the Chamber over the Hall wch Bedd I have heretofore used to lye myself before my sickness that I
have tooke me.

Item I gyve and bequeth to Margaret my daughter,
one Trundle bedd with all the furniture therunto belonging, as it standeth in the said upper Chamb^r over
the Hall, with the new Coverlet.

Item I will, and my mynd is, and by this my Testament doe gyve unto my Executo's all my goods
Catells, Moveabl^s & unmoveabl^s whatsoever, except
all my Moveabl^s of houshold stuff, and other my
ymplements w^thin the inward house, to the paieng
my debts.

Item my will and mynd is that all my moveables
of houshold stuff not heretofore gyven in this my
will, I doe bequeth the houshold stuff, namely Bedding, lynnen, Wollen, Pewter, Brasse, Stoles, Cofers,
and Deirie vessels, and all other things in the Chief
Mansion or in set house, both in deirie hall Chambers and butrye, to be equallie pted amongest my
saide Children. John, Richard, Susane, Elizabeth,
& Margaret, by my supvis^er of this my last Will and
Testament, according to his discretion as he shall
think it most mete and convenient as my trust is in
hym.

Item I doe make and ordein the said John my
sone to be sole Execut'r of this my last will and Testament, and to see the same trewlie pformed and

executed, as I doe Co͞mgt my whole trust in hym, and as he shall answere before god at the laste daye.

Item I doe mak and ordein Henrye Spachett of Romberough aforesaid Supvisor of this my last Will and Testament, for his aide and trouble herein I gyve hym tenne Shillings of lawfull Englishe Money to be paied by my Executor.

In Witness to this my last will and Testament conteyning fyve shets of paper I have sett my mark and Redd in the pᵉ͠nce of Henrie Spachett, John Fuller and me Nicholas Wright.

Proved at Beecles, by John Lawrence, June 2, 1590. Deposited at Ipswich.

WILL OF RICHARD LAWRENCE OF RUMBURGH
Younger brother of John of Wisset, a copy of whose will is given above

Be it knowne unto all men by these pˢnts that I Richard Lorance being of good and pfitt Memorye, doe make and ordayne this my last will & Testament.

First I bequeathe my soule into thandes of God, and my body to be buryed.

First I am to receyve of my brother John Lorance the some of Thirtie Pounds of good and lawfull monye of Englande, at Mychaelm's next, more he hath of myne, a posted bedsted with a fether bedd and thinges longe thereto, a greate Chest, a Coffer and in the Coffer a paire of Vellwie Venicians,[1] a table, too stooles, twoo chayres, one Copper Kettle, three pewter dishes, one Salter booke, xij yards of

[1] Velvet hose.

blacke frieze, paier of gersie nether stockes, one paier of boots, twoo ewin bowes & a paier of arrowes I have at Pateriches, twoe pewter dishes, Francis Watling owe unto me fortie shillings, Richard Batila owe unto me for one paier of gersie netherstock v^s viij^d George Gorlinge owe unto me eight groats. James Reading owe unto me fortie shillinges. Robt. Darnye have in his hand vj^{li} of good and lawfull money of England. I am to receave for the house of Thomas Calie at Michaellmas next xvij^s and so xvij^s a quarter till Michaellmas next after. I owe unto Thomas Mose two & fortie shillings, I owe unto Bartholomew Warrant x^{li} to be payd at Michaellmas next. I owe to the saide Patericke aforenamed xxviij^s I owe unto Thomas Gooches wyfe tenn groates. I owe unto the wyfe of Tongett fifteen shillings. I will and my meanynge is that all my debts be paide and fullye satisfied, then I will that whatsoever Remaynethe I give unto my brothers, and systers to be equallie devyded amonge then ptt and part lyke. More I give unto the saide Patericke aforenamed, half a crowne of good and lawfull monie of England. I make my brother John Lorance my full & whole Executor to take my debts and to paye my debts and discharge my will. Whatsoever is in my Coffer unrehearsed, I will that it be devyded as in before saide. Thomas Howarde owe me tenn stillings.

Witnessith Willm Bamford and Robert Darnye.

Proved in the Bishops Court of Norwich, June 30, 1596.

WILL OF JOHN LAWRENCE OF WISSET

Grandfather of the emigrant ancestor of the same name

In the name of God amen, the second day of June in the year of o^r lord god 1606.

I John Lawrence of Wisset in the county of Suff. yeoman, being sick of body but of good and pfect Remembrannc, thanks be given unto Almighty God, doe ordeyn and make this my last will & testament in man^r & forme following. But principally I give and comend my soule into the hands of Allmighty god, desiring him most mcifully to Receyve the same into his mcy, & my body to be buryed where my christian Brethren thinck it mete.

Item I geve & bequeath unto Johan my wife my best bedstead & bed fully furnished as it standeth upon eyther of the chambers on the plor or on the kychen, to be chosen by Johan my wife after my decease or at the Inventory making.

Item I geve unto my s^d wife one little square table in the plo^r one little Chest, one Coffer standing in the same, one great back chayer, one great buffet-stole, & one Little one, two Cushins of Birdworke & one other small^r cushin, one little back chayer next unto the best standing in the hall, my little brasse pot, one paier of pothokes to the same one broad kettle, one skillet, next the best, one little Restiron, three Bowlles, one little frying panne, one latten ladle, one pewter candlestick, one Brazen candlestick, one washing maund, one close grate, one brasse morter, wth a pestell, one Joynd forme in the Hall, thre of my best Silver spones, all my hemp & towe, twoe bere firkins & one litle kettle.

Item I geve unto my said wife my warmyng panne, & my wicker chayer to have the use of for tearme of her lyfe & after her decease I doe geve & devyse them unto Henry Lawrence my sonne.

Item I geve and bequeath unto my s^d wife my best chest standing upon the chamber, to have the use of for terme of her lyfe & after her Decease I doe give it unto Robert Lawrence my sonne.

Item I geve & bequeath unto Henry Lawrence my sonne, my best bedstead & bed full furnished wth a paier of sheets to the same as it standeth in the parlo^r my great chest, one buffet stole, my cubbard & table wth a Joynd forme to the same, one great Chayer & my best back Chayer two of my best Bird work Chushins, & one little cushin, one coffer standing in the plor chamber, my Byble, twoe silver spoones, one of them to be of the best sort, and my best Brasen candlestick, one paier of Cobirons, one great Restiron, my best Caldren of Copper being Curbled, my best kettle next unto the Brass Kettle, my great skillet, my best Brass pot, one spitt, one luchpanne, one Trendle bedstead wth a flock bed, & a flocke bolster lying upon the bed in the kitchen, one blanckit, one of my best Coverings lying upon any of my Trendle beds, one paier of Holland sheets, & one Holland Band cloth wch were myne before I was marryed, one paier of Malt quernes, one paier of Musterd Quernes, two paier of sheets half a dozen table napkins, & one long Towell, my best Milk tub churne, one whay kealer, my best chese bord upon the Dayry chamber, one other Chese Bord belowe in the Dayry lying on the south syde of the s^d Dayrye wth the Trestles thereunto belonging, my best salting Keler, my best chese presse & my best chese salt and chese Brede thereunto belonging, six milck bolles & one Butter keler.

Item I geve & bequeath unto Robert Lawrence my sonne, my Lyvery bedstead standing in the kichen wth my best cov^{r}ing, Fether bed & Fether bolster pillow blanckits & one paier of sheets unbequeathed, my table in the kichen wth the Trestles thereunto belonging, one Joynd stole & one long forme standing in the Hall, one great chayer & one little chayer twoe Bird work cushins, one little cushin, twoe silver spones besydes his owne whereof one to be of the best sort, one pewter candlestick, one great old chest Standing in the plor chamber, twoe paire of sheets, half a dozen table napkins, & one little Towelle, one Caldron next unto the best, one Braw Brasse panne, one Lyttle kettle, one little skillet, one old Cubbard, two chese boards, six milck bolles, one chese presse one chese salt & Bread next unto the best.

Item I geve & bequeath unto Margery Whiting my daught^r one trendle bedstead with a fetherbed, a bolster, a pillow, a cov^{r}ing, a paier of sheets, twoe silver spones, & v^{lb} to be pd wthin half a yere after my decease.

Item I geve & bequeath unto Arthur Whiting my grandchild xx^s

Item I geve Roger Whiting my grandchild xx^s

Item I geve & bequeath unto Katherin Shacker my daughter one trendlebedstead, one litle fetherbed, one bolster, one Covering, one blankit, one paier of sheets, one pillowe, & two silver spoones.

Item I geve & bequeath unto the sd Katherin Shacker my daughter, the some of v^l to be pd her wthin one wholle yere next after my decease, if that my executors do think it may convenyently be spared.

Item I geve unto Katherin Shacker my grand-child xx^s.

Item I doe geve & devyse unto Johane my wife all my lynnen unbequeathed. Also I do devise & my woll & mynd is that all my pewter unbequeathed shalbe evenly devysed betwixt Johane my wife & Henry & Robert Lawrence my sonnes, be even por-cons. Also my will & mynd is that all the rest of my dayry vessels that is unbequeathed shall be evenly devyded amongst all my children.

All the rest of my moveable goods, chattels, uten-siles & Implements of household or household stuff, after my debts, legac^s pbats & funerall expenses satis-fied & discharged, viz. my Corn Haye, Cattles, Uten-sills & implements of household stuffs of what kynd, nature or quality soev^r they be of, being unbe-queathed, shalbe sold by my executors hereafter to be named, & the mony that shall increwe & aryse upon the sale of my s^d goods, I will & my mynd is that fower score pounds shalbe put out by my execu-tors hereafter to be named during the life of Johane my wife, & to paye unto the s^d Johane my wife the some of seven pounds yere & Yerely during her s^d naturall Lyfe, viz. at the feast of the Anñcacon & St. Michaell tharchangell by even porcons, The first paym thereof not to begyn untill the feast day of Thanñcacon of o^r lady next after it be Raysed by the

use or benefitt of the sd lxxx^{li} & after my wife's decease I will the sd lxxx^{li} shalbe & Remayne to Henry
& Robert Lawrence my sonnes, to be evenly devyded
betwyxt them wthin half yere next after my wife's
decease. Provyded always my will & mynd is that
if that Henry & Robt. Lawrence my sonnes, shall,
will & doe enter into bond unto Johane my wife
wth sufficient suretyes wthin twoe monthes next after
my deceasse, to pay unto Johane my wife the sd some
of vij^{li} yere & yearly in mann^r & forme as is Aforesd.
Then I will & my mynd is that Henry & Robt. Lawrence my sonnes shall have & take the sd lxxx^{li} after
such bond being entered unto the sd Johane my wife,
to their owne use, & then I will that my executors
shalbe acquitted and discharged of the sd lxxx^{li} as also
of the yerely Anuity unto Johane my wife lawfully by
the sd Johane my wife, Henry & Robt. Lawrence my
sonnes. The which if they will not, can not, or doe
not, discharg my executors, & my sonnes enter into
these bonds, as Aforesd, Then I will that my executors shall have & take the sd lxxx^{li} into there hands
to the use, as is Aforesd, untill half a yere next after
my wifes deceasse, & the Remaynder of mony that
shall Aryse by the sale of my goods after the lxxx^{li}
being taken out & my debts, legac^s pbats & funerall
expenses fully discharged, I will shall Remayne all
wholly to Henry Lawrence my sonne. Provided yet
further that if either of my sonnes doe dye wthout
heires & not marryed before they shall enter their
porcons, Then I will that the portion of mony to
them so geven being deceassed as aforesd, shall Remayne unto them lyving. Provyded alwayes that

my sonne lyving shall have for his pt xx^{li} & my daughters xx^{li} evenly devyded betwixt them & the rest of his porc̄on of goods to be evenly devyded amongst all my children & if that both my sonnes doe dye as Aforesd, that then their porc̄ons to Remayn unto my daughters & to their heires to be evenly devyded betwyxt them.

Item I doe ordeyn and make Thomas Morse of Frostenden my brother-in-law & Robt Mighells, of Wisset my executo^{rs}, to pform this my last will and testam^{t} according to the intent & true meanyng of the same.

In witnes whereof I have hereunt sett my hand the day & yere above written.

Signed Johis Lawrence. Delyv^{r}ed in the psence of Samuell Kake, Roger Mihells.

Proved 27 March 1607. Deposited at Ipswich.

MEMORANDA RELATING TO SEVERAL BRANCHES OF THE LAWRENCE FAMILY IN ENGLAND

John Lawrence of Ramsey, in Huntingdonshire, in the reign of Henry VIII., 1509–47, was the ancestor of the family at St. Ives, in the same county, of which Sir John Lawrence, the father of the President of the Council, was knighted at Windsor by King James I. previous to the coronation. It is from one of the younger sons of the President that the Lawrence family of Studley Park, and Hackfall in Yorkshire, are descended.

Another branch of the Lawrence family was seated at Heatingfordbury in the reign of Henry VII., and became allied to the great and illustrious, to the ambitious Dudley, Duke of Northumberland, to the Earl of Warwick, to Lord Guildford Dudley; the brilliant Leicester; and to Sir Philip Sidney. Lord Heytesbury, as heir of the Vernons, is the representative of this branch of the Lawrence family.

One of the peculiar features of the old city of London was the number of houses enriched with plasterwork, skilfully modelled in imitation of foliage, fruit, heads of men, and animals, and most prominent heraldic insignia. A house of this description bore on its front the turbot crest and arms of Lawrence, differenced by a canton, and was the residence of Sir John Lawrence, lord mayor in 1665; he was the grandson of a Fleming who left the Netherlands in the reign of Elizabeth and settled in Great Saint Helen's, where Sir John built a mansion not unworthy of Genoa, "la superba."

During the Revolutionary war no less than three hundred and twenty-four persons bearing the name of Lawrence (with many modifications of spelling) were in the military service of the Commonwealth of Massachusetts. Authority for this statement is found in the ninth volume of "Massachusetts Soldiers and Sailors in the War of the Revolution," a work published under the direction of the office of the Secretary of State. From this volume (p. 569) we take the following: "Samuel Lawrence, Groton; Corporal, Captain Henry Farwell's company of Minatemen, which marched on the alarm of April 19, 1775. Service six days. *Also* Captain Henry Farwell's (1st) company, Colonel William Prescott's (10th) regiment, muster-roll dated August 1, 1775, enlisted, April 25, 1775, service ninety eight days. *Also*, company return, probably [October, 1775]. Order for bounty, coat or its equivalent in money, dated Sewall's Point, November 16, 1775."

FROM THE "RECORDS OF THE CHURCH IN BRATTLE SQUARE, BOSTON" (1699–1872)

Admitted as Communicants:

Oct. 4, 1812. Amos Lawrence & Sarah Lawrence his wife. [By the Rev. Professor McKean.]

Dec. 6th. 1817. William and Susan Lawrence.

March 1st. 1829. Abbot & Catharine Lawrence.

Baptisms

Oct. 18, 1812. William Richards of Amos & Sarah Lawrence, by Rev. W. E. Channing.

April 17, 1814. William Boardman of William & Susan Lawrence.

June 29th, 1818. Lydia Elizabeth of William & Susan Lawrence.

Oct. 1st, 1820. Anna Bigelow of Abbot & Catharine Lawrence.

May 19th, 1822. James of Abbot & Catharine Lawrence.

June 1st, 1823. Susan Elizabeth of William & Susan Lawrence.

Sept. 21st, 1823. Mary Means of Amos & Nancy Lawrence.

March 28th, 1824. Mary Boardman of Wm. & Susan Lawrence.

Nov: 6, 1825. John Abbot of Abbot & Catharine Lawrence.

Sept. 17, 1826. Harriet Boardman of William & Susan Lawrence.

Jan. 7th, 1827. Robert Means of Amos and Nancy Lawrence.

July 1st, 1827. Timothy Bigelow of Abbott & Catharine Lawrence.

Aug. 2d 1829. Abbott of Abbott & Catharine Lawrence.

Aug. 16th 1829. Mary Frances of William & Susan R. Lawrence.

Decr 30, 1832. Catharine Bigelow Lawrence, child of Abbot & Catharine Lawrence, by Profr J. G. Palfrey.

Marriage

June 5, 1811. Amos Lawrence & Sarah Richards. By Rev. Jos. S. Buckminster.

Deaths

June 29th, 1818. Lydia Elizabeth Lawrence, Æt. 14 days; infantile.

Jan. 14th, 1819. Sarah Lawrence; Consumption.

Aug. 22d, 1819. Sarah, infant daughter of Wm. Lawrence, 4 days; lung fever; baptized by Dr. Ware.

Dec. 8th, 1828. Mary Means Lawrence; 5; lung fever.

FROM THE RECORD IN THE FAMILY BIBLE OF AMOS LAWRENCE OF BOSTON

Amos Adams Lawrence, born at Boston, July 31, 1814. Baptized by Revd John T. Kirkland in Brattle Street Church.

Susanna Lawrence, born at Boston, May 23d, 1817. Baptized at Dedham by Rev. Joshua Bates.

MORTGAGE DEED OF THE GROTON HOMESTEAD

In the month of April, A. D. 1807, Amos Lawrence attained his majority, and having finished his apprenticeship in Groton, he came to Boston to seek his fortune. To enable him to start in business with some capital, his father mortgaged the home-farm for one thousand dollars, and loaned the money to his son. Following is a copy of the original document:

Know all Men by these Presents, That I, Samuel Lawrence of Groton, in the County of Middlesex, and Commonwealth of Massachusetts, Esquire; in consideration of one thousand dollars to me paid by Benjamin Lee, of Cambridge, in the said County, Gentleman, the Receipt whereof I do hereby acknowledge, do hereby give, grant, sell and convey unto the said Benjamin Lee, his heirs and assigns forever, a certain parcel of Land lying in said Groton, about one mile from the meeting-house in said Town, with all the buildings thereon; said parcel of land is the same whereon the said Samuel now lives, and contains fifty acres, be the same more or less, bounded as follows, to wit; easterly on the highway leading by the dwelling-house in which the said Samuel now lives, southerly on the highway leading over Nashua river, so called, to Tarbell's Mills; westerly and northerly on Joseph Tufts' land, with all the privileges, [etc.] To Have and to Hold the afore-granted premises to the said Benjamin Lee, his Heirs and Assigns, to his and their Use and Behoof forever. And do covenant with the said Benjamin Lee, his Heirs and Assigns, that I am lawfully seized in Fee of the afore-granted Premises; That they are free of all Incumbrances; That I have good Right to sell and convey the same to the said Benjamin Lee; And that I will warrant and defend the said Premises to the said Benjamin Lee, his Heirs and Assigns forever, against the lawful Claims and Demands of all Persons.

Provided nevertheless, that if the said Samuel Lawrence, his Heirs, Executors, or Administrators, pay to the said Benjamin Lee, his Heirs, Executors, Administrators or Assigns, the Sum of one thousand dollars in Gold or silver coin, in three years from the date hereof, with interest annually; then this Deed, as also a certain bond, bearing even date with these Presents, given by the said Samuel Lawrence to the said Benjamin, to pay the same Sum with interest as aforesaid, at the Time aforesaid, shall both be void; otherwise shall remain in full Force.

In witness whereof, I the said Samuel Lawrence have hereunto set my Hand and Seal this first Day of September in the Year of our Lord One thousand eight hundred and seven.

Signed, sealed and
delivered in Presence of us,

WILLIAM LAWRENCE
OLIVER WENTWORTH } SAMUEL LAWRENCE. [Seal.]

Middlesex ss. Groton, Sept. 1st, 1807. Then the above-named Samuel Lawrence personally appeared and acknowledged the above Instrument to be his free Act and Deed; before me,

JAMES PRESCOTT { Just. of
Peace. }

Middlesex ss. Cambridge, 2 Sept^r, 1807. Received and Entered in the Registry of Deeds, Book 175, Page 217.

Attest,   SAM BARTLETT, Reg.

POSTSCRIPT

Written by Sarah Richards Lawrence, in a letter from Amos Lawrence to his brother Abbott, then in England; dated at Boston, May 19, 1815:

MY DEAR BROTHER, — If I were not cumber'd about many things, I should before this have written you something like a letter. Amos has left a blank space, which I readily fill to assure you that you are not forgotten by me, and that I most heartily wish for your return, even before I hear of your arrival. Return soon, and purchase me a pair of ear-rings, answerable for your own taste. The price not exceeding ten dollars. Thus you will oblige

Your affectionate sister,

S. L.

MEMORANDUM

The following is taken from a fly-leaf of the first sales-book of Amos Lawrence, wherein the first item is entered under the date Dec. 17, 1807.

Amos Lawrence's first book of sales, commenced at his store at No. 31 Cornhill (now 24 Washington Street), July, 1810, in which each day's sales are entered in detail, and the *first* entry was for *four cotton handkerchiefs* to a Cape Cod man, which proved the foundation of an extremely profitable business for the whole period of my continuing in the retail trade. This man seemed interested in me as a young beginner, and came a few days afterward with a number of his brother fishermen, and from that time they were in the habit of coming to me for their dry goods, under the belief that I would deal fairly by them, in which they were *never* disappointed. I never pretended to keep a " cheap shop," but always professed to give them a *fair equivalent for the money*, and whatever was not satisfactory to them might be returned and the money refunded; in *all* my experience with them I have no recollection of any such call from any one of them. This fact shows how true that maxim is that " Honesty is the best Policy." The whole of the Wellfleet and Chatham people were my customers for years.

Amos Lawrence.

Boston, July, 14, 1840.

ANOTHER FLY-LEAF MEMORANDUM

My brother William had overworked himself on the farm, and his health was so far impaired that he contemplated taking the office of Deputy Sheriff, which he could have had; but before doing so, he came, on the ninth day of October, 1809, to make me a visit of a few days, and has remained here to this date.

Amos Lawrence.

October 9, 1842.

CAPTAIN AMOS LAWRENCE [1716–1785]

The following is a " List of Officers Commissioned for ye 6th Regimt of Militia in ye County of Middlesex Inft, 1762."

John Bulkeley Esqr, Colonel.
James Prescott, Lieut. Col.
Phineas Gates, Major.

1st Company in Groton.
Amos Lawrence, Captain.
Joseph Sheple, Lieut.
Thomas White, Ensign.

2nd Company in Groton.
Abel Lawrence, Captain.
Nathll Parker, Lieut.
Robert Parker, Ensign.

Mass. Archives, 99 : 33.

DEACON SAMUEL LAWRENCE

In the year 1798 a direct tax on dwelling-houses and lands was levied by the United States Government, and Deacon Samuel Lawrence served as principal assessor for the district including the towns of Groton, Shirley, and Dunstable. His associates were Samuel Rockwood and Jacob Patch of Groton, Joshua Longley of Shirley, and Isaac Wright of Dunstable.

EXTRACT FROM A LETTER

Written by Baron Justus von Liebig (the distinguished scientist and professor of Chemistry in the University of Giessen, Germany) to a resident of

Cambridge, Mass., and published in the "Boston Courier," Jan., 1848. The letter has reference to the gift of fifty thousand dollars to Harvard College, by the Hon. Abbott Lawrence, to found the Scientific School, which was named in his honor.

" Although I have not the honor to know personally Mr. Abbott Lawrence, I will venture to desire you to express to him my profound respect and esteem. Men of his stamp are rare gems, and fortunate is the land that possesses them. His magnificent gift founds a scientific institution which is a necessity of the times, and which is destined to spread the greatest benefactions and blessings over your whole land. By what means, in this day, can these be more successfully promoted than by the spread of useful knowledge, the cultivation and development of the spirit by which new ideas are to be brought out and rendered practical? All progress rests upon this. Empiricism does not overstep its confines, but science creates the *knowing*, and prepares the way for the *cunning*, and gives to otherwise stagnant sap both life and motion.

" His letter, which you sent to me in the newspaper, filled me with the highest respect and the most profound astonishment. Blessings upon this noble man! His name will live in the memory of the latest generation.

"GIESSEN, December 12, 1847."

A MINUTE-MAN [1]

BY MARY FOSDICK

CHAPTER I

Captain Amos Lawrence was an estimable farmer in New England, who was born in the first quarter of the eighteenth century, and at a suitable age married Miss Abigail Abbott. She brought him as part of her dowry various handsome pewter articles, among them several large plates, or platters, on which her initials were stamped or cut, as was the fashion in her day, a handsome hall clock with mahogany case and brass face, and other articles of household furniture; though, as her father was also a farmer, it is not probable that she brought Captain Lawrence very much else beside the bedding which every bride expected to provide. As to her personal attractions I have no means of knowing. Though born in Boston's neighborhood, Captain Amos Lawrence made his way to Groton, a thriving village farther inland, and there our minute-man was born in the spring of 1754. He was a bright boy, and "did well," as people said, both as a son and brother at home and as a scholar in school; and when he had exhausted the best educational advantages the place then afforded, he went to work on a small farm, which he took on a mortgage, hoping probably to make it profitable enough to enable him to support a wife.

[1] Under this title is here given a story of Major Samuel Lawrence and the members of his family.

THE LAWRENCE FARM, GROTON, MASS., 1837

Whether he had in mind the lady whom he afterward married, I am unable to state, but in his twenty-first year he became engaged to a handsome girl, a year younger than himself, whose acquaintance he probably made while visiting his grandparents Lawrence, as her father lived in a town (Concord) adjoining the one in which his mother, Miss Abbott, had been born (Lexington); so we may naturally suppose that he desired to make the farm as successful as possible. His parents had other children, and having given him the benefit of the best educational facilities in Groton, could not afford to do more, though they must have realized that such a boy as he would have been glad to go through college, as at least two of his contemporaries did, and would be an honor to any profession, for he was beloved and respected by his fellow-townsmen as few young men of his age were, and was as fond of books as if he had been a rich Tory's son.

He was steadily making his way toward being known as a successful farmer, and toward the goal of his hopes, — marriage with his handsome sweetheart, — when the times began to grow so troublous that almost every one looked sober, and asked what was coming to the Colonies in the near future. The residents of Groton were always glad to meet Samuel Lawrence, with his bright, cheerful face, alert manner, and hearty laugh. " Don't be discouraged," he would say, " If the British want a taste of American powder, let them have it. They'll not want a great many," and he was one of the first to assist in recruiting a company of " minute-men," of which he was an officer. These minute-men were to be ready to start at a moment's warning for the seat of war, wherever it was, whenever they were notified that the British had begun to show fight. Until then, he, like many another, was a peaceful farmer, eating his bread in the sweat of his brow; and he was looking forward to building a nest for the handsome Susanna Parker, who on her part was spinning and weaving sheets and pillow-cases, as well as blankets, for its lining. He was so popular in the town that he had no difficulty in persuading others to enlist with him, and no one of them grudged him the titles or offices he held, though many of them were older men than he; and after his day's work they were drilled in a large barn belonging to one of them.

Major Samuel always had a pleasant smile and encouraging word for every one, which was remembered in after years by his townsmen.[1] " I declare for 't," one old man said years afterward, " ef Major Sam's v'ice and laugh did n't keep our hearts up, when we could n't hardly believe that the British soldiers would n't ride over us with their fine horses and uniforms, and their harnsome guns.   But he 'd allers say, ' Come now, Mr. ——, you are as good as a Tory soldier, any day, and, if I ain't as tall as Goliah, I 'm a servin' the same Lord Almighty that *David* was, so let 's go ahead, and let 'em see what Americans are made on, when the time comes.   You 've got a wife, and I 've got a sweetheart, and we don't need to fight but one day at a time.'   He was a short man, but we never thought o' that, his soul was so big.   He 'd a

---

[1] Samuel Lawrence was a corporal at the time of the Lexington alarm, and by successive promotions attained the rank of major.

shared his last crust with his men, and I only hope that when I git my discharge in this world, I shall be 'llowed ter be where I can serve with him in t'other." This was said by an octogenarian after Major Lawrence's death, and the respect in which the latter was held by the whole community increased as time went on. Whatever he did was done well, and he did a great variety of things, too, in the course of his life. He could go but seldom to see his lady-love; but when he did go he made good use of his eyes and ears, and for that reason his farm bade fair to become one of the best in the region. He had in his employ a boy, or young man, eight years younger than himself, in whom he had begun to feel interested in the first place because he seemed to have so few friends, his mother having died while Major Sam was finishing his education. When he heard that Oliver Wentworth's mother was dead, and that there was talk of apprenticing Oliver to some one, he asked his father, upon returning from school, if he would not take the boy to help him on the farm, and he brought forward so many arguments to prove that Oliver would prefer working on a farm, and that his mother would have preferred it for him, that it would be better to take the few pounds that her effects would bring and put them into something that would benefit Oliver,[1] that at length Mr. Lawrence said, " Well, Sam, have your own way. If he does well, all right, but if he does n't, he shall be apprenticed to Mr. Smith, the wheelwright." Oliver

---

[1] Whom he would employ himself as soon as he had a farm of his own.

never was apprenticed to Mr. Smith, however. He was a sturdy New England boy, and he was faithful to his duties, working with the better will because Mr. Lawrence had told him what had led him to take him. He was also much interested in Major Sam's love affairs when the young man made a confidant of the boy, then in his fourteenth year. When Major Sam — though he was only " Mr. Sam " then — took the small farm on a mortgage, Oliver's first question was, "Ain't ye goin' ter let me work for ye, Mr. Sam?" (or perhaps it was plain " Sam " until his employer had a military title, though of this I can only surmise), and when he was told that that was a part of the agreement with Mr. Lawrence, Sr., who was wont to keep his word, he said, "I'll stick to you then, as long as I live, unless you tell me to cut," which he did. He was at first quite content to attend to the farm while Mr. Sam was collecting his recruits; but at length he requested so earnestly to be allowed to "jine the militie," so as to be able to accompany him into the army, that Major Sam overlooked the fact that he was too young to be enrolled as a soldier, and told him that if he himself went to fight he would take him as a personal attendant, which was all that Oliver desired. The days went on, and Major Sam drilled his men in the large barn and kept himself and them informed of the condition of things in Boston and elsewhere so far as was possible; though we may suppose that with his usual modesty he would ask the older men for whatever information they could give, before imparting his, and that when theirs had been received he said what he had to say as briefly and simply as possible, before going about the work of drilling his men.

When he and Oliver were engaged in shelling or husking corn, or in chopping or piling wood on the small wood lot belonging to the farm, he would express to the lad his opinions regarding matters and things in general, thus gaining more and more of Oliver's confidence and affection; neither of which was ever withdrawn, and both of which were expressed when Oliver was nearing his fourscore years and ten, if not later.

Letters were few and far between in those days, but Samuel Lawrence managed to send a letter to his sweetheart now and then, and to receive some from her in return, in which she could give him bits of information as to the state of things nearer the metropolis, as well as in her own home. But the winter passed, and no blow was struck by the British which was felt to warrant the calling out of the militia. March went by, and April came, when one day as the young minute-man was busy ploughing, while Oliver guided the one horse, one of the selectmen of Groton rode up to the fence and shouted, " Samuel, notify your men. The British are coming." The young minute-man did not wait for words. He drove the plough deeper into the furrow, saying, " Oliver, free the horse, and then go as fast as you can to tell my men in the town to meet on the Common, while I notify those farther off." Oliver went, thankful that he could trust his young employer's promise to let him accompany him into the war; and as the selectman had given a general warning, the bells of the meeting-house

fronting the Common were ringing when the last man
had been told and the captain came to take command
of his little company.

It has been said that Colonel Prescott, who lived farther from the seat of war, passed them before his
brother, who was chairman of the selectmen of Groton,
with his fellow-selectmen, had given out all their arms
and ammunition; but if so, there are two reasons that
may readily account for the statement, for some of the
annals of the Lawrence family distinctly say that " in
less than two hours after the selectmen notified Samuel, he and his men were on the march for Concord,"
and Colonel Prescott could scarcely have called out his
Pepperell troops and marched them to Groton — five
miles — in less time than that, unless they were already equipped when the messenger from Concord
reached Pepperell. But local history says that the
colonel himself did not wait for his men, but order-
ing some of those in Pepperell to take word to the
rest, as well as to the minute-men in an adjoining
town, he himself at once started for Concord.   As he
was mounted, *he* would naturally pass the Groton men
before they were ready to begin the march. Another
reason, if the Pepperell men did pass through Groton
while arms, etc., were being distributed, why they
might have done so is that Groton had another company of minute-men, commanded by another man, an
older man than Samuel Lawrence, who may not have
been able to notify his command as speedily as Samuel notified the one in which he was an officer. However that may have been, it is declared by one of his
grandsons, on the authority of the minute-man's third

son, that he and his men were on the march in less than two hours, and as many of the men lived on out-lying farms it must have taken time to notify them. The ploughshare was turned into a sword, and the man who had so lately been a peaceful farmer was on the way to defend his country in her need.

The battle at Lexington and the fight at Concord were both over when he reached the latter place, and though Susanna Parker lived close to one of the roads through which they passed to join Colonel Prescott, the young minute-man did not turn to the right hand or to the left. As he lacked a few days of being twenty-one years old on that memorable day, we may imagine how great a trial it must have been for him to pass so near without being able to tell her that he was on his way to protect her; and Oliver's first real service for Captain Samuel after they left Groton *may* have been to carry a message for him to Mr. Parker's house. But if such were the case, no record of the fact has come down to the writer of this little story.

CHAPTER II

Susanna Parker was called a very handsome girl, and her portrait, painted when she was more than fourscore years old by the best portrait painter known in America at that day, shows handsome, reg-ular features and a rather stately bearing. There were later three copies of this portrait, one of which was in the possession of her daughter Elizabeth, a second owned, I *think*, by Hon. Abbott Lawrence's family, and about the third I am uncertain. The original was, I am told, the one in the possession of Mrs. Mary Woodbury, having been given or bequeathed to her by Mr. Amos Lawrence, for whom it was painted. I am under the impression that a silhouette, which I frequently saw in the house of one of the latter gentleman's sons was that of the minute-man, but I cannot be positive. It gave the profile and shoulders, with the hair drawn back and braided in a queue, and it showed regular features and a benign expression. I was so sure that it was Captain Samuel Lawrence, that I never asked about it, and it never occurred to me to doubt about the matter until I undertook to write this little narrative, which I wish to have true to facts.

Mrs. Lawrence's sons all describe her as having been a handsome and dignified woman, and it is easy to believe that she might have been a belle in the place where she was born. Of her birthplace and early connections I can say little that has not already been said, but she had so many friends after her marriage that it is probable she had a great many in her girlhood. Certainly she was very much in love with the young minute-man, in whose pathway she never put any stumbling-blocks. After he passed her by with his company, her mind was busy while her hands were spinning and weaving, and when some time later the question was raised as to how the town where she lived was to obtain its mail, she said, "Father, I can be mail-carrier, if you will let me." Mr. Parker laughed. He was a practical man and did not expect grapes of thorns, so how could he expect that the British forces would allow one of the provincials to go unmolested through their lines, even if it were a young and handsome woman? "Nonsense, Susanna," he replied; "your wanting Sam Lawrence's letters is not going to persuade the British to allow you to pass their lines and go through Charlestown into Boston, and you would not get a sight of Sam, for he is not anywhere near Boston."

"That is true enough, father," replied Susanna, when he had ceased speaking; "but will you let me take old Whitefoot and let Billy go with me on Mr. Savage's Peggy, if Mr. Savage will lend her to us, to see the commander of the British forces? I'll do the rest."

"Do you mean it, Susanna?" asked Mr. Parker, looking at her in astonishment.

"Did you ever know me to say anything I did *not* mean, father?" was her reply, and her father yielded.

"Perhaps it is just as well that you should not know my whole plan, father," she said as she thanked him. "It may save you some trouble sometime to be able to say that you did not; but I'll bring the mails." And the next day she started for Boston to interview the British commander there. No one spoke unpleasantly to her, though more than one man, as she passed through the country between her home and her destination, asked her if she knew that the British had cut everybody off from Boston.

"We know it," she replied; "but our business is urgent." Her brother Billy was a nice-looking boy of fourteen, and very proud to be the esquire of his handsome sister; but when they reached the British

lines and were ushered into the presence of the re-
doubtable commander, he felt that he should not
have been equal to the occasion, as she was.

"We have a relative living in Boston," she said,
giving the name of an aunt of her mother's, I believe,
who was old, not rich, and apparently not in a position to do anything to aid the provincials or to injure
the British cause, "and we came to ask you for a permit to go unmolested through your lines to visit her
sometimes, as she is old and lonely, and naturally
feels very sad at being cut off from her friends."

"What is your name?" inquired the officer.

"Susanna Parker," she replied, "and this is my
brother William. We live in the town of Concord."

"Ah!" said the officer, "I suppose your father and
the rest of the family are among the men who are
preparing to fight us whenever we make an onset."

"No, sir," replied Nancy; "my father is an invalid,
and this is my only brother." She did not think it
necessary to state that her father's invalidism had
been caused by a British bullet.

"Hum," said the officer, "I can give you one pass,
but it would be too much of a risk to pass two at
the same time. I will make out a permit for Miss
Susanna Parker of Concord, and whenever you
choose to present it, you will have safe transit through
our lines. If you meet with any disrespect from the
Regulars at any time, be so good as to notify me
and I will attend to the matter."

"Thank you, sir," said Susanna, making him a
dignified curtsey; "good-day, sir." And from that
time on, through snow or over ground that was often

frozen solid, twice every week until the evacuation of Boston she rode alone through the British lines to reach the house of her aged aunt. The mail from the village was sewed in small pockets made in the riding skirt which she wore, the pockets being so arranged in the facing that they could easily be sewed in and ripped out, and not likely to attract attention even if she were examined, which she never was. These letters were left to be taken in charge by a man who was interested in the American cause, who could come to the house of the old lady without exciting suspicion; and the mail for the residents of Concord was sewed into the pockets and carried back, while the few newspapers were concealed, I think, under the "postilion," as it was afterward called, of the riding jacket which she wore. She always said that she never received a disrespectful look or rough word from either British or American soldier or citizen, though she was several times stopped in Charlestown to be *smoked* or fumigated, lest she might disseminate the small-pox, of which there were some cases there. It was in this way that the people of her native town were kept informed of the progress of the war for some months, and there were doubtless many who had husbands or brothers or sons, if not lovers, in the army, who must have blessed her for her courage. Certainly her children, grandchildren, and great-grandchildren must all have felt proud to remember it, and to realize what her personal dignity must have been at the age of twenty or twenty-one. She was always a very reserved woman, never known to kiss any one outside of her own family, and rarely those within it, for she said that kissing always reminded her of Judas Iscariot. When told of the engagement of one of her granddaughters when she herself was nearly eighty-four, she said, shaking her head, —

"It is very shallow to be engaged so young!"

"Why, grandma," said the young lady, "how old were *you* when *you* were engaged?"

"I was — twenty — and a little over," replied Mrs. Lawrence with dignity, though she hesitated a little, and she made no more demur regarding the present engagement when her granddaughter responded, —

"And I am twenty-one and a half, grandma."

She was true as steel, and perhaps her reserve only made her more deeply loving; for none of her children ever felt any lack of the truest affection, which was returned without stint, her sons delighting to recall the fact that she had a habit of coming to their rooms to kneel beside their beds for a moment of silent prayer, when she supposed them to be sleeping.

She did not see her lover between the time of the battle of Lexington and some period in 1777, more than two years later, though he was, until the battle of Bunker Hill, with Colonel Prescott's troops, not many miles from her home; but his letters kept her informed as to his health, and so far as possible as to what he was doing.

Meanwhile the British forces were steadily increasing and making up their minds that victory would certainly be theirs. How could those raw recruits with small means, and more knowledge of the plough and the hoe than of gun and sword, hope to overcome

King George's well-trained troops, with their modern equipments for war, their handsome uniforms, and the king's treasury to back them? And how could they dream that their ammunition could hold out against such men as Howe and Gage? So they were coiling themselves like some huge reptile ready to make the spring which should be fatal to the poor little provincial army, which could hardly hope for many reinforcements while the other Colonies were beginning to be in danger from British soldiers and British ships. And meanwhile, too, Susanna Parker was spinning and weaving for the men who were fighting, instead of for her future home. Her letters to her lover were not such as to depress the young minute-man, and must have brought comfort to his heart, as he recalled their words while on the march, or trying to sleep when encamped somewhere for a night.

CHAPTER III

As the days passed until the 17th of June, Samuel Lawrence remained with Colonel Prescott's troops, and on the morning of that day their adversaries saw with amazement what the " raw recruits " had accomplished in the way of intrenchments in a single night. They were greatly dismayed as well as surprised, but they were not daunted, for they came steadily on to receive the terrible fire of the Americans under the command of Colonel Prescott. Samuel Lawrence was one of his aids, and it was from his daughter Mary Lawrence, who was born in 1790, and who was alert and active until her sixty-ninth year, at which time the writer was sixteen, that the following information was received, though it was also given to her some years later by one of Major Lawrence's grandsons, who was then a man of sixty one or two, and who remembered his grandfather well, having passed much time in the old homestead in his youth. Samuel Lawrence and another man stood beside Colonel Prescott almost throughout the battle, steadying him on his horse, as he was feeling ill and afraid to trust himself to keep his seat, though his eye was steady, and he gave his orders in a cool, commanding voice. There have since his day been those who tried to prove that General Putnam, being his superior in rank, must have been in command at Bunker Hill, and as a compromise some writers of history have said that both were practically in command; but the writer, who has known personally descendants of both gallant commanders, and has no reason for partisan feeling, can only say that Samuel Lawrence's daughter heard from his own lips that as Massachusetts was not the only one of the Colonies where there was trouble, General Putnam did not reach the field of action with his reinforcements until the battle was practically decided, and that when Colonel Prescott offered to relinquish command, he said, " The fight is as good as over, and you had better hold your men," which, it seems to the writer, reflects much more honor on the two officers, as well as on the battle itself, than does the idea that there was no particular head, but some parts of the battle were controlled by one, and some by another. Samuel Lawrence's grandson, when a man of somewhat over sixty, as has been said, remarked to the writer, " I don't say anything about it, for I number both Prescotts and Putnams among my friends, but that is what my grandfather always said; " — and as he was a boy of thirteen, and his father a man of forty-one when Samuel Lawrence died, they had every reason to know.

After the battle of Bunker Hill, Samuel Lawrence was one of the men of whom Washington took command under the Old Elm in Cambridge, and in 1777 he was granted a brief furlough, when he visited his sweetheart.

" Mr. Parker," he said to her father, " I wish that you would allow Susanna and me to be married before I go back to the army. We have been engaged more than two years and a half, and she is willing to marry me now if you will consent."

" And what is to become of her while you are fighting ? " inquired Mr. Parker. " You do not expect to take her with you ? "

" No," said the young lover, " by no means, Mr. Parker. I expect that you will go on letting her live with you until I come to claim her; but I should like to think of her as my wife if I should be shot by a British bullet."

Mr. Parker considered, and finally consented, saying, " Well, Susanna, you might as well be Sam's widow as his forlorn damsel, if he should lose his life," and the wedding took place, though the minute-man went almost from the marriage vows to rejoin the army; for while the service was in progress the alarm was given summoning all officers and privates back to their posts. This was in the latter part of July, 1777, and though later he was given another brief furlough, that second one was the last time he saw his wife until the term of his enlistment was over in 1778, at which period the battle-ground was no longer in Massachusetts, having taken to the south, so to speak. Upon returning to Massachusetts, he went at once to Mr. Parker's, no doubt with his heart full of longing for a sight of his wife and the son who had been born to him in the autumn of 1778.

" Well, Mr. Parker," said he, after giving his accoutrements to Oliver to carry to his room, " I have come to claim my family."

" Yes," replied Mr. Parker; " but you don't expect to camp out, do you? Where are you going to put your family, Sam?"

" That is the question," answered the major. I have preferred to think that he was called "major" by his fellow-townsmen until he was made an officer in the church at Groton, and received the more peaceful title of deacon, which at that day was considered a very honorable one by the men of New England. It gave them the right to advise the pastor; to pass the bread and wine when there was "a distribution of the Lord's Supper," as they expressed it; to pass the long-handled contribution boxes down the many pews; and to rap over the head any drowsy or inattentive boys, if it came in their way. The writer can remember those contribution boxes in Groton, though they were superseded by smaller ones when she was in her teens. The deacons walked solemnly to the communion table, a

common mahogany one such as might be seen in
the hall or parlor of some of the better houses,
and took those boxes, from just where she never
discovered, though apparently from some place beside the pulpit stairs by which the minister had
ascended to the wide reading desk, which was a few
feet, three or four at the least, from the long sofa on
which at some great occasion, like an "installation,"
as it was called, four or five reverend gentlemen
might be seen seated together, while one or two more
occupied chairs placed at the head of the two short
flights of stairs. Then with the boxes the deacons
went each to one side of the church and began by
presenting his box to the person at the inner end of
the front pew, whom the long handle easily reached,
then drawing it back to the next, and then to the
next, until each occupant had made a deposit; and
unless they were children, woe betide those who did
not put a coin or a bill in it, for the deacon waited so
long and patiently that people in the other pews
took note of the one who failed to make his or her
contribution. After visiting all the pews in the body
of the church in this manner, the deacons returned
up the aisles, presenting the boxes, which a wag of
a later day called "corn-poppers," to those in the
wall-pews, and after the last ones had been visited,
took them to the communion table, upon which they
were placed with great solemnity, and the deacons
returned to their own places, locking themselves
carefully into their pews, after the manner of all
the other worshippers, with the brass button which
was on the outside of the door. But this was long

after Deacon Lawrence's day, though it was in the same building in which he was given his office. We must go back to him, as he said, "That is the question" to Mr. Parker.

"Of course my farm is run out," he went on, "and my tools have rusted. I left my horse with one of the neighbors, who agreed to look after my cow, and the house was not fit for Susanna and the baby; but I have saved up my pay, and I will go to Groton to-morrow and look about for a proper house for them. Perhaps I can exchange my farm there for a better one, with some cash in addition to it; for some of my men had farms which were carried on by their sons or brothers while they were away. Will you be ready to leave your home here, Susanna, as soon as I can find one in Groton?"

"My home is wherever you think it best to make it, Sam," was the answer, and in due time the young couple, with their baby and Oliver Wentworth, began their housekeeping on a pleasant old farm, in a comfortable dwelling. There was land enough to enable the captain to go on in the peaceful career which he had laid out for himself as a boy, and there his second son, Samuel, was born, in 1781. A third son was born in 1783, and baptized William, and in 1786 a fourth one came and received his grandfather's name of Amos; and in them all Oliver Wentworth felt the deepest interest, while for them all he had the strongest affection. He doubtless mourned most sincerely, too, when Samuel, the second son, — and the only one of the minute-man's sons who did not outlive boyhood, — died.

" Oliver," said Major Lawrence one day, " do you know how to make shoes ? "

" Yes," replied Oliver; " I worked in a shoe-shop quite a spell afore mother died."

" Well," said the major, " I am thinking that if my children are to have shoes, I shall have to make them myself. I had to go to so much expense to stock the farm with tools and cattle, to say nothing of horse and vehicles, that I have n't made much headway."

" I can make 'em some, if you 'll git the hides," responded Oliver; " but they won't be very harnsome ones."

" I expect to help you," said Major Lawrence. " I want you to show me how, Oliver. I can get the hides, and you must tell me what else we shall need."

" Lasts," replied Oliver, " and awls and hammers, and lapstones, and luther aprons, with some coarse cloth for linin's, and shoe-thread, and I guess that's about all. I k'n make the wax and pegs myself."

" Very well," said the major. " Then I 'll be a shoe-maker in the winter, Oliver, and you can help me. We shall have to have lasts for all the boys, and I guess I 'll have to make my own boots, if not shoes for Mrs. Lawrence."

And after that nearly all the shoes worn by the former minute-man's family, and even some of those worn by his neighbor's children, were made by him and his devoted assistant until the close of the century, if not later. In 1788 a girl arrived, and was baptized Susanna for her mother; and then Major Lawrence began to think that the house in which they lived was hardly adapted to the needs of his family. "Susanna," he said one day, "this place has done very well so long as we had only boys, but if we are going down the line with a company of girls, it strikes me that we might do better."

"Yes, Samuel," replied Mrs. Lawrence, who, after having a son Sam, had begun calling her husband by the more dignified full name.

"I was thinking," went on Major Lawrence, "of the old Bolter place, where there are already so many fine trees. How would you like to live there? It is in another district, but the school is close by, and the children will have a long walk to go to school from here."

"Yes, Samuel," answered Mrs. Lawrence; "I have often thought of all you say, but can we afford to build?"

"Yes," replied the major; "I have been saving up all I could with that in my mind. Everybody does n't care as much for trees as we do, and that place is too good for some of the farmers to be able to buy it, and too far from the village for the people who could afford it. If you say so, I will make an offer for it, and begin to plan for a new house, so that we may sell this place as soon as possible. I shall build a shoe-shop in connection with it, too, so that Oliver and I can have a fire in the winter, and not need to be in your way in the house."

So the land was bought and the house built, and the family, consisting of parents and children, Oliver Wentworth and a capable colored woman named Maria Hazard, who, though young, was strong and willing, moved into it, greatly to the comfort and convenience of all concerned; for it was well built, with fine cellar, dairy, and outhouses, besides accommodation for future sons and daughters. One of the latter, who was afterward my informant regarding many of the facts contained in this narrative, appeared on the scene in 1790, and was baptized Mary. She told me that her father never interfered with the discipline of his children, saying that their mother understood such things better than he did, and that he was always an affectionate father, as well as an indulgent one so far as his means would allow. The children, as fast as they were old enough, began attending the district school, and from that went to the Academy, which he had himself been instrumental in establishing on a safe basis; but he must often have felt harassed with his small means and growing family. In 1792 a fifth son was born, and received his grandmother Lawrence's maiden name of Abbott. In 1796 a third daughter was born, and was baptized Eliza, and, in 1801, came a sixth son, who was named Samuel, the first Samuel having died early, as has been stated. At this time Major Lawrence's son Luther had graduated from Harvard College, and was a handsome young man, with the dignified stature and bearing of his mother, as well as the fair skin and fine large blue eyes of both parents. Indeed, all the five sons and two daughters, who lived until the writer's day, were considered exceptionally fine looking, and had what some called "the Lawrence blue eye," which was transmitted to their descendants, of whom I have known personally three generations. All but two of the minute-man's children were tall and finely proportioned, and those two, Mr. Amos Lawrence, and the daughter, Mrs. Mary Lawrence, whom I knew best, and who was born in 1790, were well proportioned, though one was below the medium height for a man, and the other below that for a woman. Both had remarkably fine profiles, and were so full of interest in their kind that their expression was most attractive.

CHAPTER IV

"Father," said Mr. Luther Lawrence, after returning from his last year in college, "I have made up my mind to study law with Hon. Timothy Bigelow, if you do not object."

"We will talk it over, — your mother and I," replied the major, who was still busy making shoes for his children in the winter, though his eldest son had been promoted to city-made boots and clothing ; and the result was that the young man went into Mr. Bigelow's law office, from which in due time he moved into one of his own. Not long after opening his own office, he built a nice old colonial house which still exists in Groton, though since his day it has been considered large enough to accommodate two families. But Major Lawrence could not afford to send another son through college, though, as has been said, both sons and daughters received the education gained in Groton Academy, and he was probably not sorry that his third son, Mr. William Lawrence, had a taste for farming, and was contented to assist him on the farm after leaving the Academy, in or near 1800. Mr. Amos Lawrence, the next in age, said, when it was his turn to graduate from an academic course, —

"Father, I think I'll go into mercantile life, if you can get Mr. Brazer to take me into his store."

" Ask your mother what she says, Amos," was the reply. After saying, " I hope you have considered the dangers of such a life, Amos, and will seek higher counsel than mine," she put nothing in the way of the fulfilment of his wishes. Mr. Brazer's store was the most important one for miles around, and numbered among its customers people from many of the surrounding towns, and for some time the young man remained there ; but his fellow-clerks, of whom there were five, were not altogether congenial, so with a very small sum of money in his pocket he decided to seek employment in the city, where he secured a situation as clerk with a firm with whom Mr. Brazer, who was ready to give him a good character for honesty, sobriety, industry, and capacity, had dealings frequently. There he discharged his duties with care and fidelity until invited to become a partner in the firm, when he announced his intention of going into business for himself, which he did. He was very successful, partly, no doubt, because he was true to the teachings of his father and mother, and gave away a certain portion of his income (much more than the Jewish tenth) yearly, besides adding in various ways to the comfort of his parents, so that Major Lawrence could say with truth, " Well, Susanna, we are surely very much blessed in our children."

In 1804 or 1805 Mr. Luther Lawrence, the lawyer,

married the sister of the Hon. Timothy Bigelow, with whom he had studied for his profession, and built his house in Groton, as has been stated already, where he lived for some years before removing to become an honored resident of a city of which he was mayor at the time of his death, when he left a widow and at least two daughters. A son and, I think, three other children had died before that date, which was 1839. At the time of his marriage the little shoe-shop adjoining the L of his father's house was still used by the minute-man and Oliver in the winter, and there were various little shelves existing in it when the writer was a child, on which were little blocks of wood, sawn transversely from a hardwood stick, which had been put there more than forty years before by either Major Lawrence or Oliver, to dry for shoe-pegs. I have heard that the neighbors said " Major Lawrence's pegs never drop out because he dries them so thoroughly before he uses them." But besides these little blocks and various other relics of shoemaking, — lasts, hammers, awls, etc., — the shop contained all the old iron that had accumulated in the household for as long a time as the shoe-pegs had lain there, — old gridirons, candlesticks, pots and kettles, wheel-tires, an old harrow and tools of various sorts, antiquated ploughshares, besides out-of-date lamps and a variety of old tinware, and it was for the purpose of ferreting out an old candlestick of brass or iron that the old lady who had been a baby in 1790 took me into the shop with her. I had often sat on one of the steps leading up to the door and wished that I could see inside, that being the only place so locked from intrusion, apparently; and as I had seen something, I cannot now recall what, but something that had pleased my childish fancy, which some one said had been "rummaged out of the shop," I had an idea that it was a sort of Arabian Nights cavern, and was much disappointed to find it only a rubbish room.

In 1811 Major Lawrence's son Amos was married to a city-bred young lady, whose father wore a powdered wig and silver knee-buckles, with the finest of coats and knee-breeches, an embroidered waistcoat, and lace ruffles, while her mother wore a high crepe turban and a handsome brocade dress over a satin petticoat with a hoop, or something that made her skirt very *bouffant*. I have often seen their portraits, owned by one of their grandsons. This grandson, when old and infirm, used often to sit for hours listening to his reader, with his right leg crossed over the left, holding the right ankle in his hand, exactly as his grandfather was painted, and as it had been the older man's habit to sit, according to the statement of the old lady, Mary Lawrence Woodbury, who gave me so much of the foregoing information. In fact, it was she who introduced her brother to the lady whom he afterward married; for the city girl, Miss Sarah Richards, had been one of her schoolmates in Groton Academy, having, I think, boarded in the family of the pastor of the church. It was in 1811 or early in 1812, that two young men came one day to see Major Lawrence, who was at that time called Deacon Lawrence. They had been for some time studying law with his son Luther, and

had previously been fellow-townsmen and later classmates in college, and the elder one went at once to
the point for which he had come.

"Deacon Lawrence," he said, "I came to ask you
if I may have your daughter Susanna."

"My Susanna!" exclaimed the deacon in astonishment. "Why, she's not — Why, I don't want to get
rid of her!"

"No, sir," replied the young suitor, "but I am
ready to start as a lawyer, and I love Miss Susanna.
Will you give her to me?"

"I'll ask her mother," replied Deacon Lawrence.
"She is the one to say."

And then the other young man spoke. He was
a few weeks younger than the first speaker, and he
said:

"And I came to ask you for Miss Mary, Deacon
Lawrence. I have been for a long time looking
forward to asking you. I fell in love with her when
I first heard her and Miss Susanna sing in church.
They are both fine singers, Deacon Lawrence."

"Yes, yes," replied the amazed father, "but I
haven't thought them old enough to marry yet awhile.
To be sure Mary is as old as her mother was when I
married her, and Susanna is older! Well, I'll ask
their mother and let you know. My son Luther
thinks a great deal of you, and we haven't any fault
to find with either of you."

And the result was that at as speedy a date as
possible both the young ladies were engaged. I can
well believe that a lover of music might have been
attracted by their voices, for it was recorded that a

distinguished man of that day wrote later to a friend that Deacon Lawrence's two older daughters were fine singers. The other daughter may have had a musical ear, but I never heard of her giving it vocal expression, which does not prove that she never did. If the daughter Mary sang as well for a young girl as she did for a lady of sixty, her voice must have been remarkable; for at that period and even later it was true and clear and sweet, not only in such hymns as —

> " Hush, my dear, lie still and slumber!
>   Holy angels guard thy bed.
>   Heavenly blessings without number
>   Gently fall upon thy head."

and

> " When I can read my title clear
>   To mansions in the skies,
>   I 'll bid farewell to every fear,
>   And wipe my weeping eyes,"

which she sang to an old revival tune that involved the repetition of the third line, when the fourth line came again, and then the words

> "Oh! that will be joyful, joyful, joyful,
>   Oh! that will be joyful, when we meet to part no more,
>   When we meet to part no more,
>   On Canaan's happy shore;
>   'T is there we meet at Jesus' feet
>   When we meet to part no more;"

which two hymns I often heard her sing through to her infant grandchildren; not only in these but in some spirited hunting songs which I never heard sung by any one else, her voice was well worth hearing. The songs were as follows:

" The dusky night rides down the sky,
And ushers in the morn.
The hounds all join the jovial cry,
The hounds all join the jovial cry,
And the huntsman winds his horn.
Then a-hunting we will go,
A-hunting we will go,
A-hunting we will go to-day,
A-hunting we will go.

" The wife about her husband throws
Her arms, to make him stay.
' My dear, it rains, it hails, it blows,
My dear, it rains, it hails, it blows,
You must not go to-day.'
But a-hunting we will go,
A-hunting we will go,
A-hunting we will go to-day,
A-hunting we will go.

" Sly Reynard now like lightning flies,
And speeds across the vale.
But when the hounds too near he spies,
But when the hounds too near he spies,
He drops his bushy tail.
Then a-hunting we will go.
A-hunting we will go,
A-hunting we will go to-day,
A-hunting we will go.

" Poor Reynard now to faintness worn,
In terror ceases flight.
And happy homeward we return,
And happy homeward we return,
To feast away the night.
And a-feasting we will go,
A-feasting we will go,
A-feasting we will go to-night,
A-feasting we will go."

The next one was, though I recall but one verse:

" At dawn Aurora gaily breaks,
In all her proud attire,

Majestic o'er the glassy lakes
    Reflecting liquid fire.
All Nature smiles to usher in
    The blushing Queen of Morn,
And huntsmen with the day begin,
    To wind the mellow horn,
      The mellow horn, the mellow horn,
And huntsmen with the day begin
    To wind the mellow horn."

A third was:

"A southerly wind and a cloudy sky
    Proclaim it a hunting morning.
Before the sun rises, away we'll fly,
    Dull sleep and a drowsy bed scorning.
To horse, my brave lads, and away!
    Bright Phœbus the hills is adorning.
The face of all Nature looks gay,
    'T is a beautiful scent-laying morning.
    Hark! Hark! Forward!
      Tantara, tantara, tantara!
    Hark! Hark! Forward!
      Tantara, tantara, tantara!"

And all were sung with the spirit of a young girl.

Not long after the engagement of their two daughters came the heaviest blow that had ever fallen upon the minute-man and his wife; for the eldest one, Susanna, went to visit her brother, Amos Lawrence, at his city home, was taken suddenly and seriously ill, and died before they could be informed of her illness in time to reach her. It was a very severe shock to all the family; for she was, her sister Mary told me, much like their mother, and they all looked up to her as the eldest daughter. Perhaps Mary felt her death even more than the others, and it certainly produced a great change in her views of life and in her habits. The family had been a very hospitable one, and for the times a rather gay one, as so many good-looking young people were sure to be in demand, and Susanna and Mary, as well as their brothers, William and Abbott, and very possibly their lovers, had often helped to make up a merry party which drove to some neighboring town for a ball or smaller gathering. But after her sister's death Mary preferred home to any such gayeties. Very soon, too, she had a trial of her own, to which only one other beside her older brothers had the key, and of which she never spoke to any one. The young lawyer to whom she was engaged, having in some way come into possession of land in one of the then Western States, wished to begin upon his legal career there, and expected her to go with him, which perhaps she might have done, as she was but a little over twenty-two, had not the advice of her older brothers led her to feel that, as the eldest living daughter, she had a duty to her mother, as well as to her lover. It seemed to them almost as much a cutting herself off from her parents as it would now if Australia, or at least Japan, were the country in question, and they all three said: " Father and mother are both nearly sixty years old, and Eliza is scarcely more than a child. You would regret very much going so far away from home, if anything should happen to either of them," and as her lover felt that he could not view the case with their eyes, her engagement was, by mutual consent, broken. No one of the next generation had ever heard of this engagement until one of the younger members of it, singularly enough, married a son of the rejected lover, and through her husband's father, who before his death put her in possession of some old letters, learned not only of that, but that after he had married and become a widower, he offered himself to her again years later, when she was a widow with one child. She had always disliked the idea of widows who had children marrying a second time, especially when, as in this case, there were children on the other side, and she refused him. When after having heard from the lady mentioned above the account of her early engagement, the writer asked her a meaningly leading question about a book with his name in it in her library, though she blushed like a girl, she answered as briefly as possible, which looked as if she had not altogether outgrown her early romance. Before her marriage she had refused another offer from a gentleman who was later a very prominent man in his native State, as her first lover became in his own State and in Washington also. She was said to have been remarkably good at repartee, which usually makes a pretty girl attractive, and though I was told that when young her repartees were sometimes mixed with sarcasm, she had either overcome or outgrown it before I knew her. She was a bright, alert, and kind-hearted old lady, a great reader, too, enjoying such books as Macaulay's Essays and histories, and Prescott's works, with Irving's " Life of Washington," much more than she did stories, though she was familiar with the old-fashioned novels of Miss Austen, Miss Edgeworth, and Madame D'Arblay, and was an admirer of many of Sir Walter Scott's works.

CHAPTER V

Within the next year or two another gap was
made in the minute-man's family circle by the de-
parture of his son Abbott to go into business in the
metropolis with his brother Amos, leaving but four
of the nine children he had had, still in the homestead: two sons, one of them over thirty and the
other about fourteen; and two daughters, aged respectively twenty-four and eighteen. But Amos had
been so successful, and was moreover so thoroughly
faithful to every smallest duty, as well as to the larger
ones, that it was doubtless a constant source of thank-
fulness to his parents that his younger brother could
be with him, instead of going to a stranger. Certain
it is that the younger brother also showed remarkable capacity in business affairs, as well as in whatever he undertook, and was a power in his day. In
1819 he married a niece of his eldest brother's wife,
Miss Katharine Bigelow, daughter of Hon. Timothy
Bigelow, before mentioned, and considered by every
one an unusually " good match," as the saying was,
for any one.

The young lawyer who had been engaged to Miss
Susanna Lawrence had been so much overcome by
her death that he gave up his legal profession and
studied for the ministry, going, after his ordination,
to be settled over a small country parish at some distance from Groton; but he had always kept up by
correspondence and otherwise his connection with
Deacon Lawrence's family, certainly with Mr. Luther
Lawrence, and five years after his fiancée's death he

came to Groton for a visit. Either then or shortly afterward he found the younger daughter, Mary, who had given up his friend, so attractive, that he asked her to marry him, and as his parish was not so far from her parents that she could not go home easily in case of emergency, as her sister was now a grown woman, and, furthermore, as the experience of the past few years had deepened her own character, making her more thoughtful of the needs of others than she was at the time of her earlier romance, and more desirous to do something for the spread of religion, she accepted him after due consideration, was married in the late summer of 1818, and went to be the mistress of a small country parsonage, with only one young girl as assistant.

And then another sorrow fell upon the minuteman and his wife; for in the following spring a chaise arrived at their door, and in answer to the "Who's there?" which Deacon Lawrence called from his chamber window, his daughter's voice said, "It is Samuel [Rev. Samuel Woodbury] and I, father; Samuel is ill." He hastened to admit them, but the minister, who had inherited, as people thought in that day, the seeds of consumption, was so worn out from the inroads it had made upon him that early in July he died in the house where ten months before he had been married, and where late in September his little daughter was born. His widow had no other home from that time until her death more than forty-one years later, for after the death of both her parents three of her brothers bought the estate, and three years after, one; seven years after, the second, and ten years after, the third, arranged by will that she should have a home there for life, if she wished, besides leaving her such large legacies that she was able to live in affluence. Her little girl, the only one of Deacon Lawrence's granddaughters who ever passed much time in the house before his death, was a great pleasure and pet for both him and his wife, who were both nearing their threescore and ten years, he being sixty-five and Mrs. Lawrence sixty-four when she was born; and I remember hearing her say more than once that they were most gentle and affectionate grandparents, neither of them ever interfering with her mother's methods of bringing her up, excepting that he would sometimes wish to give her at the table something that he considered a dainty, and if her mother objected, would respond, " Tut, tut, it will do her good, Mary," though he forebore to proffer it again. As in one instance, at least, it was a bit of bacon, and her mother had to the end of her days a horror of every sort of fatty food, it is not strange that the little girl was not fed upon such dainty morsels, which would hardly have left her the beautiful, clear, red and white complexion shown in a portrait of her painted at sixteen by the same artist who painted those of her grandmother and her mother, a man quite noted at that day. This portrait she never liked herself; for she had, I have heard, a remarkably beautiful smile, which the painter desired to catch for his picture, to which end he told her some amusing stories, and paid her some audacious compliments, producing a result which most people admired, but which she and her mother also always declared to be unnatural. I have heard that she was considered a very handsome girl, not only in her native town, but by those who saw her at the homes of her uncles in the metropolis. When she was born, she was Deacon Lawrence's tenth grandchild; as he already had three grandsons, — one being the son of his eldest son Luther, and the others Amos's sons, aged respectively seven and a half and five and a half years; while Luther had had four daughters, one of whom died in infancy, Amos one, and Abbott one. In 1822 there were eleven grandchildren, another, a boy, having been born in Abbott's household, and during that year William Lawrence, who had, soon after his brother Abbott's marriage, left the farm and gone to Boston to become a successful merchant, married the only daughter of his partner in business, a rich man who was past sixty and willing to have the business in younger hands.

In 1823 there was another grandson in Deacon Lawrence's family line, for William's first child was born. During that year Miss Eliza Lawrence, who must have been a strikingly handsome young woman, as she had perfectly regular features, large blue eyes, and wavy hair, with a tall and dignified form in her later years, was married to a very fine looking young man of old and aristocratic antecedents, whom she had met while visiting her brothers in the city, and the home family was reduced to the two old people and the widow and her little daughter; for the youngest son had some time previously left the nest to fit himself for a business life.

Oliver Wentworth was still one of the household,

though growing old like his employers, and he felt a most affectionate interest in the rising generation of Lawrences. The sons of Mr. Amos Lawrence, and some of the other grandsons of Deacon Lawrence, always spoke of him and addressed him as *Uncle* Oliver in his later years, and gradually that became the name by which he was alluded to by many others of the minute-man's descendants, who as long as he lived were in the habit of going to see him, and have a little chat with him about old times, whenever they were near enough.

There was also a colored woman, a descendant, or at least a connection of the Maria Hazard who had been in Mrs. Lawrence's service in the early days of her housekeeping, who had been the nurse of the widowed Mary's little daughter, and who remained in the family in some one capacity or another for several years. Her brother, whom the writer remembers as the oldest negro she ever saw, and a most respectable man, who was as regularly in a seat in one of the wall-pews at the right-hand side of the pulpit as the minister was in his place in the pulpit itself, was, so far back as 1823, often called upon for various services in the Lawrence household, and once saved a grandson of the Deacon's — a somewhat venturesome little lad — from drowning, by jumping into the river on which the boy had gone out in a leaky boat, and swimming ashore with him. The victim of the accident, Amos Adams Lawrence, told me the circumstances himself, saying that at the time the reproofs which he received from his grandparents and aunts made much more impression upon him than did the fact that he

owed his life to the kind-hearted negro; but if that were
so, he made up for it in later years, for he bought and
gave to Peter Hazard the little farm which he (Peter)
had hired and become attached to, and when Peter was
too old to be able to work it, sent a sum of money regularly to a responsible person in Groton, to be used for
Peter's support until the old colored man died at the
age of one hundred years. It was questioned by some
of the residents of the town whether Peter would have
been so regular an attendant at public worship had it
not been that his benefactor, in his desire to make up
to him for the lack of helpful surroundings, kept Mrs.
Joshua Green (Deacon Lawrence's youngest daughter, who had, after living for a few years in the interior of the State, come to occupy a pleasant house in
Groton, which was in 1850, or thereabouts, replaced
by a more convenient and handsomer one) supplied
with tobacco, of which she was instructed to give Peter a certain amount whenever he had been at church
and came to claim it after the services were over.
However that may have been, his well-dressed and
well-built figure was seldom missing in its accustomed
seat when I attended what was called the *Orthodox*
Church in Groton; but as Mrs. Green was also a
most charitable person, and doubtless supplemented
her nephew's gift with tea, sugar, and even with more
substantial things, as I have heard she did, it must
have been a powerful addition to the attraction of his
seat in the meeting-house. His wife was included in
his benefactor's bounty, as his support and hers as
well were considered in its amount, and both Mrs.
Green and Mrs. Woodbury were in the habit of visit-

ing them, and keeping their nephew informed regarding them, though when he passed a day in Groton he always went himself to see him. Peter's sister, Lucy Hazard, once told the little girl whose nurse she had been, and who repeated it to me herself, that she would thankfully be skinned alive if she could only turn white by the means; which shows how much unhappiness Noah's second son was probably accountable for.

The minute-man lived on his quiet, useful life, beloved and respected by every one, and helping, so far as lay in his power, every good cause, until the year 1827, when he had an attack of apoplexy or paralysis, — I think the latter, as his illness was a brief one, — and he died in November of that year, at the age of a little over seventy-three years and six months. He had lived to see all his five sons successful and honored in their various positions; three of them were on the way to be ranked among the richest men of their day, and one of them was destined to serve his country in a high office; while there was not one of his children who could not count " hosts of friends " among the cultured and the educated, the rich and the poor, the honored and the unknown. What wonder if he said to the wife who had shared his joys and his sorrows, his cares and his successes, for within a few months of half a century, " Susanna, we have had the best blessings of this world, and we will look forward to sharing some of those which the next can give." He rested from his labors, and his works followed him. After his death his sons felt that it was not right for their mother and sister to have the care

of Oliver in his old age, especially as he had begun
to be sadly afflicted with rheumatism. As he himself expressed it, when asked by people in the town,
" How are you nowadays ? " " I 'm pretty well as
to my *bodily* health, but I 'm most eat up with the
rheumatiz." So they built a convenient little house
for him on the grounds and fronting the road, as did
the homestead, and gave the rent of it to a respectable
widow with three daughters, with the understanding
that he was to have the best of care. That he received it there is no reason for doubting, and there
until his death, which took place at the age of ninety-
five, Deacon Lawrence's children, grandchildren, and
even some of his great-grandchildren, often visited
him. I myself saw him more than once in the pleasant room which had been designed especially for his
own use; but at that time he was so infirm that if I
had asked him any questions as to the past he would
hardly have been able to give me much information,
and I can only remember that he said, " So Miss
Woodbury said you might come to see me ! Well,
well."

As I have said so much about this one of Deacon
Lawrence's family, Mrs. Mary Lawrence Woodbury,
whom I knew best, it seems right to add something
about those of his other children whom I remember.
Mr. Luther Lawrence died before I was born; but I
recall perfectly seeing his widow in 1849, at which
time I was five years old and living in Groton, where
she came with Mrs. Woodbury to call on my mother,
who had been an intimate friend of a daughter of
hers, whose death had occurred a year or so before.

She won my heart by having brought me an exquisite little fan, with carved ivory sticks and a delicate gilt pattern on a white ground for the fan part, and, though I was not allowed to use it, excepting on the very infrequent occasion of a children's party, I was exceedingly proud of it. I recall her as tall, rather portly, dressed in the deepest black I had ever seen, with a long crêpe veil. Mrs. Woodbury always wore black, but it never impressed me as did Mrs. Luther Lawrence's. Mr. William Lawrence I can just remember, though I fear I should have no recollection of his handsome, kindly face, had it not been for a portrait and bust seen later. His figure I seem to see perfectly as it looked when I was between three and four years old, nearer three than four. He had asked my parents to bring my older brother and myself to see a procession which was to pass his house, fronting Boston Common, and on our way thither we had stopped to call on a friend of my mother's who had a little boy a few months younger than my five and one-half year old brother. This boy was in his nursery, playing with a large Noah's ark, which he showed to us, and when we left he very politely presented me with a green bird which had attracted my fancy. I can see it now, stiff and unshapely and of a peculiar shade of green which I do not think any bird's plumage ever exhibited, but at the time I thought it beautiful, and when, as I sat in my mother's lap in Mr. William Lawrence's window, watching the procession, with my hands on the sill, it suddenly slipped from my grasp and fell into the little grassy yard, inclosed with an iron fence, below,

I was quite heartbroken. I can remember crying, and that my mother tried to hush me, and I can distinctly recall Mr. Lawrence's figure as he climbed over the iron railing which ran up the steps, and then climbed back again with the little bird. He was then sixty-six years old, and though I did not until I was older know that all those who saw him were much distressed that a man of his years, and as heavy as he was, should attempt such a feat, I always loved him from that day. I do not think I ever saw him again, for he died in the following year; but even a child of the age I had reached remembers such a kindly act. His widow I remember seeing once afterward, when I may have been seven or eight years old, and I recall a gentle, sweet-faced woman; but as she was delicate, her companion devoted herself to me while my father talked with her. This companion, a handsome young lady, whose father, a rich and prominent Southerner in his lifetime, had died, leaving two accomplished daughters thrown upon their own resources, I always recalled with great regard; for she not only gave me some very delicious candies on that occasion, but she more than once sent some boxes of confectionery to my brother and myself, and I remember being greatly pleased when some time later I was told that she was engaged to be married to a cousin of my mother's.

Mr. Amos Lawrence I remember seeing once or twice before his death in 1852, but he was an invalid at that time. Both my brother and I had to thank him for more than one entertaining book in our juvenile library. His widow I saw in 1864, when

she was so gratified by a spontaneous call which I
paid her, which she said she should not have expected from a young girl not quite out of her teens,
that she gave me some money with the request that
I would buy a handsome hand bag, as she was an
invalid and could not go out to select it. She was
not Mr. Lawrence's first wife, but his children all
respected her and treated her as they would have
treated their own mother, who had died when the
eldest was a boy of but seven years old. She died in
the late fall of 1866.

The next one to Mrs. Woodbury, of Deacon Lawrence's children, Mr. Abbott, was, I believe, the hand-
somest one of all, and certainly I never saw a man of
his age as handsome as he was in 1854, when I saw
him last. Even at ten years of age, he struck me as
a very remarkable looking man, with his beautifully
cut features, which, however, had nothing of effemi-
nacy about them, his fine eyes, smooth face, well-
proportioned figure, and elegant manners. He had
then but lately returned from a high diplomatic
position in Europe. His wife I saw once or twice
after his death, and both my brother and I had a
number of things which were proofs of her thought-
fulness of others. Among other things there were
a small book, with several illustrations in colors of a
" Lord Mayor's Show " which she had witnessed in
London, and in which there were Beef-eaters and
Highlanders, and others, so accurately depicted, that
I at once recognized one of the former (who admitted me with some friends to the Tower in 1885), and
a " Thumb Bible," a tiny book about two inches

square with an embossed leather binding and silver clasp. This little book contained a verse from every book in the Bible, each one being put down in its order, — Genesis, Exodus, etc. I was told by an English lady in 1895 that it would command a high price in England then; for there had never been but the one edition, which was gotten up by an enterprising bookseller just after America's celebrated dwarf, Tom Thumb, had paid his first (and last, I think) visit to England, and had been presented by Queen Victoria with the little coach and two white ponies with which he entered Groton in 1850, a little before Mrs. Abbot Lawrence sent from London by mail the two books mentioned above.

Mrs. Joshua Green comes next in order to Mr. Abbott Lawrence. As I have said, she was a very handsome woman, and after her death I was told that in her youth her hand and arm were considered particularly beautiful, both in shape and proportion. I know that her hands were beautiful, even in old age, and I admired her very much. Her gifts to me were apt to be flowers, of which even as a child I was very fond; but there were few with whom she had even a speaking acquaintance who could not have told of some kindness received from her. Her husband was always more or less of an invalid, but he was a strikingly fine looking man till the close of his life, or until I saw him last in 1870, after which time I never saw Mrs. Green, who died in 1874.

Mr. Samuel Lawrence, the last of the minute-man's children, died in 1880, in his eightieth year. He was also a very fine looking man, and one of the tallest of the brothers. One of his daughters and I had been playmates and warm friends as children; but I did not see her for seventeen years, until, in 1872, a cousin, or rather a second cousin, of mine went to live in the place where Mr. Samuel Lawrence soon after took a house, and in the spring of 1874 I was invited to visit my old playmate. I had always heard that Mr. Lawrence had a peculiarly winning manner, and a power of attracting people to him, and one could not be in the house with him without becoming aware of it. Genial and affectionate, unselfish, and with a cheerfulness that had borne up against business disappointments, as well as other personal trials, it was a delight to talk with him, and to witness the respect in which he was held by the residents of the pretty country town in which he had come to end his days, and apart from his unvarying kindness to myself there were many things which drew out my respect and affection. I recall, for one thing, that he was late for dinner one Sunday, a most unusual thing with him, for he was, and liked to have others, perfectly punctual. Upon coming in after the meal had been some time under way, he answered his wife's remark that she should have been anxious about him in a few moments, with, " You see I wanted to be sure that that little Comstock girl was not seriously ill, and it was farther than I thought." The little girl in question — the daughter of a man who owned a saw-mill in the place — had been faint and her parents took her out of church and did not return, so that old gentleman of nearly seventy-four had walked a long distance to see about her. I can only wish

that the minute-man might have lived to see this
son's beautiful wife, the only one of those who married into his family whom he did not know; but Mr.
Lawrence did not marry as early as most of his brothers and sisters did. In 1833 he married a Baltimore
lady (Miss Alison Turnbull) of a little over twenty,
who was the light of his eyes and the joy of his heart
for almost fifty years. Lovely in face and character,
accomplished and winning, she made innumerable
admirers in her Northern home, which she gave
up bravely to share her husband's misfortunes when
a sudden shock overthrew his business; and in a
smaller sphere she won the love and admiration of
all, and my every recollection of her is of a most
beautiful woman, a tender and devoted wife, a loving
and sympathetic mother, and a bright, entertaining
friend, while the latter part of my acquaintance with
her gave me an insight into the deep religious principle which had sustained her through more trials
than fall to the lot of most.

I might go on to relate pleasant things about the
grandchildren and two other generations of descendants of the minute-man, and their husbands and
wives, but they numbered so many that I must re-
frain, merely stating that his lineal descendants in
1844, when his widow was still living, were forty-five,
while those who had married into the family were
fourteen. In 1889 the former had increased to one
hundred and seventy, and the latter to fifty-one,
there being seventy-two of his great-great-grandchil-
dren. His faithful wife died in 1845, having outlived
him eighteen years, so that she was in her ninetieth

year. Her strongest wish, at her life's close, was that her children, grandchildren, and great-grandchildren should serve the same Master who had been her's and her husband's, and surely they had every right to " arise and call her blessed."

INDEX

INDEX

The numbering of the Genealogy is reproduced in this Index in heavy-faced figures.

Douglas, Elizabeth, 215.
William, 215.
Dudley, Ann, 233.
Eleazer A., 233.
Thomas, 233.
Duncan, Mary, 147.
Peter, 147.
Dwight, Dorothy, 248.
Joseph, 248,

Eames, Hannah, 248.
Robert, 248.
Edgar, Mary Edmundson, 196.
Elliott, Ann, 197.
Robert, 197.
Ellis, Caleb, 25, 192.
Nancy (Means), 25, 28, 192.
Emlen, Elizabeth, 174.
Emmons, Lydia, 170.
Endicott, Martha, 241.
John, 241.
Samuel, 241.
Evans, Joanna, 224.
Everard, Judith, 118.

Faulkner, Francis, 248.
Rebecca, 248.
Fitch, Elizabeth (Grimes), 234.
Elizabeth (Walker), 234.
Mary, 178.
Mary, 234.
Sally, 225, 234.
Samuel, 234.
Samuel, Jr., 234.
Sarah (Lane), 234.
Zachariah, 225, 234.
Zachary, 234.
Fletcher, Rebecca Chamberlain, 165.
Fosdick, Christina Dakin (Caryl), 41.
Charles, 34, 42.
Charles Mussey, 36, 42,
David, 44, 44.
Lucy, 46, 44.
David, 47.
Dea. David, 47, 48.
Rev. David, 41, 45, 48.
Elsie Woodbury, 37, 42.
Frederick, 39, 43.
Frederick Woodbury, 40, 43.
George, 33, 42.
James, 46, 47.
James, Jr., 46, 47.
Joanna (Skelton), 47.
John, 45.
Lucy, 46, 44.

Fosdick, Lucy Maria (Hill), 43.
Margaret Willis, 35, 42.
Marion Lawrence, 38, 42.
Mary, 32, 42.
Mary Louise (Snow), 42.
Mercy (Pickett), 46.
Miriam Eddy, 43, 43.
Nellie, 41, 43.
Rose, 45, 44.
Richard Coffin, 42, 43.
Samuel, 46.
Capt. Samuel, 46.
Samuel Woodbury, 31, 41.
Sarah, 47.
Sarah Lawrence (Woodbury), 30, 41, 49.
Sarah Woodbury, 47, 45.
Stephen, 45.
William, 47.
Foster, Abigail (Poor), 248.
Abraham, 248.
Alfred Dwight, 249.
Dorothy Dwight, 243, 247.
Dorothy (Dwight), 248.
Dwight, 248.
Dwight (2d), 249.
Ephraim, 248.
Ephraim, Jr., 248.
Hannah (Eames), 248.
Harriette Story (Lawrence), 168, 247, 250.
Henrietta Perkins (Baldwin), 249.
Jedediah, 248.
Lawrence, 244, 247.
Lydia (Stiles), 249.
Mary, 239.
Mary (Neale), 188.
Maxwell Evarts, 246, 247.
Rebecca (Faulkner), 248.
Reginald, of Boxford, 239, 240.
Reginald, " the first," 248.
Reginald, 247, 249, 250.
Reginald, 245, 247,
Ruth, 242, 247.
Sarah, 6.
Sarah, 221.
Fowle, Joanna, 210.
Ruth (Ingalles), 210.
Zachary, 210.
Franklin, Martha, 124.
Frothingham, James, 47.
Mary, 47.
William, 47.

Gardiner, Hannah, 215.

www.ingramcontent.com/pod-product-compliance
Lightning Source LLC
Chambersburg PA
CBHW070548270326
41926CB00013B/2242